FEARS
OF A
SETTING
SUN

THE DISILLUSIONMENT OF
AMERICA'S FOUNDERS

DENNIS C.
RASMUSSEN

PRINCETON UNIVERSITY PRESS
PRINCETON & OXFORD

PUBLISHED BY PRINCETON UNIVERSITY PRESS
41 William Street, Princeton, New Jersey 08540
99 Banbury Road, Oxford OX2 6JX

press.princeton.edu

ALL RIGHTS RESERVED
New paperback printing, 2022
Paperback ISBN 9780691241418
Cloth ISBN 9780691210230
ISBN (e-book) 9780691211060

British Library Cataloging-in-Publication Data is available

Editorial: Rob Tempio and Matt Rohal
Production Editorial: Sara Lerner
Text Design: Chris Ferrante
Production: Erin Suydam
Publicity: Maria Whelan and Kate Farquhar-Thomson
Copyeditor: Kathleen Kageff
Cover design: Emily Weigel
Cover images from top to bottom: *The Williamstown Portrait*, Gilbert Stuart. *Alexander Hamilton*, John Trumbull. *Official Presidential portrait of John Adams*, John Trumbull. *Thomas Jefferson*, Rembrandt Peale.

This book has been composed in Adobe Caslon and The Fell Types
The Fell Types are digitally reproduced by Igino Marini.
www.iginomarini.com

PRINTED IN THE UNITED STATES OF AMERICA

FOR SAM

CONTENTS

CONTENTS

ACKNOWLEDGMENTS

LIKE MANY AMERICANS, I have long enjoyed reading popular biographies of the founders—the kind that academic historians sometimes deride as "founders chic." Until fairly recently my own research centered on the Scottish and French Enlightenments—Adam Smith, David Hume, Jean-Jacques Rousseau, Montesquieu, Voltaire—so these books on the founders mostly served as a pleasant diversion. It often struck me, however, that while the stories were generally meant to be inspiring and uplifting, the endings were never entirely happy. On the contrary, almost all the leading founders ended up being, for one reason or another, rather disappointed in the government and the nation that they had helped to create. This seemed like a point worth pursuing, and I was surprised to find that no one had done so in a systematic way. I decided to have a go at it myself, and this book is the result.

As a relative newcomer to the study of the American founding, I benefited enormously from the voluminous scholarship on the period, above all the magnificent collections of the major founders' papers. I hope that my intellectual debts are made clear in the notes, but special mention must be made of Gordon Wood, whose dual biography of Adams and Jefferson, *Friends Divided*, was one of the immediate inspirations for this book, and who reassured me at the outset that the disillusionment of the founders was a topic worth pursuing. Jeremy Bailey, Ian Boyko, Ari Kohen, Howard Lubert, Peter McNamara, Peter Onuf, Rich Rasmussen, John Rhodehamel, Jean Yarbrough, and an anonymous reviewer all generously provided comments on the manuscript, for which I am deeply grateful. I am also thankful for the support of my colleagues at Tufts University, where I began this project, and at Syracuse University, where I completed it. My editor Rob Tempio has been an enthusiastic backer of this project since the day I conceived it, and I appreciate all that he and the whole team at Princeton University Press have done to bring it to fruition.

ACKNOWLEDGMENTS

As always, my deepest debts are to my family and friends for all their love and support. My first three books were dedicated to my parents, my wife, and my friends, respectively, so it is only appropriate that I dedicate this one to my son, Sam. Watching him grow up gives me greater confidence in the future than the founders ever had.

A NOTE ON QUOTATIONS

When quoting letters and other texts from the eighteenth and nineteenth centuries, I have retained the original spelling, punctuation, and capitalization, even where they differ—as they often do—from present-day norms.

PROLOGUE

A RISING OR A SETTING SUN

O N SEPTEMBER 17, 1787, the delegates to the Constitutional
Convention gathered one last time in the Assembly Room of
what is now Independence Hall.[1] They had spent four long
months—six days a week, five hours a day, not counting the many
smaller gatherings that took place after hours in Philadelphia's taverns
and boardinghouses—hashing out the structure and powers of a proposed new national government. Most of the forty-one delegates in
attendance that day longed for nothing more than to conclude their
business and decamp from the city as soon as possible. After the en-
grossed Constitution was read aloud, Benjamin Franklin rose to signal
his intention to address the group. Franklin—the oldest delegate at
age eighty-one, and the most eminent save the convention's president,
George Washington—was nearly crippled by gout and kidney stones
and found it difficult to stand up for long.[2] His speech, which he had
written out in advance, was accordingly delivered by his Pennsylvania
colleague James Wilson in his distinctive Scottish burr. Franklin began
his carefully crafted set piece by confessing that "there are several
parts of this Constitution which I do not at present approve," but he
quickly noted that "the older I grow, the more apt I am to doubt my
own judgment, and to pay more respect to the judgment of others."
He urged any of the delegates who may have had qualms about the
proposed government to make allowances for their own fallibility and
to endorse the charter that the group had crafted so painstakingly. For
his own part, he declared, "I consent . . . to this Constitution, because
I expect no better, and because I am not sure, that it is not the best."[3]

Franklin likely hoped that this speech would serve as the convention's poignant culmination, but it was not to be. Nathaniel Gorham

I

of Massachusetts stepped forward to propose a last-minute tweak that would open the door for more representatives in the House. When the proposal was supported by none other than Washington himself—the only time during the entire convention that he made a substantive recommendation—it passed without opposition; no one in the room would have even considered defying the general's express wishes so directly and openly. Yet the harmony was not total. Three holdouts—Edmund Randolph, Elbridge Gerry, and George Mason—refused to sign the document, and the former two occupied more of the group's time with extended explanations of their internal struggles. The signing was then postponed still further by discussion of what to do with the official journals of the convention; the delegates agreed to leave them under Washington's care. It was late afternoon by the time the thirty-eight signers finally lined up to put their names to the document, starting with New Hampshire and moving south down the Atlantic Seaboard to Georgia.[4]

Yet Franklin managed to get the last word after all, at least according to the record kept by James Madison—a coda even more poetic than the one that he had planned. As the last delegates were affixing their signatures, Franklin called attention to the high-backed mahogany chair that Washington had occupied at the head of the room all summer, which had a decorative half sunburst carved into the crest (and which is still on display at Independence Hall—see the frontispiece of this book for a photograph of the crest). Franklin remarked that painters often found it difficult to differentiate, in their compositions, a rising sun from a setting sun. "I have," he said, "often and often, in the course of the session, and the vicissitudes of my hopes and fears as to its issue, looked at that [sun on the chair] behind the President, without being able to tell whether it was rising or setting: but now at length, I have the happiness to know, that it is a rising and not a setting sun."[5]

Whatever sense of hope the founders may have felt at the new government's birth, almost none of them carried that optimism to their graves. Franklin survived to see the government formed by the Constitution in action for only a single year, but most of the founders who lived into the nineteenth century—or even to the dawn of the new century, like Washington—came to feel deep anxiety, disappoint-

ment, and even despair about the government and the nation that they had helped to create. This book tells the story of their disillusionment.

Americans no longer deify the "Founding Fathers" in quite the way we once did. We are keenly aware of their manifold and manifest flaws with regard to slavery and their treatment of the American Indians, for example. Yet we do still tend to exalt and even venerate what the founders founded, namely the Constitution and the American form of government. The US Constitution is the oldest extant charter of national government, and arguably one of the most successful. Whatever their political gripes, few Americans would even contemplate jettisoning any of the basic features of the constitutional order: the separation of powers into three branches, the checks and balances among those branches, the bicameral Congress, the division of sovereignty between national and local authorities, the Bill of Rights, and the like. This order has, after all, enabled the country to survive, grow, and generally prosper for well over two centuries—in fact, to develop into history's greatest economic and military power. Moreover, when our politics go awry we tend to assume that it is because we have failed in some way to live up to the founders' vision—that if we could somehow fulfill their expectations then all would be well.

It comes as something of a surprise, then, to learn that the founders themselves were, particularly by the end of their lives, far less confident in the merits of the political system that they had devised, and that many of them in fact deemed it an utter failure that was unlikely to last beyond their own generation. This point has been made before, to be sure. No less an authority on the period than Gordon Wood has written that the bustling democratic society that the American Revolution unleashed "was not the society the revolutionary leaders had wanted or expected. No wonder, then, that those of them who lived on into the early decades of the nineteenth century expressed anxiety over what they had wrought. Although they tried to put as good a face as they could on what had happened, they were bewildered, uneasy, and in many cases deeply disillusioned. Indeed, a pervasive pessimism, a fear that their revolutionary experiment in republicanism was not working out as they had expected, runs through the later writings of

the founding fathers."[6] Yet for all the tremendous amount that has been written on the founders, the fact that most of them ended up disillusioned with the country that they created is a fact that is little known among the general public and seldom emphasized even by scholars of the period. It is admittedly impossible to canvass everything that has been written on the founding and the early republic within a single lifetime, but a reasonably thorough search did not yield a single book, article, or even book chapter that takes the disillusionment of the founders as its theme.

This book focuses principally on four of the preeminent figures of the period: George Washington, Alexander Hamilton, John Adams, and Thomas Jefferson. These four lost their faith in the American experiment at different times and for different reasons, and each has his own unique story. As we will see, Washington became disillusioned above all because of the rise of parties and partisanship, Hamilton because he felt that the federal government was not sufficiently vigorous or energetic, Adams because he believed that the American people lacked the requisite civic virtue for republican government, and Jefferson because of sectional divisions that were laid bare by conflict over the spread of slavery.

Washington, Hamilton, Adams, and Jefferson were the most prominent of the founders who grew disappointed in what America became, but they were certainly not the only ones. As we will see very briefly in chapter 13, *most* of the other leading founders—including figures such as Samuel Adams, Elbridge Gerry, Patrick Henry, John Jay, John Marshall, George Mason, James Monroe, Gouverneur Morris, Thomas Paine, and Benjamin Rush—fell in the same camp. The most notable founder who did *not* come to despair for his country—the proverbial exception that proves the rule—was the one who outlived them all, James Madison. Madison did harbor some real worries from time to time, particularly during the nullification crisis (1832–33), but on the whole he remained sanguine about the nation and its politics all the way until his death in 1836. The final two chapters explore why Madison largely kept the republican faith when so many of his compatriots did not.

To say that the great majority of the founders became disillusioned is not to deny that some of them experienced moments of real hope

and optimism, even in their later years. Perspectives naturally ebb and flow along with changing events and even daily moods. Yet the strains of pessimism and disappointment in the founders' later letters and other writings are far deeper and more persistent than is generally realized. This pessimism did not stem merely from the disgruntlement of old age: it is true that Washington and Jefferson did not grow disenchanted with America's constitutional order until they were fairly old men, but Hamilton and Adams began to lose hope when they were much younger. Though some of these figures suffered from occasional bouts of depression, often brought on by personal insults or ailments, this was not the whole story, either. Their anxieties about the nation that they had founded were simply too enduring, too well reasoned, and too closely connected to their deepest aspirations and beliefs to be chalked up to momentary low spirits. Nor is there need for any kind of guesswork or hazy inferences in establishing this point: there is a vast historical record attesting to the founders' disillusionment. Much of the evidence comes in private letters rather than in public speeches or writings, but the founders were all keenly aware that their correspondence would be pored over by future generations. For all their concern about posterity's judgment, their growing disappointment was not something that they even tried to hide.

An underlying premise of this book—one that seems fairly obvious once it has been stated, but that is nonetheless underappreciated—is that the founders' thinking about politics did not somehow terminate with the ratification of the Constitution in 1788 or the Bill of Rights in 1791. Although an immense amount has been written on the outlooks of each of the leading founders, the majority of it focuses on their views during the founding period itself—say, from 1775 to 1791. There are perfectly good reasons for the emphasis on this period: this was, after all, when the country achieved its independence and when the charter by which we still live was devised and ratified. Yet the founders' views of the pitfalls and possibilities of republican government continued to develop over the succeeding decades, shaped by the struggles and successes of the constitutional order that they had created. Given our continued attraction to the founders—our perpetual efforts to recover their ideas and renew their ideals—it seems sensible to try to achieve the fullest possible understanding of their outlooks, rather

than confine ourselves to a snapshot taken at one moment in time. While their views during the founding period are eminently worthy of our attention, so too are their views in the succeeding years, which were, after all, shaped by greater real-world experience.

Franklin provided another famous quip about the outcome of the Constitutional Convention, in addition to the one about the rising sun. The story goes that as he left the hall after the signing of the Constitution, Elizabeth Powel—a close friend and advisor of Washington—accosted him to ask whether the delegates had proposed a republic or a monarchy. "A republic," Franklin replied, "if you can keep it."[7] The founders were keenly aware of just how difficult it would be to "keep" their republic, for a host of historical and theoretical reasons. To begin with, republican government had never before succeeded on a large scale. The only republican governments at the time were either small city-states like Venice and San Marino or confederations of city-states like the Netherlands and Switzerland. There had never been a republic the size of even the original thirteen states in all history. Ancient Greece had its democracies, and Rome had been a republic for a time, of course, but the founders generally saw these precedents less as models to follow than object lessons of what to avoid. As Hamilton bluntly put it in *Federalist* number 9, "it is impossible to read the history of the petty Republics of Greece and Italy, without feeling sensations of horror and disgust at the distractions with which they were continually agitated, and at the rapid succession of revolutions, by which they were kept in a state of perpetual vibration, between the extremes of tyranny and anarchy."[8]

There were also a variety of standard explanations that had been honed and rehearsed by political philosophers for centuries as to why republican rule could not succeed in a large country. Large populations and large geographic areas are likely to contain a good deal of economic, cultural, and religious diversity, and all these factors, it was assumed, would prevent the people from really *being* a people. In a large country, that is to say, the people would not feel sufficiently united; they would not know or care enough about those who were far away or very unlike themselves. As a result, they would also not know

or care enough about the government, or have much desire to dedicate themselves to the public good. The representatives in such a country would almost inevitably be very different from their constituents— since they would likely have to stand out in terms of fame or wealth to get elected—and many would have to move far away from their home districts to a distant capital city, so their views and interests would be sure to diverge from the people's views and interests. And it would be difficult for these representatives to develop a uniform set of laws, since different parts of the country would have contrasting needs and conditions. Such arguments had endured since the ancient Greeks and had recently received the imprimatur of Montesquieu, whose book *The Spirit of the Laws* was hugely influential during the founding era. All this is why the founders frequently described them-selves as engaged in an "experiment," one designed to demonstrate the viability of republican government on a large scale after more than two thousand years of failure.

We tend to think of the founders as hardheaded pragmatists rather than starry-eyed idealists, and in some senses they were. It was quite simply impossible for northerners and southerners, large states and small states, nationalists and localists to get everything that they wanted and remain part of the same union, so compromise was inevitable. In other respects, though, the founders self-consciously set out to achieve the unprecedented. Given that the United States has now emerged as history's greatest superpower and that republi-can government has now spread across much of the globe, it takes a real act of historical imagination to see the audacity—indeed, the presumptuousness—of the founders' expectation that their actions would prove to be a world-historical event, that these thirteen states huddled against the Atlantic could get right what everyone else in history had gotten wrong.

Madison declared matter-of-factly at the Constitutional Con-vention that their deliberations "would decide for ever the fate of republican government."[9] Hamilton proclaimed in *Federalist* number 1 that "it seems to have been reserved to the people of this coun-try, by their conduct and example, to decide the important question, whether societies of men are really capable or not, of establishing good government from reflection and choice, or whether they are forever

destined to depend, for their political constitutions, on accident and force."[10] Adams agreed that "the people in America have now the best opportunity and the greatest trust in their hands, that Providence ever committed to so small a number, since the transgression of the first pair."[11] And Washington announced in his First Inaugural Address that "the preservation of the sacred fire of liberty, and the destiny of the Republican model of Government, are justly considered as *deeply*, perhaps as *finally* staked, on the experiment entrusted to the hands of the American people."[12] These are not statements of individuals who limited themselves to small, easily achievable goals.

Because they saw themselves as playing for history's highest stakes, the founders were thoroughly absorbed with the fate of their experiment and ever wary of anything that might dampen its chances of success. Their eventual disillusionment with America's constitutional order was especially profound precisely because of the transcendent importance that they attached to it. This disillusionment eventually ran so deep that their complaints and laments can seem overwrought— even hysterical—to modern readers.

As partisanship began to arise within his cabinet and around the nation in the early 1790s, Washington bemoaned the "internal dissentions" that were "harrowing & tearing our vitals" and making it "difficult, if not impracticable, to manage the Reins of Government or to keep the parts of it together." Unless the partisan bickering abated, he warned Jefferson, the republic "must, inevitably, be torn asunder— And, in my opinion the fairest prospect of happiness & prosperity that ever was presented to man, will be lost—perhaps for ever!"[13] When the partisanship did not abate—on the contrary, it grew continually worse—Washington's outlook became ever more bleak. During his retirement he grew convinced that "party feuds have arisen to such a height, as to . . . become portensious of the most serious consequences" and that they were unlikely to "end at any point short of confusion and anarchy."[14] By the end of his life, Washington was certain that the country was "moving by hasty strides to some awful crisis."[15]

Hamilton, for his part, worried from the outset that the federal government formed by the Constitution would be too feeble to survive for long. Over the course of the 1790s he devoted most of his considerable energy to bolstering the government as much as possible,

but he was never convinced that he had managed to do enough, and any remaining hopes that he may have had were dashed in 1800 when his archenemy Jefferson was elected president with a mandate to pare down its powers still further. "In vain was the collected wisdom of America convened at Philadelphia," Hamilton wailed in 1802. "In vain were the anxious labours of a Washington bestowed."[16] Though he was felled by Vice President Aaron Burr's bullet at age forty-nine, by that point Hamilton had already come to deem the Constitution a "frail and worthless fabric" and to conclude that "this American world was not made for me."[17] He died believing that "every day shews more and more the much to be regretted tendency of Governments intirely popular to dissolution and disorder."[18]

Misgivings about the virtue of the American people, and hence their fitness for republican government, suffuse Adams's correspondence from the Revolutionary War onward. As early as January 1776 he remarked that "there is So much Rascallity, so much Venality and Corruption, so much Avarice and Ambition, such a Rage for Profit and Commerce among all Ranks and Degrees of Men even in America, that I sometimes doubt whether there is public Virtue enough to support a Republic."[19] It was not long until these lingering doubts were thoroughly confirmed: his fellow citizens would not in fact put the public good ahead of their own self-interest, Adams came to believe, and so republican government could not be expected to endure for long in the United States. "Oh my Country," he exclaimed in the midst of his long retirement, "how I mourn over thy follies and Vices, thine ignorance and imbecillity, Thy contempt of Wisdom and Virtue and overweening Admiration of fools and Knaves! the never failing effects of democracy. I once thought our Constitution was quasi a mixed Government, but they have now made it, to all intents and purposes, in Virtue, Spirit and effect a democracy. We are left without resources but in our prayers and tears."[20] To his son John Quincy, he predicted that "the Selfishness of our Countrymen is not only Serious but melancholly, foreboding ravages of Ambition and Avarice which never were exceeded on this Selfish Globe ... the distemper in our Nation is so general, and so certainly incurable."[21]

For most of his life Jefferson was the most optimistic of the founders, harboring a seemingly unshakable confidence in the wisdom and

goodness of the American people, but in his final decade even he lost heart. During the Missouri crisis (1819–21) he famously proclaimed that the conflict between North and South over the expansion of slavery, "like a fire bell in the night, awakened and filled me with terror. I considered it at once as the knell of the Union. . . . I regret that I am now to die in the belief that the useless sacrifice of themselves, by the generation of '76. to acquire self government and happiness to their country, is to be thrown away by the unwise and unworthy passions of their sons, and that my only consolation is to be that I live not to weep over it."[22] Nor was this an isolated moment of anguish: the centralization of political power kept Jefferson mired in the depths of despair for the nation. Just months before he died he bemoaned "the evils which the present lowering aspect of our political horison so ominously portends." He had expected, he confessed, that "at some future day, which I hoped to be very distant, the free principles of our government might change . . . but I certainly did not expect that they would not over-live the generation which established them."[23]

Such statements can seem extravagant today, because we know how the founders' experiment turned out: the Constitution is very much still with us, and despite the frequently dysfunctional and ugly nature of its politics, the American republic has survived well into the twenty-first century. The founders did not have the advantage of hindsight, however, and the nation's first few decades provided plenty of very real causes for worry. We sometimes picture the early republic as a time when wise patriots in powdered wigs and knee breeches came together to rationally determine the country's best interests, but in fact this period was marked by an unusually high level of both acrimony and uncertainty.[24] The chaos of this era was, of course, small potatoes compared to the upheavals produced by the French Revolution, much less the bloodbaths that followed the Russian and Chinese Revolutions, but it seemed far from insignificant at the time. As Joseph Ellis rightly remarks, in the United States "the politics of the 1790s was a truly cacophonous affair. . . . In terms of shrill accusatory rhetoric, flamboyant displays of ideological intransigence, intense personal rivalries, and hyperbolic claims of imminent catastrophe, it has no equal

in American history. The political dialogue within the highest echelon of the revolutionary generation was a decade-long shouting match."[25]

One cause of all the rancor and anxiety was that there was, as of yet, little sense of stability or permanence attached to the fledgling government. Not only was republican rule assumed to be impossible in large countries, it had rarely lasted for long even in small ones and so was widely regarded as inherently fragile. Nor did the first effort at nationwide governance inspire much confidence: the Articles of Confederation had produced an utterly feckless government that had been abandoned in less than a decade.[26] Who was to say that its replacement would fare any better? It was yet to be seen whether a national authority could command the loyalty of the diverse American populace and corral the actions of thirteen hitherto-sovereign state governments that remained jealous of their own powers. The Constitution had barely survived vicious ratifying fights in some of the biggest and most important states (Virginia, Massachusetts, and New York) and was still opposed by many influential figures.[27] Moreover, the document was deliberately but disconcertingly ambiguous on a number of key points, particularly with regard to federal-state relations and the separation of powers; its ratification did not so much settle the country's political disputes as provide a new arena in which to fight them. There were few precedents or fixed poles to guide the nation's lawmakers, administrators, and judges as they set out to implement the new system, and the very fate of republican liberty seemed to them to hinge on their every decision. No wonder a sense of crisis pervaded the era, and no wonder the founders' correspondence was littered with predictions of imminent collapse.

It took almost no time at all for American politics to become far more fractious—indeed, far more nasty—than the framers could have imagined. Bitter sectional and partisan antagonisms emerged by the end of Washington's first term as president, and they reached a rolling boil by the end of his second. The two main parties saw and treated each other not just as opponents who advocated the wrong policies, but rather as enemies of the Constitution who actively sought to subvert the basic principles of the Revolution: the Republicans regarded the Federalists as monarchists and tools of the British crown, while the Federalists regarded the Republicans as Jacobins bent on

instituting mob rule. Their newspaper polemics included "some of the ripest vituperation in American literary history," in the words of one scholar.[28] Cries of treason entered virtually every political debate, fears of foreign plots abounded, and physical violence was lamentably commonplace.

A low point was reached in 1798, in the midst of the "Quasi-War" with France, when the governing Federalists used their power to clamp down on dissent through the Alien and Sedition Acts, while the Republicans responded with implicit threats of secession in the Virginia and Kentucky Resolutions. Members of Congress brawled on the floor of the House of Representatives with canes and fire pokers, and the violent mobs roaming the streets of Philadelphia induced President Adams to smuggle arms into the executive mansion as a precautionary measure. At this point the country seemed to many to be on the verge of civil war. By 1800 the British foreign secretary was confidently predicting that the "whole system of the American Government" was, as the British had always expected, "tottering to its foundations."[29]

Nor did the acrimony dissipate entirely in the early decades of the nineteenth century, when the Republicans' ascendancy led to an era of something close to one-party rule. On the contrary, the specter of disunion and civil war haunted the entire period. When reading the history of these years it sometimes seems as if every major political event—whether it was Hamilton's financial program (1790–91), the Whiskey Rebellion (1794), the Jay Treaty (1795), the prospect of anyone other than Washington becoming president (1796), the Alien and Sedition Acts (1798), the army buildup associated with the Quasi-War (1798–1800), Jefferson's election (1800), the Louisiana Purchase (1803), the Embargo Act (1807), the War of 1812 (which lasted until 1815), the Missouri crisis (1819–21), the contested 1824 presidential election, or the nullification crisis (1832–33)—caused one group or another to threaten the breakup of the union.

These threats seemed all the more real and ominous because of the continual turmoil that prevailed in Europe during this period, which so often devolved into anarchy and terror or culminated in autocratic rule.[30] As one historian reminds us, "Of all the monarchs of important states in 1789, not one remained securely seated on his throne in 1815.

The changes had often been violent—the king of France, guillotined; the king of Sweden, shot; the czar of Russia, strangled in his bed. The crowned heads of England and Portugal had lost their reason; the ruler of the Sicilies had lost his throne. Republics had fared no better— Venice, Switzerland, the Low Countries, all subverted or subdued."[31] The United States enjoyed no automatic immunity from such a fate, particularly in its young, fragile, and fractious condition.

America's prospects seemed so doubtful to the founders during the nation's early years because, in fact, they were.

WASHINGTON

CHAPTER I

THE DEMON OF PARTY SPIRIT

FOR AN OBSERVER looking back on it, the level of trust, respect, and indeed veneration that the founding generation accorded to George Washington is startling.[1] No American has enjoyed greater or more enduring prestige during his lifetime. To his contemporaries Washington's preeminence seemed self-evident. Elections were little more than formalities when he was involved. In 1775 he was the unanimous choice of the Continental Congress to command the Continental Army; in 1787 he was the unanimous choice of the Constitutional Convention to preside over its deliberations; and in both 1789 and 1792 he was the unanimous choice of the presidential electors to occupy the new nation's highest office. For the first decade and a half of the country's independence, the greatest figures in an age full of great figures almost instinctively submitted their wills to his.[2] It was no exaggeration to say that he was "first in war, first in peace, and first in the hearts of his countrymen."[3] Without Washington's unifying presence, it seems exceedingly improbable that the states could have remained sufficiently united to win the war for independence, that the Constitution could have received sufficient support to reach the threshold for ratification, or that the new government could have weathered the trials and tribulations of its early years. He was the one truly indispensable figure of the founding era.

As "The Father of His Country," Washington's foremost wish for his progeny was that it remain free of political parties and partisanship.[4] All the founders at least professed an aversion to factions, as they were frequently called—this was a stock theme of eighteenth-century political discourse—but none loathed them more fiercely, consistently, and sincerely than he did. As Washington saw it, partisans

are necessarily *partial*, meaning that they favor the interests of a parochial group over the public good. Whether that parochial group was centered on a geographic region, a socioeconomic class, a profession, a culture, an ideology, a religious sect, or some combination thereof was immaterial: any form of favoritism was incompatible with the kind of disinterested virtue that Washington prized above all else. Partisans could not be true patriots. Parties were also, in his view, fatal to republican government. By sowing conflict, they divided the community and subverted public order; by opposing the government's actions, they prevented its effective administration; by favoring some over others, they opened the door to political corruption and foreign influence. From the beginning of the Revolution to the end of his life, Washington counseled anyone who would listen that factions were the gravest threat that the young nation faced. "If we mean to support the Liberty and Independence which it has cost us so much blood & treasure to establish," he warned just a year into his presidency, "we must drive far away the demon of party spirit."[5]

To be sure, Washington was not entirely blind to the inevitability of dissent. "To expect that all men should think alike upon political, more than on Religious, or other subjects," he admitted, "would be to look for a change in the order of nature."[6] Nor did he believe that it was always wrong for like-minded individuals to band together to further specific ends. But he expected that such alliances would be temporary; when their chosen end was achieved, they would naturally disband and assimilate back into the body politic. The idea of a standing opposition party whose entire purpose was to challenge and resist the administration's measures filled him with disgust.

If this sounds impossibly naïve, we should recall that the Constitution itself not only makes no mention of political parties, but was devised under the assumption that they would never emerge. (The Twelfth Amendment, ratified in 1804, implicitly recognized the existence of parties for the first time by stipulating that candidates for president and vice president would be listed and voted for separately, thereby making it more likely that they would hail from the same party—as well as preventing an electoral tie of the kind that occurred in 1800 between Thomas Jefferson and Aaron Burr.) Moreover, two aspects of Washington's past made him more prone than most to

believe in the possibility and necessity of transcending partisanship. First, his political coming-of-age occurred in 1750s and 1760s Virginia, which was one of the least faction-ridden times and places in colonial America. Second, and even more importantly, his experience commanding the Continental Army during the Revolutionary War convinced him that unity was an essential precondition for any grand undertaking—whether it be winning independence or launching a new government.[7]

As president, then, Washington sought above all to play a unifying role, both within his administration and on behalf of the country as a whole. He did not expect or even desire immediate unanimity within his cabinet, but he did assume that he and his advisors could reason impartially together, and thereby reach a consensus, on any given issue. When that proved impossible with regard to certain controversial topics, he endeavored to do the impartial reasoning himself by gathering facts and opinions from all sides—either in person or via written reports—and mediating among them. Vice President John Adams, for one, thought that Washington generally succeeded in this regard, attesting that "he seeks information from all quarters and judges more independently than any man I ever knew."[8] Washington also continually sought ways to encourage the public to follow his own evenhanded and open-minded example. In virtually every action that he took and every policy that he supported—whether it was declaring neutrality in the war between Britain and revolutionary France or promoting the idea of a national university—he did so with an eye toward whether it would diminish the incipient divisions among the American people. The baleful effects of party spirit was one of the foremost themes of his public pronouncements, from his First Inaugural Address to his Farewell Address.

Washington did manage to keep the country intact during its treacherous first eight years, which is perhaps more than any other individual could have achieved in the same role, but in the end he failed utterly to keep partisanship at bay. The parties that emerged in the 1790s—the Federalists and Republicans—were not quite like modern political parties, with their formal mechanisms for selecting candidates, devising platforms, raising money, and waging campaigns, but they were nonetheless recognizable ideological groupings that

fought each other with a venom that would make some of the most ardent partisans of today blush. Indeed, the 1790s has been described as "the most fervently partisan decade in American history."[9] The two sides were led by a pair of bitter enemies within Washington's own cabinet, Secretary of the Treasury Alexander Hamilton and Secretary of State Thomas Jefferson. Historians still debate whether Washington himself was actually a president "above party," as he sought to be, or whether he was in fact a partisan Federalist in all but name.[10] The fairest conclusion seems to be that he managed to stay largely above the partisan fray for a number of years, but that by the end of his second term he did indeed drift into the Federalist camp.

To this day Americans are more likely than the citizens of almost any other democracy to echo Washington's fears and aspirations on this score—to denounce the very idea of political parties and to demand that their politicians rise above mere partisanship. On the other hand, political scientists are quick to point out that parties serve a number of crucial roles in democratic politics: they aggregate and articulate interests, channel politicians' ambitions, provide an organized locus for dissent, mobilize supporters, structure voters' choices, and provide collective accountability to those voters. In fact, it is now widely believed that "democracy is unthinkable save in terms of parties."[11] For our purposes, however, it matters little whether Washington's ideal of nonpartisan, disinterested politics was a noble aspiration or a naïve pipe dream. Either way, it was one of his fondest hopes for his country, and its disappointment cut him to the core. By the end of his life, we will see, Washington regarded both the government and the citizens of the United States as irretrievably partisan. In his own view, then, his political career represented something like the reverse of his military career: in politics he won most of the battles—the elections, the policy disputes—only to lose the broader war.

Throughout the early-to-mid-1780s, when the Articles of Confederation were in effect, Washington was in an almost continual state of alarm about the nation's future. He was no longer in the habit of making public pronouncements, having returned to his farm and his plow after the war like a modern-day Cincinnatus, but the correspon-

dence that poured forth from Mount Vernon made it crystal clear that he regarded the Confederation Congress as woefully inadequate to meet the needs of a dynamic, growing country.[12] Only a stronger, more effective national government could bring America back from "the brink of a precipice" and save it from plunging into "inextricable ruin," he emphasized time and again.[13] He was accordingly one of the prime movers, along with Alexander Hamilton and James Madison, in calling for the convention in Philadelphia in 1787. Washington's exertions were all behind the scenes, as it were, but the mere knowledge that he planned to attend the gathering conferred on it a sense of legitimacy that it would not otherwise have had.

Having (inevitably) been chosen to preside over the convention, Washington participated very little in its deliberations, which suited the laconic general just fine. He found the delegates' perpetual bickering and intransigence rather trying, however. In the middle of the summer he wrote to Hamilton (who had returned to New York for a time), "I *almost* dispair of seeing a favourable issue to the proceedings of the Convention, and do therefore repent having had any agency in the business."[14] A number of the compromises that the delegates forged left Washington dissatisfied, above all the Connecticut Compromise, according to which representation in the House of Representatives would be based on population while each state would be represented equally in the Senate. Like the other Virginia delegates, he regarded the latter half of the bargain as an ill-advised concession to the small states that would severely weaken the national character of the new government.[15]

Washington's attitude toward the Constitution at the close of the convention is difficult to discern, as there is little record to go by. James Madison later recalled that "no member of the Convention appeared to sign the Instrument with more cordiality than he did," and there was never any doubt that Washington supported ratification, given that the alternative—continuing to muddle through under the Articles of Confederation—was, to him, unthinkable.[16] On the other hand, Abraham Baldwin, a delegate from Georgia, reported that Washington told him on a morning stroll around this time that "he did not expect the constitution would exist more than 20 years."[17]

Washington's letters over the ensuing months reflect a similar ambivalence. A week after the convention's close he forwarded a copy of the

proposed charter to several leading Virginia politicians, commenting, "I wish the Constitution which is offered had been made more perfect, but I sincerely believe it is the best that could be obtained at this time."[18] Given that it would always be possible to amend the document in the future if needed, he told one of his aides-de-camp from the war years, "I think it would be wise in the People to adopt what is offered to them."[19] To the Marquis de Lafayette—whom he regarded almost as an adopted son—Washington enthused that "it appears to me ... little short of a miracle, that the Delegates from so many different States (which States you know are also different from each other in their manners, circumstances and prejudices) should unite in forming a system of national Government, so little liable to well founded objections." Yet he still felt compelled to stipulate that he was not "such an enthusiastic, partial or undiscriminating admirer of it, as not to prerceive it is tinctured with some real (though not radical) defects."[20]

Though Washington's correspondence made clear where he stood on the question of ratification, he never said a word in public on behalf of the Constitution during the state ratification debates. Having presided over the convention, he believed that it was his duty to at least formally continue playing the role of neutral arbiter. He may have also worried that speaking out in favor of the Constitution might smack of self-promotion, since his election as the nation's first president, in the event that the new government in fact materialized, was certain.[21] Still, the common knowledge that he supported ratification, and the assumption that he would abandon his retirement if called on by the nation to do so, were key factors in the debates. When the Constitution squeaked through the Virginia ratifying convention in the face of intense opposition from Patrick Henry and others, James Monroe wrote to Thomas Jefferson in France, "be assured [Washington's] influence carried this government."[22]

Washington was pleased by the Constitution's ratification, as well as by the fact that supporters of the new charter won an overwhelming majority in the initial congressional elections. He reported happily to Lafayette that "federal sentiments seem to be growing with uncommon rapidity. . . . This encreasing unanimity is not less indicative of the good disposition than the good sense of the Americans," adding, "I think, I see a *path*, as clear and direct as a ray of light" leading to the

nation's "permanent felicity."[23] Yet Washington was also filled with a sense of foreboding. Partly this was because he was genuinely reluctant to reenter the public arena. When he had resigned his commission as commander of the Continental Army in 1783 he had assumed—and indeed pledged to the world—that he would be retiring for good. Now he felt that he was past his prime and was being forced to go back on his word and risk his cherished reputation, all to "quit a peaceful abode for an Ocean of difficulties." He told Henry Knox—who had taken over command of the army upon Washington's resignation, and who would soon become his secretary of war—that "my movements to the chair of Government will be accompanied with feelings not unlike those of a culprit who is going to the place of his execution."[24] Washington knew that he had little real choice in the matter, as the country needed his presence and leadership, but he hoped to sit at the head of the government for as short a time as possible—ideally less than a full four-year term.

Washington's sense of foreboding was redoubled by the daunting prospect that awaited him upon his inauguration in April 1789.[25] The new government had to be developed almost from scratch, with only the fuzziest blueprint to guide the newly elected officeholders. A bill of rights needed to be added to the Constitution to placate its opponents. Commerce was lagging, and the nation and many of the states faced crushing debts. The western frontier was far from secure, and the peace with Britain remained precarious. Moreover, the young republic initially encompassed only eleven somewhat disjointed states, as North Carolina and Rhode Island had yet to ratify the Constitution— nor was it entirely clear when, or even if, they would. (North Carolina ultimately ratified that November, while Rhode Island held out until May of the following year.) Washington hinted at his greatest fear of all in his Inaugural Address: that "local prejudices" or "party animosities" would "misdirect the comprehensive and equal eye which ought to watch over this great Assemblage of communities and interests"— that is, the newly reconstituted American republic.[26]

Given the many challenges that it faced, America's constitutional experiment got off to a surprisingly promising start, from Washington's

perspective: the first few years of his first term went remarkably smoothly.[27] As Congress set about creating the various executive departments and approving what would become the Bill of Rights in its initial session in the summer of 1789, all was tranquil enough in New York—the temporary capital—for Washington to occupy himself mostly with questions of presidential etiquette: Should he throw parties? Make or receive visits? How often, in what style, and under what circumstances? He also settled on an exceptional group to form his small cabinet, including Henry Knox at the War Department, Alexander Hamilton at Treasury, Thomas Jefferson at State, and Edmund Randolph as the attorney general.[28] (Jefferson was still serving as minister to France at the time but eventually took up his post in March 1790.) Washington's closest advisor during these early days, however, was the leading figure of the new House of Representatives, James Madison—the separation of powers be damned.[29] Washington could not know that the seeds of future discord lay hidden within this group of luminaries, for they remained mostly dormant for the first year or two. Indeed, in June 1790 he informed Lafayette that "I feel myself supported by able Co-adjutors, who harmonise extremely well together."[30]

As far as Washington was concerned, then, the new government's first year was a marked success. As he embarked on a tour of the northern states—all but recalcitrant Rhode Island—in October 1789 he informed Gouverneur Morris, who had gone to France on business, that "the national government is organized, and as far as my information goes, to the satisfaction of all parties. . . . Opposition to it is either no more, or hides its head."[31] Back in New York in January, he added to the English historian Catharine Macaulay Graham that "so far as we have gone with the new Government (and it is completely organized and in operation) we have had greater reason than the most sanguine could expect to be satisfied with its success."[32]

That same month Hamilton submitted to Congress the first major component of his financial program, the Report on Public Credit, which produced the earliest hints of serious division within Washington's circle of close advisors. Hamilton proposed, among other things, that the federal government should assume and fund all outstanding

government debts—both national and state—at full value, but Madison balked at the idea of repaying all debt holders equally. Many of the government-issued certificates, after all, were no longer in the hands of the deserving soldiers who had initially earned them, since they had been snapped up at deep discounts by speculators hoping to turn a profit. Conflict also emerged over the as-yet-undetermined site of the new, permanent national capital: most northerners backed Philadelphia or New York, while most southerners preferred a location on the Potomac River. Washington found that during Congress's second session "the questions of assumption—Residence—and other matters have been agitated with a warmth & intemperence; with prolixity & threats; which it is to be feared has lessened the dignity of that body, & decreased that respect which was once entertained for it." Such "jealousies & distrusts," he feared, would "have a most unhappy tendency to injure our public affairs—which, if wisely conducted might make us (as we are now by Europeans thought to be) the happiest people upon Earth."[33]

The two main sources of discord were, however, resolved in a grand bargain whose basic outlines were worked out during a now-famous dinner at Jefferson's house in June: Madison would allow the assumption bill to pass in the House in exchange for Hamilton's support for a capital on the Potomac.[34] The Compromise of 1790, as it is often called, delighted Washington, not just because he was a firm supporter of both sides of the deal—the full funding of government debts and the erection of a national capital conveniently near Mount Vernon—but also because it seemed to promise a reduction in the nascent divisions that so alarmed him. "The two great questions of funding the debt & fixing the seat of the government have been agitated, as was natural, with a good deal of warmth as well as ability," he wrote that August. "These were always considered by me as questions of the most delicate & interesting nature which could possibly be drawn into discussion. They were in more danger of having convulsed the government itself than any other points. I hope they are now settled in as satisfactory a manner as could have been expected; and that we have a prospect of enjoying peace abroad, with tranquility at home."[35] Washington's vision of amicable, disinterested politics seemed realizable once again.

Moreover, Hamilton's assumption bill soon helped to stabilize the nation's public credit, and with it the government itself. Washington told Thomas Paine, who was then in London, that "our new government answers its purposes as well as could have been reasonably expected. . . . We are gradually overcoming the difficulties which presented themselves in its first organization, and . . . our prospects in general are growing daily more favorable."[36]

Just as the national capital moved to Philadelphia in December 1790—its second temporary site, where it would remain for a decade as Washington, DC, was being built—Hamilton issued the second of his great reports, this one proposing the establishment of a national bank. This proposal elicited even more strident opposition than the first one had, with Madison and Jefferson contesting it on constitutional as well as prudential grounds. Madison argued in the House, and Jefferson contended within the cabinet, that Congress did not have the authority to establish a bank, but Hamilton convinced Washington otherwise in a classic brief for an expansive reading of the Constitution. Yet even after this somewhat rancorous exchange Washington felt mostly heartened by Congress's third session. At the close of the session he commented that "especially on the subject of the Bank, the line between the southern and eastern interest appeared more strongly marked than could have been wished. . . . But the debates were conducted with temper and candor." Moreover, he went on, "our public credit is restored—our resources are increasing—and the general appearance of things at least equals the most sanguine expectation that was formed of the effects of the present government."[37]

Washington then embarked on a tour of the South, and his warm reception throughout the country further convinced him that all was well and that the future was bright. His letters from the summer of 1791 positively radiate with confidence. "The United States enjoy a scene of prosperity and tranquillity under the new government that could hardly have been hoped for under the old," he told Catharine Macaulay Graham.[38] The next day he added to his friend David Humphreys that "each days experience of the Government of the United States seems to confirm its establishment, and to render it more popular."[39] To Lafayette he predicted that "the attachment of all Classes of citizens to the general Government seems to be a pleasing presage

of their future happiness and respectability."[40] And he rhapsodized to the French diplomat the Chevalier de la Luzerne that "it appears that the United States are making great progress towards national happiness, and if it is not attained here in as high a degree as human nature will admit of its going—I think we may then conclude that political happiness is unattainable."[41] Washington would not retain this unclouded optimism for long.

———————◆———————

Washington's long-term disillusionment began to set in during the election year of 1792. The prior autumn Jefferson and Madison had, unbeknownst to Washington, started taking steps to organize opposition to the Hamilton-led Federalist program.[42] Their most consequential move was to reach out to Philip Freneau, a college classmate of Madison's and a fiery journalist. Jefferson offered Freneau a sinecure as a translator in the State Department, and they gently suggested that he might also wish to start a national newspaper. Jefferson and Madison rightly regarded the leading periodical of the time, John Fenno's *Gazette of the United States*, as a staunchly pro-Hamiltonian outlet—it received a sizable chunk of its advertising directly from the Treasury Department—and they hoped to counter its effects on public opinion with more critical commentary.

Freneau launched the *National Gazette* in October 1791, and within a few months it emerged as a fawning admirer of Jefferson and a vicious critic of Hamilton. Freneau was unrelenting in his attack: every aspect of Hamilton's financial program was depicted as a deliberate ploy to fleece everyday Americans and further enrich greedy merchants, as well as a dangerous power grab on behalf of the federal government that would inevitably pave the road toward monarchy. It is difficult to see the covert initiation and ongoing subsidizing of a virulently anti-administration newspaper as anything other than an act of gross disloyalty on the part of Madison, who remained one of Washington's close advisors, and especially Jefferson, who was an integral member of his cabinet. Certainly Washington would have seen it that way, had he known about their actions.

Freneau was soon joined in his onslaught by Benjamin Franklin Bache, also known as "Lightning Rod Junior," a nod to his celebrated

grandfather. Bache's *General Advertiser* (later renamed the *Aurora*) was, if anything, even more vehement than the *National Gazette* in its criticism of Hamilton and his sins against republicanism. Together these periodicals helped to galvanize the opposition to the Federalist program and unite it around a common creed. In response, the pro-administration papers grew ever more strident and colorful in their denunciations of the emerging Republican party. The result was an increasing spiral of invective, scandalmongering, and bald-faced lies that makes much of today's "fake news" appear rather tame by comparison. As Gordon Wood comments, "the partisan newspapers were truly scandalous. Indeed, never in American history has the press been more vitriolic and more scurrilous than it was in the 1790s."[43] By the fall of 1792, with congressional and presidential elections looming on the horizon, the latent divide among Washington's advisors had broken out into the open.

It was against this backdrop of increasingly visible and bitter partisanship that Washington pondered his own future. He had initially hoped to relinquish the presidency before serving even a full four-year term, but the pull of events had prevented him from doing so. Now as he felt himself growing old (he had just turned sixty), increasingly hard of hearing, and weary of the fatigues of office, Mount Vernon beckoned all the more. There was no question, of course, that he would win reelection in a landslide if he were willing to serve another four years, but he desperately hoped that he would be able to avoid doing so.

In the early months of 1792, Washington told his coterie of advisors—Hamilton, Jefferson, Knox, Madison, and Randolph—that he planned to step down at the end of the present term. Their immediate and unanimous response was that he could not. Hamilton and Jefferson agreed on little else, but they spoke with one voice in insisting that the country needed Washington's unifying presence now more than ever. Hamilton stressed that Washington's departure would be "deplored as the greatest evil, that could befall the country at the present juncture," and Jefferson memorably declared that "North & South will hang together, if they have you to hang on."[44] At least initially, Washington remained unconvinced. In May he asked Madison to help him prepare a valedictory address informing the people of his intention to retire. He wanted the address to stress in particular that

"we are *all* the Children of the same country" and that "our interest, however deversified in local & smaller matters, is the same in all the great & essential concerns of the Nation."[45]

As the summer progressed, however, Washington's stance began to soften. He asked his private secretary, Tobias Lear, who was traveling through New England, to assess the mood there about whether he ought to serve a second term, and Lear replied that the public preference remained beyond doubt: "no other person seems ever to have been contemplated for that office."[46] Washington was even more moved, however, by the palpable growth in party spirit within his cabinet and around the nation. A small part of him longed to quit his post in disgust, but his sense of duty was ultimately too strong: deep down he knew, as his advisors had been telling him all along, that the fragile equilibrium within the still-new government would be impossible to maintain without him to manage the helm. Given how badly he wanted to return to Mount Vernon, the fact that Washington eventually consented to serve a second term is a testament to the depth and immediacy of his fears.

In late August, Washington sent long, heartfelt, and very similar letters to Jefferson, Hamilton, and Randolph, begging them to adopt a more conciliatory spirit and stressing that nothing less than the fate of the nation was at stake. To Jefferson he bemoaned the "internal dissentions" that were "harrowing & tearing our vitals," calling them "serious," "alarming," and "afflicting." "Without more charity for the opinions & acts of one another in Governmental matters," he insisted, "it will be difficult, if not impracticable, to manage the Reins of Government or to keep the parts of it together: for if, instead of laying our shoulders to the machine after measures are decided on, one pulls this way & another that, before the utility of the thing is fairly tried, it must, inevitably, be torn asunder—And, in my opinion the fairest prospect of happiness & prosperity that ever was presented to man, will be lost—perhaps for ever!"[47] To Hamilton he expressed his hope that "liberal allowances will be made for the political opinions of one another; and instead of those wounding suspicions, and irritating charges with which some of our Gazettes are so strongly impregnated . . . there might be mutual forbearances and temporising yieldings *on all sides*. Without these I do not see how the Reins of

Government are to be managed, or how the Union of the States can be much longer preserved ... Melancholy thought!"[48] To Randolph he complained that the "attacks upon almost every measure of government with which some of the Gazettes are so strongly impregnated" were in danger of "rending the Union asunder. The Seeds of discontent—distrust & irritations which are so plentifully sown—can scarcely fail to produce this effect and to Mar that prospect of happiness which perhaps never beamed with more effulgence upon any people under the Sun."[49]

The shrill replies that Washington received from Hamilton and Jefferson could have only deepened his anxiety. They both expressed regret about Washington's apprehensions but then quickly moved on to insist that *they* were the more injured party, to lay out a list of grievances, and to suggest that changes might have to be made to the cabinet soon. "I *know* that I have been an object of uniform opposition from Mr. Jefferson, from the first moment of his coming to the City of New York to enter upon his present office," Hamilton complained. "I *know*, from the most authentic sources, that I have been the frequent subject of the most unkind whispers and insinuating from the same quarter. I have long seen a formed party in the Legislature, under his auspices, bent upon my subversion."[50] Jefferson, for his part, protested that "I will not suffer my retirement to be clouded by the slanders of a man whose history, from the moment at which history can stoop to notice him, is a tissue of machinations against the liberty of the country which has not only recieved and given him bread, but heaped it's honors on his head."[51] So much for cooperation, or indeed civility.

By not withdrawing his name from consideration, Washington implicitly consented to serve another term, and he was duly reelected on a unanimous vote in November 1792. At this point he was astonished by the level of rancor between his two brilliant lieutenants and worried that the republic itself was at risk, but far worse was yet to come.

CHAPTER 2

FAREWELL TO ALL THAT

T HE PARTISAN DIVIDE that emerged during Washington's first term grew ever deeper during his second. As we have seen, the first fissures within the highest echelons of American politics appeared even before Jefferson's return from France, when Madison opposed aspects of Hamilton's Report on Public Credit, but it was the Jefferson-Hamilton rivalry that widened these fissures into an unbridgeable chasm. Jefferson and Hamilton had never met before they took up their posts as the highest-ranking officials in Washington's administration, but the mutual hatred between them quickly grew both deep-seated and distinctly personal. The personality clash was an unusual one in many respects. Hamilton was (and is) often regarded as a champion of the economic elite while Jefferson self-consciously cast himself as the apostle of humble farmers, yet Jefferson was a rich, well-connected slaveholder who looked down on Hamilton—a self-made immigrant—as a presumptuous upstart seeking to exalt himself above his proper station. Such condescension was almost perfectly calculated to infuriate the proud Hamilton, who regarded Jefferson's populism as sheer hypocrisy.

The two were, as Jefferson later recalled, "daily pitted in the cabinet like two cocks."[1] Neither was able to gain reliable ascendancy over the other, as Henry Knox typically supported Hamilton's positions and policies while Edmund Randolph usually (though not always) sided with Jefferson. The even split among his advisors both enabled and required Washington to mediate between the two sides himself. By the time Jefferson left the State Department on December 31, 1793, he and Hamilton could hardly stand to be in the same room. The fact that Washington managed to keep them together in the

administration for as long as he did—nearly four years—was itself a noteworthy accomplishment; one can only imagine how vitriolic the enmity between them would have grown without his steady presence at the helm.

Far more than discordant personalities were at play, however: the Hamiltonian Federalists and Jeffersonian Republicans had very different policy visions for the new government. Hamilton's expansive financial program—which included the assumption and funding of government debt, the institution of import duties and excise taxes as reliable sources of government revenue, the creation of a national bank and mint, and the promotion of manufacturing—was not just the first but also one of the most enduring flashpoints for partisan controversy. Whereas the Federalists regarded such measures as commonsense steps designed to put the government on a sound economic footing, Republicans depicted them as part of a vast conspiracy undertaken by scheming moneymen and "stockjobbers" (one of Jefferson's favorite terms) to corrupt the young nation—the serpent in America's agrarian paradise. More generally, whereas Hamilton and his followers advocated a robust exercise of federal power, especially by the executive branch, Jefferson and his devotees advocated a more limited scope for federal authority and placed greater trust in the state governments and the people's branch, Congress. Though slavery was not a paramount political issue during the 1790s, there was also a hint of fear among some Republicans—many though certainly not all of whom were southerners—that northern Federalists would eventually use a strong federal government to meddle with their single most valuable asset.

Beneath these policy disagreements lay an even deeper divide over matters of basic principle. Each party deemed itself, and itself alone, to be the true and proper guardian of the new American republic. The names adopted by the two sides offer a revealing indication of how they viewed each other. The Federalists tended to regard their opponents not just as advocates of a more limited government but rather as unreconstructed Anti-Federalists—which is to say, opponents of the Constitution and hence the government under which they were living. The Republicans, in turn, saw their opponents not just as advocates of a stronger federal government but rather as antirepublicans—which is to say, monarchists who were, as Jefferson put it, "preaching up and

panting after an English constitution of king, lords, and commons."[2] ("Monocrat" was another standard Jeffersonian epithet for his adversaries.) Put another way, each side feared catastrophic retrogression at the hands of the other: the Republicans were, in Federalist eyes, seeking to overturn the constitutional settlement of 1787–88 and thereby risk a revival of the near anarchy that the country had endured under the Articles of Confederation, while the Federalists were, in Republican eyes, seeking to overturn the revolutionary principles of 1776 and thereby reintroduce the kind of tyranny that they had endured as colonists under British rule. Mutual suspicions of treason did not exactly foster the kind of reasonable compromise that Washington hoped for and expected.

Foreign affairs too helped to inflame partisan antagonisms, particularly during Washington's second term. The conflagration that was to engulf France, and indeed much of Europe, over the course of the 1790s was set off just after Washington's inauguration in 1789. Jefferson was still in Paris at the time, and he immediately became an ardent champion of the revolutionaries' dreams of liberty, equality, and fraternity. For many years—even after the onset of the Terror—he and his fellow Republicans remained convinced that France was not just America's first but also its natural ally, a sister republic that was following in America's revolutionary footsteps. Indeed, many Republicans came to regard the French Revolution as a sort of safeguard for their domestic priorities. "I consider the establishment and success of their government as necessary to stay up our own," Jefferson wrote to George Mason in February 1791, "and to prevent it from falling back to that kind of Halfway-house, the English constitution."[3]

Hamilton and his followers, by contrast, favored Britain as the true bastion of stable, constitutional government and hence the better model for emulation. The United States and Britain shared a common language, history, and set of traditions, the Federalists often noted, and Britain was easily America's most important trading partner. Particularly as the turbulence in France grew bloodier over the course of the 1790s, many Federalists came to see the Republicans as slavishly devoted to a revolution gone badly awry, and at times even as radical Jacobins bent on setting up guillotines on America's own shores. The Republicans, in turn, regarded the Federalists' partiality for

Britain—so recently America's oppressor and adversary—as evidence of their longing to reinstitute hereditary rule. ("Anglomen" was yet another of Jefferson's frequent sobriquets.) Though both sides desired peace for the young American republic, they were also alarmed by the prospect of victory by the wrong side in Europe's wars—and above all by what such a victory would mean at home.

All these sources of discord were intensified by the fact that almost no one at the time regarded parties as natural or even defensible features of republican politics. Parties were, again, widely seen as factions—parochial groups seeking to advance their own selfish interest at the expense of the public good. As a result, when parties in fact emerged, neither side was able or willing to recognize the legitimacy of the other. The Federalists tended to view Republicans who opposed their program not as well-intentioned fellow citizens with different views or even as rivals for power but rather as disloyal foes of the people's duly elected representatives, and hence the American government itself. Jefferson, Madison, and their followers did eventually come to accept that they had formed an opposition party, but they hoped and believed that it would be a temporary one. As soon as they rescued the American republic by removing the stockjobbing, monocratic Anglomen from power, they assumed, parties and partisanship would no longer be necessary and would naturally fade away. Few foresaw the day when two standing parties would routinely alternate in power without upending the regime. Ironically, then, the fact that almost no one believed in the legitimacy of political parties made the partisanship of the 1790s all the more bitter.

Washington had his own political principles and his own domestic and foreign policy preferences, of course, many of which leaned in a Federalist direction. Yet he categorically rejected the lurid, conspiratorial view that the two sides in America's first party war frequently took of one another: he had no fear that Jefferson and the Republicans wanted to overturn the Constitution, set up guillotines, and turn America into a tribute state of revolutionary France, any more than he feared that Hamilton and the Federalists wanted to turn him into a new King George. His real fear was that the young republic would be torn apart by factionalism, and his second term only heightened that anxiety.

Washington embarked on his second term with a sense of grim resignation.[4] The deposed Louis XVI had been beheaded on the Parisian streets in January 1793, and the French Revolution grew increasingly radicalized over the following months. Britain joined the anti-French coalition right around the time when Washington delivered his curt, four-sentence Second Inaugural Address in March. Washington immediately recognized that it would be ruinous for the United States to become embroiled in the European war. The nation was still far too weak and fragile to have much influence on the war's outcome, and its involvement would inevitably raise partisan passions to an even more intolerable pitch.

After consulting with his cabinet, Washington issued a proclamation of neutrality on April 22. This unilateral action quickly elicited howls of protest from the Republican press. In choosing neutrality over support for America's revolutionary ally, they charged, Washington had finally revealed his true, Hamiltonian—that is to say, monarchist—colors. Thus began a trend that would continue throughout the next four years: whereas the press had generally observed an unspoken moratorium on direct criticism of Washington during his first term, it declared open season on him during his second. Hurt and angry at this unexpected rebuke, Washington complained that "the publications in Freneau's and Beach's [i.e., Bache's] Papers are outrages on common decency" whose tendency "is too obvious to be mistaken by men of cool & dispassionate minds."[5] These "infamous Papers" were, he insisted, "calculated for disturbing if not absolutely intended to disturb, the peace of the community."[6]

Even greater disturbances were provoked over the course of the summer by Citizen Edmond-Charles Genêt, the new French envoy to the United States. After landing in Charleston in April, the flamboyant Genêt traveled the country, whipping up popular enthusiasm for France and recruiting American privateers to fight against the British, in flagrant violation of Washington's policy of neutrality.[7] The rapturous welcome that Genêt received sometimes bordered on outright violence. John Adams later recalled, with at least a touch of hyperbole, "the Terrorism, excited by Genet, in 1793. when ten

thousand People in the Streets of Philadelphia, day after day, threatened to drag Washington out of his House, and effect a Revolution in the Government."[8] Headstrong and indiscreet, Genêt ended up wildly overplaying his hand by threatening to appeal over Washington's head to Congress and ultimately the American people if the president would not join the revolutionary cause. When word of this affront leaked the people quickly rallied to Washington's side, and by August even Jefferson concluded that such antics were indefensible and that any further support for Genêt would only sink the Republican party along with him. The cabinet unanimously advised Washington to demand Genêt's recall. When it became clear that the newly installed Jacobins back in Paris would arrest and likely behead Genêt on his return, however, Washington magnanimously granted him asylum in the United States.

By the end of the year Jefferson decided that he had had enough. Though Washington had, as he saw it, made every effort to adjudicate between his two principal advisors in an evenhanded manner, Jefferson felt that Washington always sided with Hamilton. Convinced that his counsel was not sufficiently valued, that he was having little impact, and that he could no longer in good conscience support the administration's policies, Jefferson tendered his resignation and withdrew to Monticello. Jefferson's departure was a blow to Washington, for a host of reasons. He lost not just a capable advisor but also one of the key weights that kept the scales of the cabinet in balance. From this point forward Washington would find it increasingly difficult to remain the neutral, unbiased umpire that he always aspired to be. He also lost one of the most conspicuous public signals that his administration *was* above partisanship. Finally, while it was true that Washington would no longer have a member of his cabinet conducting guerrilla warfare from within, Jefferson would now be free to go into outright opposition as the chief inspiration, theorist, and propagandist of the Republican resistance, with Madison in the House acting as his equally adept strategist and organizer. Each successive incident and each successive year, it seemed, just fanned the flames of partisanship still further.

Washington had long worried that partisan discord would weaken popular respect for the government and the law, and the events of the summer of 1794 only augmented that concern. Hamilton's financial program included a federal excise tax on distilled spirits that proved deeply unpopular, particularly in backcountry regions where whiskey was an integral part of the local economy. (In addition to its inimitable value as an intoxicant, whiskey was far more portable and durable than corn and wheat and was sometimes even used as a medium of exchange.) In July 1794 opposition turned into violence in western Pennsylvania, where mobs attacked tax collectors, destroyed the stills of farmers who had paid their tax, and shuttered the federal courts. Some seven thousand insurgents marched on the army outpost at Pittsburgh.[9]

The Whiskey Rebellion was the most substantial display of armed resistance to the federal government until the Civil War, and it was made all the more ominous by the ideological backdrop: the rioters waved tricolor flags and set up mock guillotines to signal solidarity with the French revolutionaries and their Republican admirers. The tumult that had enveloped so much of Europe seemed to many to be poised to invade the American heartland. "What may be the consequences of such violent & outrageous proceedings is painful in a high degree even in contemplation," Washington brooded, adding that "if the Laws are to be so trampled upon—with impunity—and a minority (a small one too) is to dictate to the majority there is an end put, at one stroke, to republican government; and nothing but anarchy and confusion is to be expected thereafter."[10]

Unwilling to brook open defiance of federal authority, Washington called thirteen thousand state militia into service in August and marched them westward in September. This was a bigger force than he had ever commanded during the Revolutionary War, and it remains the only instance of a sitting American president exercising his role as commander in chief in the field. In the face of such an overwhelming display of force, the insurgency melted away without a shot being fired. Washington felt triumphant: he had managed to avoid bloodshed, a huge proportion of the citizenry had rallied to the government's side, and the federal authority had proven itself capable of acting decisively. "The spirit with which the Militia turned

out, in support of the Constitution, and the laws of our country," he wrote, had proven "that republicanism is not the phantom of a deluded imagination: on the contrary, that under no form of government, will laws be better supported—liberty and property better secured—or happiness be more effectually dispensed to mankind."[11] His old fears had not completely subsided, however: a mere two paragraphs later he remarked that "jealousies, & prejudices (from which I apprehend more fatal consequences to this government than from any other source) . . . always oppose themselves to efficient measures."[12] The opposition newspapers continued to snipe at Washington, objecting that he had deployed a massive army in peacetime to cow civilians, but his actions met with broad popular approval.

Though Washington believed that the pacification of the Whiskey Rebellion would serve to strengthen the country's republican institutions, the same cannot be said for the groups that he regarded as the ultimate source of the uprising: the Democratic Societies. These partisan, pro-Republican political clubs were reminiscent of the Sons of Liberty chapters that had proliferated in the wake of the Stamp Act in 1765, but they also resembled—Federalists were quick to point out—the Jacobin clubs of France. These societies worked on a local level to hold demonstrations, draft petitions, campaign for candidates, and aid the opposition press. They began to spring up around the country in the summer of 1793 to express support for Genêt, France, and its revolutionary armies, and there were some thirty-five of them by 1795.[13]

Washington grew almost obsessed with these groups and the danger that he thought they posed to the republic.[14] These "self-created societies," he protested time and again, not only sought to arrogate to themselves—a relatively small faction—the right to speak for the popular will but did so in direct opposition to the people's duly elected officials. Moreover, they were deliberately undermining his administration's policy of neutrality—not to mention the nation's interests—by seeking to draw the United States into war on behalf of France. Instituted in order to "sow the Seeds of Jealousy & distrust among the people, of the government, by destroying all confidence in the Administration of it," he wrote in August 1794, they would, if left to their own devices, "shake the government to its foundation."[15]

The next month he added that nothing could "be more absurd—more arrogant—or more pernicious to the peace of Society, than for selfcreated bodies, forming themselves into *permanent* Censors, & under the shade of Night in a conclave, resolving that . . . *this act* [of Congress] is unconstitutional—and *that act* is pregnant of mischief, & that all who vote contrary to their dogmas are actuated by selfish motives, or under foreign influence; nay, are pronounced traitors to their Country."[16] If these clubs "cannot be discountenanced," he worried, "they will destroy the government of this Country."[17]

Later that autumn Washington decided to take an indirect shot at the Democratic Societies in his Sixth Annual Message to Congress (the precursor of today's State of the Union). He told the assembled representatives—and beyond them, the reading public—that the Whiskey Rebellion had been "fomented by combinations of men, who, careless of consequences . . . have disseminated, from an ignorance or perversion of facts, suspicions, jealousies, and accusations of the whole Government."[18] This remark, with the weight of Washington's enormous prestige behind it, had its intended effect: almost all the Democratic Societies either receded into innocuousness or shuttered altogether by the end of the following year. Yet Washington's remark was regarded by many as an unwarranted attack on legitimate democratic dissent and a declaration of war on the Republican party itself. Madison called it "perhaps the greatest error of [Washington's] political life" and lamented that the illustrious general had lapsed into the mere head of a faction.[19]

Washington never took any official action against the Democratic Societies, believing that prosecutions would only galvanize the opposition; political trials and purges of the kind that were omnipresent in revolutionary France were both wrong and counterproductive. Still, this was one of the first instances in which Washington's fears and frustrations got the better of him. He exaggerated the threat posed by the Democratic Societies and, by taking them on in his speech, diminished his carefully crafted aura of Olympian detachment. Washington's uncharacteristic overreaction was yet another sign of just how deeply worried he was about the stability of the young republic in the face of partisan opposition.

The next major blow to national unity came from abroad, not in the form of an army but in that of a treaty. On the very day that Washington criticized the Democratic Societies in his Message to Congress—November 19, 1794—John Jay signed a treaty with Britain in an attempt to resolve a number of issues that had been left outstanding since the end of the Revolutionary War. The details of the agreement, which involved trading and shipping rights, wartime debts, the continued British occupation of forts in the Northwest Territory, and the impressment of American sailors into the Royal Navy, are somewhat arcane and need not detain us here. Though most observers at the time regarded the terms as distinctly lopsided in Britain's favor, historians have generally deemed the treaty a reasonably good bargain for the United States, if only because it postponed war between the two countries for nearly a generation at a time when America was woefully unprepared for further combat. The furor that the treaty provoked, however, would prove to be the single greatest crisis of Washington's presidency.[20]

The Jay Treaty, as it has come to be known, reached Washington in March 1795. He initially balked at some of its provisions but soon concluded that swallowing the agreement, shortcomings and all, was preferable to being cornered into fighting an unwinnable war. Knowing that the terms of the accord would provoke opposition, Washington kept them quiet until June, when the Senate reconvened to debate whether to ratify the document. The Republicans exploded in outrage when they finally read it. They had, the previous year, been dismayed that Washington agreed to negotiate at all with Britain, and they were further horrified when he chose Jay, whom they regarded as a brazen Anglophile, as an envoy; now they were livid at how much Jay had given up and how few concessions he had managed to obtain. As Jefferson, Madison, and their followers saw it, the British had never really stopped treating the United States as a colony, and the Jay Treaty came perilously close to renouncing America's independence altogether. Washington remarked that "the cry against the Treaty is like that against a mad-dog," and Jay claimed that he could

travel the entire Eastern Seaboard at night by the light of his own burning effigies.[21]

The Federalist-controlled Senate ultimately approved the treaty by a vote of twenty to ten—exactly the two-thirds majority that was required—but this calmed neither the Republicans' outrage nor Washington's anxieties. The week after the vote Washington warned Hamilton, who had stepped down as secretary of the treasury at the beginning of the year, that the "foes of order, & good government . . . are always working like bees, to distil their poison."[22] Noting that the popular opposition to the treaty was emboldening the French, Washington remarked to Edmund Randolph, who had moved from his post as attorney general to replace Jefferson as secretary of state, that "I have never, since I have been in the Administration of the government, seen a crisis . . . from which more is to be apprehended."[23]

Randolph was soon forced to resign his new position under a cloud of suspicion—he was accused of treason on behalf of France—and Washington's difficult, protracted search for a suitable replacement only redoubled his woes. In an unsuccessful bid to woo Patrick Henry to join the cabinet, Washington emphasized the gravity of the current situation: "I persuade myself, Sir, it has not escaped your observation, that a crisis is approaching, that must, if it cannot be arrested, Soon decide whether order and good Government Shall be preserved, or anarchy and confusion ensue." The "partisans of Great Britain or France" would, if their frenzy did not abate, "Create dissensions; disturb the public Tranquility; and dissolve, perhaps forever, the Cement which binds the union."[24]

Unwilling to back down, the Republicans sought to challenge the treaty with the one arm of the federal government that was then in their control: the House of Representatives. The Constitution grants the president the power to make treaties with the advice and consent of the Senate, with no mention at all of the lower chamber in this connection, but Madison and his followers were undeterred. Appealing to their control over the nation's purse, they insisted that the portions of the treaty that relied on funding for their implementation required House approval. A new milestone in the rise of partisanship was reached in March 1796 when House Republicans formally caucused

for the first time, demanding that Washington hand over a copy of the instructions that Jay had carried with him to London. Washington refused, thereby marking another first: the earliest invocation of executive privilege. Washington felt that the House Republicans' attempt to subvert the plain meaning of the Constitution had "not only brought the Constitution to the brink of a precipice, but the Peace, happiness & prosperity of the country into eminent danger."[25]

As with virtually every policy dispute that he faced, Washington won this one: the Jay Treaty went into effect, and it was duly funded by the House. It remained politically impossible to best Washington in a head-to-head confrontation. Yet the backlash against the treaty was like nothing he had experienced before. With Hamilton out of office, the Republican press turned its sights squarely on the once-untouchable president, utilizing every term of abuse that it could muster and leveling every charge that it could concoct, no matter how implausible. Washington was senile; he was a blasphemer; he was a womanizer; he had embezzled public funds; he was a tool of the British crown or desired a crown of his own; Hamilton not only controlled him behind the scenes but was also his illegitimate son; he had been a secret British agent during the Revolutionary War, and his efforts to betray the patriotic cause were foiled by Benedict Arnold beating him to the punch. Some newspapers ludicrously called for his impeachment. "If ever a Nation was debauched by a man," Benjamin Franklin Bache told his readers, "the American Nation has been debauched by Washington."[26] Washington complained to Jefferson that he had been criticized "in such exagerated, and indecent terms as could scarcely be applied to a Nero; a notorious defaulter; or even to a common pickpocket."[27]

It was not simply Washington's feelings that were hurt by all this political invective: the union itself appeared to be in danger. The Jay Treaty provoked the most serious rumblings yet of secession in the South. According to Jefferson's notes, Washington expressed alarm that there could be "a separation of the Union into Northern and Southern," in which case "he had made up his mind to remove and be of the Northern."[28] As Washington neared the end of his second term, he was closer than ever to despair at the future of the American republic.

Though many urged him to do so, Washington scarcely even considered serving a third term. Upon entering the presidency in 1789 he had intended to stay in office just long enough to allow the new government to settle into a stable trajectory, never imagining that it would take more than eight years. Some of his close associates appealed to the same motive now. "Remain with us at least while the Storm lasts," Jay pleaded, "and untill you can retire like the Sun in a calm unclouded Evening."[29] But Washington no longer believed that a clear political sky was a real—certainly not an immediate—possibility. He replied that "serious misfortunes, originating in misrepresentation ... fill my mind with much concern, and with serious anxiety. Indeed the trouble & perplexities which they occasion, added to the weight of years which have passed upon me, have worn away my mind more than my body; and renders ease and retirement indispensably necessary to both, during the short time I have to remain here."[30]

Washington was, truth be told, bewildered and aghast at what the American republic had become in the space of just seven years. "Until within the last year or two," he told Jefferson in July, "I had no conception that Parties Would, or even could go, the length I have been Witness to."[31] Two days later he added to Charles Cotesworth Pinckney—a by-then-rare southern Federalist—that "unless the virtuous, and independent men of this Country will step forward, it is not difficult to predict the consequences. Such is my decided opinion."[32]

To verify that partisanship had pervaded every arena of American political life, Washington needed only to look at his own cabinet. For his entire first term he had been advised by a stellar and balanced quartet, but now he was surrounded by mostly second-rate figures, all rock-ribbed Federalists: Timothy Pickering as secretary of state, Oliver Wolcott Jr. as secretary of the treasury, James McHenry as secretary of war, and Charles Lee as the attorney general. Jefferson had left office of his own accord, and Washington had had little choice but to accept Edmund Randolph's resignation, but he was unable to find a suitable Republican to replace either of them. Partly this was due to the difficulty of finding *anyone* who would take on these taxing posts that as yet conferred little prestige; by the end of his second term

Washington was willing to take almost whomever he could get to fill his cabinet. Yet by this point he was also reluctant to appoint anyone whose politics were too far removed from his own. Washington told Pickering that he would not "bring a man into any Office, of consequence knowingly whose political tenets are adverse to the measures which the *general* government are pursuing," remarking that "this, in my opinion, would be a sort of political Suicide."[33] Thoroughly estranged from Jefferson and Madison, Washington had unwittingly drifted toward the Federalist camp. Though he certainly would never have described himself as a partisan, his ideal of disinterested leadership was becoming increasingly difficult to realize.

By the end of his second term, then, Washington presided over a republic that was so deeply divided that even he could not straddle the chasm that separated the two sides. The objective of national unity now seemed utterly hopeless. Somber, bitter, at times even despondent, Washington was only too eager to say farewell to the presidency, and to politics.

CHAPTER 3

SET UP A
BROOMSTICK

WASHINGTON'S FAMOUS FAREWELL ADDRESS is often read as a warning about potential dangers that he feared the country might someday face, but it was just as much a lament about ills that he was sure had already beset it.[1] Back in 1792, when he was contemplating retiring at the end of his first term, Washington had asked Madison for help preparing a valedictory address; this time, he turned to Hamilton. In May 1796 Washington sent Hamilton the draft that Madison had composed four years earlier, along with his own thoughts about how it could be amended and augmented to fit the current political climate. Hamilton responded with two options: an edited synthesis of Madison's and Washington's drafts and an entirely new composition that drew broadly on Washington's outline as well as advice from John Jay.[2] Washington preferred the latter version, which he painstakingly reworked to hit the right tone and points of emphasis.[3]

The resulting tract was not delivered as a speech, but instead published in the *American Daily Advertiser* of Philadelphia on September 19, after which it—and the stunning news of Washington's imminent retirement—quickly swept the nation. Though many of the words of the Farewell Address are Hamilton's, the message is pure Washington. This was not just the longest exposition that he ever published, but also the one to which he devoted the most care and energy—the self-conscious capstone to his public life. As the considered legacy of the greatest of the founders, the Farewell Address is justly regarded as a classic of American political thought, ranking alongside the *Federalist* essays and Abraham Lincoln's great speeches and behind only the Declaration of Independence and the Constitution themselves.

Beyond the stately cadences and the aura of hard-won wisdom that pervade the address, the most striking thing about it is the form that it took: a rumination on the threats to the American experiment in self-government—"the disinterested warnings of a parting friend," as Washington put it.[4] He could just as easily have marked his exit with a sort of victory lap celebrating all that had been accomplished under his auspices. The new government was up and running and had attained a widespread sense of popular legitimacy; the Bill of Rights had been added to the Constitution; five new states had been added to the union (North Carolina, Rhode Island, Vermont, Kentucky, and Tennessee); the nation's disastrous finances had been put in order, and its prosperity was reaching unprecedented heights; the country had managed to avoid involvement in Europe's wars while maintaining its honor; overwhelmingly popular treaties with Spain and with a coalition of American Indian tribes in the Northwest Territory (both in 1795) had procured Americans free navigation on the Mississippi River and helped to secure the western frontier. Especially given the daunting challenges that the young republic had faced, it is at least arguable that even to this day no president has accomplished more.

Yet such was Washington's mindset at the end of his second term that he chose to take his leave with a warning about the forces that might doom the republic—forces that were manifest all around him. Up to this point Washington had mostly confined his concerns about America's future to private letters and conversations; as president it behooved him to put as good a face on the country's prospects as possible, so his public addresses had remained relatively upbeat. Now he broadcast his worries for all to see.[5]

Predictably, the great theme of the Farewell Address was the dangers of factionalism in its various guises: political parties, geographic divisions, and the ways in which foreign entanglements exacerbated both. Without a unified populace, Washington admonished his fellow citizens, neither the Constitution nor the union of the states could last. And if the republic were to be torn asunder, the peace, freedom, and prosperity that America had enjoyed for the last seven years would surely vanish along with it. Washington made it clear from the outset that this would be his central message. In his initial draft of the address—the one that included Madison's 1792 version along with

some updates—he disclosed the "most ardent wishes of my heart," the first of which was "that party disputes, among all the friends and lovers of their country may subside, or, as the wisdom of Providence hath ordained that men, on the same subjects, shall not always think alike, that charity & benevolence when they happen to differ may so far shed their benign influence as to banish those invectives which proceed from illiberal prejudices and jealousy."[6] His most heartfelt wish, that is to say, was that the very nature of American politics would change in a fundamental way.

The final version of the address chronicled the problem in much greater detail. Beginning with the perils of sectional antagonisms, Washington counseled his compatriots that the "national Union" is "the Palladium of your political safety and prosperity" and that "the name of AMERICAN, which belongs to you, in your national capacity, must always exalt the just pride of Patriotism, more than any appellation derived from local discriminations." All parts of the country—North and South, East and West—had the same broad interests, but that had not prevented "designing men" from seeking "to excite a belief that there is a real difference of local interests and views." "You cannot shield yourselves too much against the jealousies and heart burnings which spring from these misrepresentations," Washington insisted, for "they tend to render alien to each other those who ought to be bound together by fraternal affection."[7] At least since the Revolutionary War his outlook had been resolutely continental, and he was obviously disturbed that not everyone shared his expansive vision.

Washington reserved his harshest language and his most solemn warnings, however, for political parties themselves. Acknowledging that "the spirit of party . . . is inseparable from our nature, having its root in the strongest passions of the human mind," he nevertheless emphasized that in popular governments this spirit "is seen in its greatest rankness and is truly their worst enemy." His catalog of the evils of partisanship is relentless: parties "distract the Public Councils and enfeeble the Public Administration"; they agitate the community with "ill founded jealousies and false alarms" and occasionally even foment "riot and insurrection"; they open the door to "foreign influence and corruption"; actuated by "the spirit of revenge," they perpetrate "the most horrid enormities" against one another; they serve

as "potent engines, by which cunning, ambitious and unprincipled men . . . subvert the power of the people" by replacing the national interest with their own narrow agendas. These warnings were all, of course, inspired by problems that Washington's own administration had faced, from the rise of the increasingly vicious partisan press to the Whiskey Rebellion and the Democratic Societies to the various intrigues promoted by, and on behalf of, Britain and France. Responding directly to the contention that "parties in free countries are useful checks upon the administration of the Government, and serve to keep alive the spirit of Liberty," Washington responded that "within certain limits" this "is probably true," but that the spirit of party should still be discouraged since "there will always be enough of that spirit for every salutary purpose." The fires of partisanship cannot be altogether quenched, so "it demands a uniform vigilance to prevent its bursting into a flame, lest, instead of warming it should consume."[8]

The section of the address that is perhaps best known today, Washington's caution against permanent alliances with foreign nations, was itself part and parcel of his broader warning about the ills of factionalism. He treated foreign affairs largely as a domestic problem, as he believed that political, ideological, and emotional attachments to foreign nations would—and had—fostered the geographical and partisan divisions that he so regretted. Predilections of the kind that Republicans harbored for France and that Federalists harbored for Britain, he claimed, supply countless opportunities for foreign powers "to tamper with domestic factions, to practice the acts of seduction, to mislead public opinion, to influence or awe the Public Councils."[9] In response Washington advocated not head-in-the-sand isolationism but rather engaged independence: increased commercial and diplomatic ties across the globe along with an avoidance of unnecessary wars and permanent alliances with individual nations. (The famous phrase "entangling alliances" comes from Jefferson's First Inaugural rather than Washington's Farewell, but it describes well enough what he hoped to avoid.)[10]

As for the larger problem of domestic factionalism, Washington offered little in the way of remedy beyond the hope that the promotion of morality, religion, and education might help to foster moderation. He was under no illusion that his warning about the evils of parti-

sanship would produce the kind of disinterestedness that he believed was necessary. He confessed that "in offering to you, my countrymen, these counsels of an old and affectionate friend, I dare not hope they will make the strong and lasting impression I could wish; that they will controul the usual current of the passions, or prevent our nation from running the course which has hitherto marked the destiny of nations." The best that he could hope for is that his counsels "may be productive of some partial benefit, some occasional good; that they may now and then recur to moderate the fury of party spirit, to warn against the mischiefs of foreign intrigue, to guard against the impostures of pretended patriotism."[11] That the fury of party spirit might now and then be moderated was not exactly a cheering vision; Washington seemed to all but admit here that factionalism would prevail, and eventually rend the republic. Little did he know that the problem would grow still more intense during his few remaining years.

One divisive issue that Washington refrained from mentioning in his Farewell Address—or in any other public forum during his lifetime, for that matter—was slavery.[12] For most of his life Washington was a fairly conventional southern slaveholder, apparently little troubled by the institution. As he grew older he came to find it increasingly objectionable, prompted both by his conscience and by a concern for his future reputation. Washington inherited ten enslaved people at the decidedly tender age of eleven, and by the time of his death he held more than three hundred human beings in bondage. Over the course of the 1780s he gradually came to see slavery as a cruel and inefficient system, but his initial response was to try to *sell* his slaves, thereby profiting from their continued enslavement—and he could not find a way to make even this halfhearted move, given his commendable aversion to separating family members. Near the end of his life Washington declared himself to be "principled against . . . traffic in the human species" and made elaborate arrangements to liberate in his will those whom he had enslaved.[13] Even this posthumous effort was not a clean one, as many of the slaves at Mount Vernon were attached to an estate that legally belonged to Martha's heirs, but he freed those whom he could and made provisions for the young, old,

and infirm. Washington was the only major slaveholder among the leading founders to take such a step.

It was not until Washington's will was published after his death, however, that the public got its first inkling that he had had any reservations about holding human beings in bondage; throughout his lifetime he resolutely refused to act, or even speak out, against slavery. In private Washington professed to hope for its eradication. In 1786 he declared that it was "among my first wishes to see some plan adopted, by the legislature by which slavery in this Country may be abolished by slow, sure, & imperceptable degrees" and indeed that "there is not a man living who wishes more sincerely than I do, to see a plan adopted for the abolition of it."[14] Of course, such talk was cheap when Washington was out of politics and had no authority to introduce or champion such a plan. As president he did little to fight the institution; on the contrary, in 1793 he signed a Fugitive Slave Act that allowed slaveholders to cross state lines to recover their runaway chattel. To be fair, Washington's failure to take political action against slavery did not distinguish him from the vast majority of his contemporaries. Even most northerners who despised the institution and were not themselves slaveholders, such as Hamilton and Adams, generally refrained from pushing for concrete steps toward emancipation, fearing that doing so would destroy the fledgling republic in its infancy. Though Washington and his fellow founders hoped and expected that the stain of slavery would eventually be eliminated from the American fabric, ending it was simply never a top or immediate priority for any of them.

During the Missouri crisis (1819–21), we will see, Jefferson became convinced that conflict over slavery would ultimately doom the republic. Washington died long before the fate of slavery became a subject of major political controversy, but even in the 1790s he anticipated that it had the potential to wreak havoc on his beloved union. He predicted, for instance, that slaves would be "found to be a very troublesome species of property 'ere many years pass over our head" and that a gradual emancipation plan "might prev[en]t much future mischief."[15] An English visitor recalled him saying in 1798, "I can clearly foresee that nothing but the rooting out of slavery can perpetuate the existence of our union, by consolidating it in a common bond of principle."[16]

Washington did not express such apprehensions as forcefully or as frequently as Jefferson later did, but these statements suggest that he too saw slavery as not only a great moral failure but also a threat to America's future.

The announcement of Washington's retirement set in motion America's first real presidential contest, which pitted Adams and the Federalists against Jefferson and the Republicans. Though not quite as vicious as the election of 1800 would prove to be, the election of 1796 was accompanied by enough partisan strife to darken Washington's outlook still further. Nor was he alone in his sense of gloom: many wondered how the nation would survive without Washington's towering presence in the executive mansion. Even as he established the precedent for voluntarily stepping down from the nation's highest office, Washington continued to play his accustomed role of the caring father, assuaging the worries of his friends and fellow citizens. On his last full day in office, he assured one of his old aides-de-camp from the Revolutionary War that "altho we [Americans] may be a little wrong, now & then, we shall return to the right path, with more avidity. I can never believe that Providence, which has guided us so long, and through Such a labirinth, will withdraw its protection at this Crisis."[17] Still, he found it difficult to hide his disappointment at how divided the nation had grown—note his description of the present juncture as "this Crisis"—and his eagerness to escape Philadelphia and withdraw to Mount Vernon was palpable in nearly every letter that he penned.

As he commenced his retirement Washington felt old and tired, and he correctly assumed that he had only a few more years to live.[18] He devoted his initial summer as the nation's first ex-president to what he frequently called "rural amusements": managing his farms, upgrading his house, and building a large and profitable whiskey distillery—with all the real labor done by enslaved people, of course. He kept abreast of politics through avid newspaper consumption and extensive correspondence, neither of which did anything to cheer him. Much of the news pertained to rising tensions with France; the conflict between the United States and its erstwhile ally served to further disaffect Republicans from the new Adams administration

and ultimately culminated in the Quasi-War of 1798–1800.[19] In May 1797 Washington lamented "the threatning clouds" looming on the political horizon, and the next month he added that "nothing short of a general Peace in Europe will produce tranquillity in this country, for reasons which are obvious to every well informed, or observant man, among us."[20] By the following March, Washington had concluded that "misrepresentation & party feuds have arisen to such a height, as to ... become portensious of the most serious consequences. Where, or when they will terminate; or whether they can end at any point short of confusion and anarchy, is *now*, in my opinion, more problematical than ever."[21]

Partisanship had, indeed, reached a new peak during the early years of Adams's presidency. Vice President Jefferson noted that in the capital "men who have been intimate all their lives cross the streets to avoid meeting, and turn their heads another way, lest they should be obliged to touch their hat."[22] By the early months of 1798 the atmosphere in Congress was so caustic that Matthew Lyon, a Republican from Vermont, spat in the face of Connecticut Federalist Roger Griswold, after which the pair scuffled on the House floor, with Griswold brandishing his cane and Lyon employing a fire poker.

Washington was aghast, of course, but he himself was not immune from the rising partisan fever. Though he took no public actions and made no public statements, he now corresponded almost exclusively with Federalists. The political opinions that pervaded his letters grew ever more fiery and one-sided, to the point that he came to adopt the somewhat paranoid, conspiratorial view of the Republicans that the Hamiltonian "High Federalists" had long harbored. He began to refer to Republicans as "the French Party" and drew a bright line between "true Americans" and "those who are stimulating a foreign nation to unfriendly acts, repugnant to our rights & dignity."[23] In other words, Washington now saw Republicans as pawns of the French at best, outright traitors at worst. Fearing that their actions threatened the security and even the independence of the United States, he described them as "the curse of this country."[24]

Washington's suspicions may have been couched in exaggerated terms, but they were not entirely unwarranted. As Joseph Ellis notes, "Jefferson and Madison *had* in fact been orchestrating a concerted

and often covert campaign against the Federalists since 1791. They *had* played politics with foreign policy during the debate over the Jay Treaty. They *had* paid scandalmongers to libel Hamilton and Washington. And they *had* on several occasions (as in the Genet affair . . .) engaged in skullduggery that would have been regarded as treasonable in any modern court of law."[25] Yet it was now clear, if it had not been earlier, that Washington was no longer above the partisan fray.

Unfortunately for his peace of mind and his posthumous reputation, Washington was destined to reenter the public arena one last time. Tensions with France reached a boiling point in March 1798, when it was revealed to the American public that Talleyrand, the French foreign minister, had demanded substantial bribes from American diplomats for the privilege of entering into formal negotiations over their differences. The XYZ Affair—named after the initials used to conceal the identities of French agents in the American commissioners' dispatches—caused a sensation. Republicans were put squarely on the defensive by this glaring affront and found that they could do little to hush the drumbeat for war, especially since on the high seas French privateers were already seizing American merchant vessels by the dozen. Fearing further aggression and hoping to maintain the nation's honor, in May the Federalist-controlled Congress authorized the raising of a 12,500-man "New Army" designed to prevent Napoleon and his seemingly invincible troops from invading the American homeland.

Over the ensuing months, Hamilton and the members of Adams's cabinet—all of whom had been retained from Washington's administration—warned Washington that in the event of a war the American people would expect him to once again abandon his retirement and lead the nation's forces. In early July Adams named Washington the commander of the new army without even bothering to consult him about the appointment. Washington protested, as usual, that he was too old and unequal to the task, but he seems to have been, if anything, *less* genuinely reluctant to take on this role than he had been to assume the presidency in 1789. His explanation of his decision to Secretary of War James McHenry reveals just how

deep his anger and his fears ran: "The principle by which my conduct has been actuated through life, would not suffer me, in any great emergency, to withhold any services I could render, required by my Country; especially in a case where its dearest rights are assailed by lawless ambition and intoxicated power; contrary to every principle of justice, & in violation of solemn compact, & Laws which govern all Civilized Nations. And this too with obvious intent to sow thick the Seeds of disunion for the purpose of subjugating the Government, and destroying our Independence & happiness."[26]

Washington's main stipulation, in assuming the role, was that he would not actually take the field unless and until it was absolutely necessary, meaning that his second in command would be the de facto commander in the meantime. Washington wanted Hamilton for the post, but Adams objected, both on grounds of seniority—Henry Knox, for instance, had vastly outranked Hamilton during the Revolutionary War—and because he distrusted and despised Hamilton. Washington effectively forced Adams's hand, however, by threatening to resign unless he got his way—an act of insubordination that he would have never tolerated when he himself was president. This was not his finest hour. In fact, this entire chapter of Washington's career reads like a combination of tragedy and farce. Though the idea of an imminent transatlantic invasion was inconceivable outside of the Federalists' fevered imaginations, Washington spent untold hours, including a five-week trip to Philadelphia in November and December, working with Hamilton to organize an army to meet one. He devoted an unusual amount of attention to ensuring that the officers' uniforms would be sufficiently handsome. As for the officers themselves, he wanted only Federalists: anyone who had displayed "general opposition to the Government" or "predilection to French measures" was ruled out.[27]

Meanwhile, hard-line Federalists in Congress exploited the prevailing war hysteria by passing the now-infamous Alien and Sedition Acts.[28] These laws allowed the president to deport foreign-born residents with little cause, made it more difficult for immigrants to become naturalized citizens, and criminalized public criticism of federal officials. Though enacted in the name of national security, the acts were plainly intended to intimidate and silence Republicans, many of whom were immigrants and newspaper editors. Nothing has done

more to tarnish the Federalists' historical reputation than these repressive measures.

Washington certainly had no hand in proposing, passing, or publicly defending the Alien and Sedition Acts, but he did tacitly endorse them in private. During his presidency Washington never made any attempt to silence his critics, no matter how exasperated he became with the Republican press, but now he feared that the Republicans would conspire with the French enemy if given a chance, so he approved of the prosecution of journalists who stoked opposition to administration measures. He had never before advocated taking any kind of action against foreigners, but now he suggested that it seemed "time & expedient to resort to protecting Laws against aliens ... who acknowledge *no allegiance* to this Country, and in many instances are sent among us (as there is the best circumstantial evidence) for the *express purpose* of poisoning the minds of our people; and to sow dissentions among them; in order to alienate *their* affections from the Government of their choice, thereby endeavouring to dissolve the Union."[29] Washington's uncharacteristic approval of censorship and discrimination is both disappointing and a testament to his sense of crisis.

In February 1799, Adams sought to put an end to the hostilities by declaring his intention to send another peace commission to France. The move shocked and angered Adams's fellow Federalists, but it succeeded in curtailing the prospect of a full-scale war as well as the need for the new army, which petered out over the succeeding months. Washington's final retirement was accompanied by little fanfare from the public and even less optimism from Washington himself. During the Quasi-War his unmatched integrity, judgment, and independence had given way to the kind of blinkered partisan animus that he had so long abhorred. It was a sad end to an illustrious public career.

Washington's final year was not a happy one. In addition to the usual ailments and indignities of what then passed for old age—he was all of sixty-seven—he continued to grow increasingly frustrated with the character of American politics. On Christmas day of 1798 he complained to Lafayette that "a party exists in the United States ... who

oppose the government in all its measures, and are determined (as all their conduct evinces) by clogging its wheels . . . to subvert the Constitution. To effect this, no means which have a tendency to accomplish their purposes, are left unessayed." Left to their own devices, the Republicans would turn the Constitution into "a mere cypher."[30] The next day he told William Vans Murray, who was helping to broker the peace with France, that while the Republicans were up in arms about the Alien and Sedition Acts, "any thing else would have done; and something there will always be, for them to torture, and to disturb the public mind with their unfounded and ill-favored forebodings."[31]

The Republicans' most notable response to the Alien and Sedition Acts came in the Virginia and Kentucky Resolutions, which were secretly drafted by Madison and Jefferson, respectively. These resolutions not only denounced the Federalists' measures as unconstitutional but also staked out a case for states' rights that was sufficiently extreme to itself threaten the constitutional order. Viewing the Constitution as a compact formed by the states rather than the American people, Madison and Jefferson insisted that when the states deemed federal laws abusive they had the right to "interpose" against those laws (Madison's term) or even to "nullify" them (Jefferson's term).[32]

As Washington saw it, this view of federal-state relations was a certain recipe for rapid disunion. In hopes of countering the Virginia Resolutions he urged Patrick Henry to stand for election to Virginia's General Assembly, commenting to Henry that it would be "vain . . . to look for Peace and happiness, or for the security of liberty or property, if Civil discord should ensue; and what else can result from the policy of those among us, who, by all the means in their power, are driving matters to extremity, if they cannot be counteracted effectually?" He concluded by apologizing for the entreaty, which was driven by nothing less than "my fear, that the tranquillity of the Union, and of this State in particular, is hastening to an awful crisis."[33] Henry did agree to run and was duly elected, though he died of stomach cancer before he was able to take office. Washington also applauded the elections of John Marshall and Henry "Light-Horse Harry" Lee to Congress; he had never before supported specific candidates for office, but now he enthusiastically backed any Federalist who had a shot at winning in Virginia. He warned his nephew Bushrod Washington, who had

recently joined the Supreme Court, that there could be no "relaxation on the part of the Federalists. We are sure there will be none on that of the Republicans, as they have very erroneously called themselves."[34]

By the summer of 1799 many political minds were already starting to turn toward the next presidential election, and some anxious Federalists implored Washington to allow himself to be drafted once again in order to head off the possibility of a Jefferson administration. Washington's rebuff was swift and firm: it was his "ardent wish and desire that, no eye, no tongue, no thought, may be turned towards me for [that] purpose."[35] The reasons that he gave for his refusal were telling: not only would standing for office prevent him from enjoying his long-desired retirement, and not only would he be accused of "irresolution," "concealed ambition," "dotage," and "imbicility"; he was also "thoroughly convinced I should not draw a *single* vote from the Anti-federal side." It was no longer individuals and their virtues, he insisted, but parties and their ideologies that determined the outcome of elections. "Let that party [i.e., the Republicans] set up a broomstick, and call it a true son of Liberty, a Democrat, or give it any other epithet that will suit their purpose," he told Connecticut governor Jonathan Trumbull, "and it will command their votes in toto!"[36] Read in the context of his lifelong battle against parties and factionalism, this letter reads like an admission of defeat. Washington recognized that not only Congress but also the American people had become thoroughly and irretrievably partisan.[37]

A storybook version of the ending would have the aged Washington sitting on his porch at Mount Vernon, savoring "the sweet enjoyment of . . . the benign influence of good laws under a free government," as he had described his fondest hope in the conclusion of the Farewell Address.[38] But it was not to be. Washington's vision of nonpartisan harmony was already an exceedingly distant one when he stepped down from the presidency, and now it had been exposed as a mirage. Throughout his life Washington had usually succeeded whenever he threw his energy and influence into an enterprise, but he failed at what was, to him, one of the most important: despite his mightiest efforts, he was unable to prevent the tides of partisanship from engulfing the country. And he had always insisted, since his days at the head of the Continental Army, that republican government

could not survive for long under such conditions. As he neared the end of his life, then, Washington had good reason to fear that the "sacred fire of liberty" that had been entrusted to the American people might soon flicker out.[39] Just weeks before his death, he wrote to James McHenry: "I have, for sometime past, viewed the political concerns of the United States with an anxious, and painful eye. They appear to me, to be moving by hasty strides to some awful crisis; but in what they will result—that Being, who sees, foresees, and directs all things, alone can tell."[40]

In Washington's view, in short, his great failure was also the nation's. "The Father of His Country" ended up being decidedly discouraged about his progeny's future.

HAMILTON

CHAPTER 4

<hr>

NO MAN'S IDEAS

PERHAPS THE IDEALISTIC Washington was disappointed by the sometimes ugly realities of the new American government, one might think, but surely the more worldly, hard-bitten Alexander Hamilton must have been more pleased by it.[1] Hamilton was, after all, the principal author of the greatest defense of the Constitution—*The Federalist*—and as the nation's first treasury secretary he arguably did more than any other single individual to give shape and substance to the government that emerged from the Constitution during its early years. In fact, however, Hamilton was among the most disappointed in the national charter even at the outset. At the end of the Philadelphia Convention he resolved to defend the proposed constitution as better than nothing, but he told his fellow delegates that (as James Madison's notes have it) "no man's ideas were more remote from the plan than his were known to be."[2] Though Hamilton's outlook overlapped with Washington's in many respects, his chief worry was slightly different: the main problem, as Hamilton saw it, was that the federal government would not have sufficient vigor or "energy," particularly in relation to the state governments. Of the major founders, Hamilton was easily the most consistent and unabashed proponent of a strong national authority.

The very notion of centralized power ran squarely counter to the intellectual culture that had fueled the Revolution. One of the key principles that the colonists appealed to in order to discredit British rule in America, after all, was that political power should, as far as practicable, be exercised on a local level so as to enable the people to govern themselves rather than be ruled by an elite in a distant capital city over whom they had little influence. So potent was this legacy that the term "consolidation" continued to have sinister overtones well into the nineteenth century. Hamilton and the supporters of a

vigorous federal government were quick to point out, however, that this proclivity for decentralization had been embodied in the Articles of Confederation, which had by all accounts proved disastrously ineffective; if the Articles had been sufficient, then the Constitution would never have been needed in the first place. Today many Americans—especially but not exclusively on the political right—assume that the Constitution's primary purpose was to limit the national government through various checks and balances and thereby prevent the tyrannical exercise of power, but in fact the principal impetus for the convention was less to forestall tyranny than to avoid anarchy. The immediate problem that the framers faced in 1787 was not an overbearing King George but rather an impotent Confederation Congress, so they gathered in Philadelphia in order to make the national government *stronger* and more effective—and Hamilton was convinced that they still did not go nearly as far as they should have.

It is easy enough to speculate about why Hamilton became such an uncompromising nationalist. First, he was born and spent his childhood in the West Indies. Given that he was well into his teen years by the time he immigrated to the United States, he lacked the strong sense of state loyalty that many native-born Americans almost instinctually felt. Just as importantly, Hamilton's experience during the war—as a soldier, as Washington's aide-de-camp, and eventually as a field commander—convinced him of the need for national unity and an effective central power. As one historian writes, "during the War of Independence, the army was the school of nationalism: the men who went hungry, ragged and unpaid for years on end were not apt to share civilians' fears of strong government or to decry the authority of the Continental Congress."[3] Still further, Hamilton's predominant character trait was an all-consuming sense of ambition, which he felt on behalf of the nation as well as himself. His foremost dream for the new United States was that it would eventually achieve the kind of international prominence, military might, and economic prosperity that he saw embodied in the great European monarchies, particularly Britain. He yearned for America, no less than himself, to one day play a brilliant part on the world stage.

Hamilton spent the bulk of his political career championing the institutions that he believed would breed such national greatness.

The first item on his wish list was a strong executive, since any great nation needed a great leader at its head. Hamilton sought to justify a powerful presidency with his indefatigable pen—above all in his essays in *The Federalist* and as "Pacificus"—and to utilize his pivotal role in Washington's cabinet to develop an assertive executive branch. In particular, as treasury secretary he was well placed to establish the economic institutions that he believed were necessary to ensure the nation's future prosperity: a national bank, a robust taxing power, a funded debt, expanded manufacturing, and the like. Hamilton also desired a vigorous military, and he sought to make the most of crises such as the Whiskey Rebellion and the Quasi-War with France to build one. An active judiciary was yet another aspiration; he hoped that the federal courts would use the power of judicial review to ensure national supremacy by striking down state laws that were incompatible with the union's interests. Hamilton placed less stress on the need for a powerful legislature, but he did advocate a wide scope for congressional action, which he saw as entirely compatible with a strong executive and judiciary. His vision was that Congress would pass far-reaching laws for the president and his appointees to vigorously implement. The precise organization of the government was not of the first importance to Hamilton, however; it was more crucial simply that it be accorded as much authority as possible, particularly in relation to the state governments.[4] This would, he believed, serve to cement the union, bind the American people to it, and eventually allow the nation to compete with Europe's imperial powers on their own terms.

Although some of Hamilton's contemporaries—Jefferson being the foremost example—worried that a powerful federal government would threaten individual liberty, Hamilton insisted that it would be impossible to maintain a regime of liberty without one. His ideological and partisan opponents were so suspicious of the exercise of political power, he believed, that they had blinded themselves to the need for stability and energy in order for liberty to endure. This was most obviously true on the international stage: if the decentralizing impulse were to prevail and the union were to break up into multiple competing confederacies, then they would be easy prey for the European monarchies.[5] Even in the domestic sphere, however, Hamilton

insisted that the federal government needed to be strong enough to ensure order and carry out its duties, precisely in order to protect liberty. The feebleness of the Confederation Congress was a textbook example of the dangers of a stripped-down government: under the Articles the national government was unable to collect taxes, and so its debts went unpaid; the army was continuously undermanned and undersupplied during the war; and social unrest pervaded the country (the most famous case in point being Shays's Rebellion). It was a constant refrain of Hamilton's writings that an impotent government is often a greater threat to liberty than a strong one and that a dearth of effective political power is frequently more dangerous than an excess of it.[6]

Hamilton was, we will see, deeply disappointed in the Constitution as it emerged from the convention. He believed that the narrow interests of the small states and the widespread but unwarranted apprehensions about centralized power had prevailed even within the group of (mostly) nationalist Federalists that had gathered in Philadelphia. Hamilton spent most of the 1790s, both in and out of office, seeking to strengthen the government in every way that he could think up, but he was never satisfied that he had done enough. Though he lived only a few years into Jefferson's presidency, by the time of his premature death Hamilton was convinced that the Republicans had already done irreparable damage to an already-weak government and that little but disorder and dissolution could be expected thereafter.

Given Hamilton's emphasis on the advantages of a robust federal authority, it is unsurprising that his criticisms of the Articles of Confederation were as extensive and harsh as those of any figure of the era. In *The Federalist*, he proclaimed that under the Confederation Congress the country had "reached almost the last stage of national humiliation" and that its political order was so "radically vicious and unsound" that it was well on its way to becoming "one of the most execrable forms of government that human infatuation ever contrived."[7] Hamilton resolved to do everything in his power to transform this feeble league into a true national government, one that could pursue grand projects and operate directly on the American people without

having to rely on the state governments as intermediaries. At the Annapolis Convention, held in September 1786 in a futile attempt to tackle the protectionist trade barriers among the states that had contributed to the country's economic plight, Hamilton drafted the concluding report that called for a convention to be held the following summer in Philadelphia that would seek to "render the constitution of the Federal Government adequate to the exigencies of the Union."[8] He then persuaded the legislature in his home state of New York to send a delegation to the Philadelphia Convention and to appoint him as a member.

At the convention itself, however, Hamilton played a fairly minor role. He contributed to the debates infrequently and was absent from Philadelphia altogether for most of the crucial months of July and August. There are several plausible explanations for Hamilton's uncharacteristic reticence. One was his relative youth and inexperience; given that he was still in his early thirties at the time, he may have felt obliged to let the more distinguished and seasoned delegates lead the way. Perhaps even more important, however, was his awkward position within the New York delegation. The other two delegates, John Lansing Jr. and Robert Yates, were both determined opponents of a stronger federal government. They were convinced from the outset that the convention was exceeding its authority in devising an entirely new national charter, and they walked out after only six weeks. Hamilton was therefore in the distinct minority within the delegation in the early weeks of the convention and had no authority to cast a vote for New York thereafter, since the state's legislature had stipulated that at least two delegates needed to be present in order for New York to cast a vote. Indeed, at the end of the convention he was forced to sign the Constitution as an individual rather than on behalf of his state. Washington's diary entry for the day noted that "the Constitution received the Unanimous assent of 11 States and Colo. Hamilton's from New York."[9] (Rhode Island had declined to send a delegation.)

Yet another reason for Hamilton's reserve at the convention was that his political views diverged fairly sharply from those of the other delegates, as he made clear in his only major address to the assembly. This address represented a reversion to Hamilton's customary audaciousness: it was the longest speech of the entire summer—taking up

the entire session of June 18—and arguably also the most radical.[10] At this point the New Jersey Plan, which was favored by the small states, had been proposed three days earlier as an alternative to the Virginia Plan, which Madison and his compatriots had introduced at the outset of the convention. Hamilton took it on himself to suggest that neither plan went nearly far enough in strengthening the national authority. He told his fellow delegates that he would "give my sentiments of the best form of government—not as a thing attainable by us, but as a model which we ought to approach as near as possible."[11] And he left no ambiguity as to what his preferred model was: "In his private opinion," Madison records Hamilton as saying, "he had no scruple in declaring, supported as he was by the opinions of so many of the wise & good, that the British Govt. was the best in the world: and that he doubted much whether any thing short of it would do in America."[12]

Hamilton's celebration of the British constitution would come back to haunt him later in life, and many of the delegates were shocked that someone would hold up the government of their recent foe as a model for emulation, but perhaps they should not have been. The British constitution was, after all, revered by virtually every American up until the mid-1760s—and by most right up to 1776 and even beyond—and it was depicted by Montesquieu, the authority who was cited most frequently and favorably on both sides of the ratification debates, as the very exemplar of political liberty. Nor was Montesquieu an outlier: the vast majority of Enlightenment thinkers throughout Europe admired Britain and its balanced constitutional order. Hamilton was not wrong to suggest that his judgment on this score was "supported . . . by the opinions of so many of the wise & good."

Hamilton went on, in his speech, to outline his vision of an ideal political system for the United States, and the plan that he laid out was extraordinary. He advocated a single executive who, once elected, would serve for life—or at least "during good behavior," meaning "unless impeached." This executive (read: George Washington) would have an extraordinary set of powers at his disposal, such as a veto over legislation that could not be overridden and wide-ranging control over foreign affairs and the military, including "the direction of war, when authorized or begun."[13] Such an executive would essentially be a monarch, Hamilton admitted, though an "elective" one.[14] He

proposed a bicameral legislature in which the representatives of the more popular branch would be elected for three-year terms, but for the Senate too he backed the idea of service during good behavior. The upper house that he envisioned was explicitly modeled on Britain's House of Lords, which he described as "a most noble institution" since its members had "nothing to hope for by a change, and a sufficient interest by means of their property, in being faithful to the national interest" that "they form a permanent barrier agst. every pernicious innovation, whether attempted on the part of the Crown or of the Commons. No temporary Senate," he went on to insist, "will have the firmness eno' to answer the purpose."[15] Hamilton's model government was rounded out by a judiciary whose members would also serve during good behavior, meaning that all government officers beyond the members of one house of one branch would effectively be elected or appointed for life.

There was one notable omission from Hamilton's plan: the state governments. According to the version of the speech recorded by his New York colleague Robert Yates, Hamilton proclaimed that "we must establish a general and national government, completely sovereign, and annihilate the state distinctions and state operations; and unless we do this, no good purpose can be answered."[16] Madison's version has him declaring that if the state governments "were extinguished . . . great economy might be obtained by substituting a general Govt. He did not mean however to shock the public opinion by proposing such a measure. On the other hand he saw no *other* necessity for declining it. They are not necessary for any of the great purposes of commerce, revenue, or agriculture."[17] These comments apparently caused a stir, for the next day Hamilton tried to correct a potential misunderstanding: he had not meant to suggest that the states should be entirely *abolished*, he now insisted—only reduced to insignificance. The federal government must have "indefinite authority," since "if it were limited at all, the rivalship of the States would gradually subvert it." The states could remain as "subordinate jurisdictions," as long as they remained essentially toothless.[18] Wiping them off the map altogether could wait for a later day. Instead of the large-state plan from Virginia or the small-state plan from New Jersey, Hamilton preferred in essence a no-state plan.[19]

Hamilton's marathon speech, which lasted for more than five hours, had little immediate impact on the course of the convention: the next day the delegates carried on with their debate over the New Jersey Plan almost as if he had not even spoken. It is difficult to guess what effect, if any, Hamilton's proposal may have had on the minds of the delegates who were wavering between the plans then on the table—whether its extremeness made the Virginia Plan seem moderate and reasonable by comparison, for instance, or whether on the contrary it tainted all advocates of a stronger national government as radicals bent on eliminating the states.[20] What Hamilton's speech makes crystal clear is just how far his perspective diverged from those of the other delegates, and from the constitution that they ended up proposing. According to Yates's notes, Hamilton observed approvingly at one point that the American people were "gradually ripening in their opinions of government" and beginning to be "tired of an excess of democracy." (By "democracy" Hamilton meant less a form of government than a spirit of populism or licentiousness.) Yet "what even is the Virginia plan," Yates records him as asking, "but *pork still, with a little change of the sauce.*"[21] And the Virginia Plan that Hamilton found so grievously insufficient in fact incorporated a far *stronger* national authority than the final version of the Constitution did—including, for instance, proportional representation in both houses of Congress and a congressional veto over state legislation. Plainly, Hamilton did not get anything close to what he wanted out of the convention.

Hamilton's June 18 speech would later be cited by his political opponents as proof of his partiality for monarchy and his desire to introduce a system of king, lords, and commons to the United States. He always responded, correctly, that he had never advocated any of the usual trappings of monarchy such as hereditary power, titles, or privileges, or property qualifications for voting or officeholding. His plan was "republican" in the sense that under it all officeholders would be elected directly or indirectly by the people. Still, given Hamilton's strident praise for the British constitution and his proposal that all officeholders beyond those in the lower house be elected effectively for life, his opponents could be forgiven for regarding his plan as little more than constitutional monarchy in sheep's clothing. Hamilton *did* think that too much "democracy" was incompatible with stable,

orderly, effective rule. In his own notes for the speech he ruminated about how the American government might be "rescued from the democracy" and suggested that the other plans on the table were manifestly inadequate. In both, "a democratic assembly is to be checked by a democratic senate, and both these by a democratic chief magistrate. The end will not be answered—the means will not be equal to the object. It will, therefore, be feeble and inefficient."[22]

Hamilton recognized, even before delivering his infamous June 18 discourse, that his vision was utterly unrealizable in the America of 1787, but it was not in his nature simply to surrender. The remainder of his contributions to the convention were aimed at persuading his fellow delegates to "tone their Government as high as possible," as he put it the following week. If they could not find a way to imbue republican government with "due stability and wisdom," he warned them, "it would be disgraced & lost among ourselves, disgraced & lost to mankind for ever."[23] As the summer wore on, he found it impossible to hide his dismay at the direction in which the convention was heading. He absented himself from Philadelphia in late June, and on arriving in New York he wrote to Washington that he was "seriously and deeply distressed at the aspect of the Councils which prevailed when I left Philadelphia. I fear that we shall let slip the golden opportunity of rescuing the American empire from disunion anarchy and misery. No motley or feeble measure can answer the end."[24] After a weeklong return to the convention in the middle of August, Hamilton departed once again and did not resume his seat for good until early September. When he did, he opened his first speech back—which centered on the mode for electing the president—with the comment that "he had been restrained from entering into the discussions by his dislike of the Scheme of Govt. in General; but as he meant to support the plan to be recommended, as better than nothing, he wished . . . to offer a few remarks."[25]

On the final day of the convention, according to Madison's report, Hamilton "expressed his anxiety that every member should sign" the proposed constitution. While "no man's ideas were more remote from the plan than his were known to be," he implored, "is it

possible to deliberate between anarchy and Convulsion on one side, and the chance of good to be expected from the plan on the other[?]"[26] A "chance of good" is hardly a ringing endorsement, but Hamilton had made his calculation: even if the government that they were proposing was not nearly as energetic as he would prefer, it was still an immense improvement over the Articles of Confederation. After the convention's close he quickly became one of the Constitution's most unflagging and capable defenders. Indeed, it is difficult to think of anyone who worked harder to get the new charter ratified and the new government up and running, Madison not excepted.

In a series of cleverly crafted letters, Hamilton helped to assuage Washington's worries about reentering the public arena and to prod the retired general to accept his inevitable and indispensable role as the nation's first president. At the New York state ratifying convention in Poughkeepsie he turned in what was, by all accounts, a valiant performance, helping to push one of the key Anti-Federalist strongholds over the edge toward ratification. And, of course, he was the driving force behind *The Federalist*: he conceived of the idea of writing an authoritative series of essays on behalf of the proposed constitution; persuaded Madison and John Jay to join the project; wrote the bulk of the pieces—fifty-one of the eighty-five—himself, often at a breakneck pace; and oversaw the organization and publication of the rest, all while keeping up his legal practice. Even for someone with Hamilton's boundless energy, it was a Herculean effort.

Hamilton's contributions to *The Federalist*, written under the pen name "Publius," are among his most famous and influential writings, but they are not the best sources for obtaining insight into his own outlook, especially taken alone. The overriding purpose of the essays, after all, was to persuade skeptics of the proposed constitution—nearly all of whom thought that the government outlined in the document was far too powerful—to support ratification. It is clear from Hamilton's correspondence and convention speeches that his own concerns about the proposed government were exactly the reverse of those of the audience that he was seeking to reach, so he was hardly likely to flaunt either the direction or the depth of his misgivings in such a forum. Still, throughout the essays he sought to explain why an energetic national government was both safe, if properly constructed,

and necessary. His aim was to convince his fellow citizens not only to ratify the Constitution—which he might have done more effectively by playing down the powers that the new government would wield—but also to view the issues as he did.[27]

In his first article as Publius, Hamilton remarked that "the vigour of government is essential to the security of liberty" and that "a dangerous ambition more often lurks behind the specious mask of zeal for the rights of the people, than under the forbidding appearance of zeal for the firmness and efficiency of government. History will teach us . . . that of those men who have overturned the liberties of republics the greatest number have begun their career, by paying an obsequious court to the people, commencing Demagogues and ending Tyrants."[28] A few weeks later he added that "the circumstances that endanger the safety of nations are infinite; and for this reason no constitutional shackles can wisely be imposed on the power to which the care of it is committed."[29]

Hamilton's most forceful pleas on behalf of an energetic government, however, came in his essays on the presidency. He opened *Federalist* number 70 by tackling the "idea, which is not without its advocates, that a vigorous executive is inconsistent with the genius of republican government." If this were true, he argued, then it would be a damning indictment of the very idea of republican government: "A feeble executive implies a feeble execution of the government. A feeble execution is but another phrase for a bad execution: And a government ill executed, whatever it may be in theory, must be in practice a bad government." Hence, Hamilton found it impossible to avoid the conclusion that "energy in the executive is a leading character in the definition of good government."[30] Even as he endeavored to assure his readers that the proposed constitution incorporated enough checks and balances to prevent tyranny, then, Hamilton also sought to persuade them of the necessity of a strong central government, including a powerful presidency.

Hamilton proclaimed in his final *Federalist* essay that the proposed constitution was "the best which our political situation, habits and opinions will admit" and insisted that it would be "the extreme of imprudence" to reject it "in the chimerical pursuit of a perfect plan."[31] This was a sincere statement: while the Constitution that Hamilton

and his collaborators had been defending was far from his own preferred model, he realized that it was the closest approximation to a
sufficiently vigorous government that the American people would
then accept.

We know from his private writings, however, just how precarious
Hamilton thought the new government's prospects were. In a note
written in the wake of the convention, he predicted what would likely
happen if the Constitution were to be adopted. On the plus side, he
observed, "it is probable general Washington will be the President of
the United States. This will insure a wise choice of men to administer
the government and a good administration. A good administration
will conciliate the confidence and affection of the people and perhaps
enable the government to acquire more consistency than the proposed
constitution seems to promise for so great a Country." Yet he worried
that even this would not be enough. If "the *organs* of the general
government" were not strengthened, he fretted, then "in the course
of a few years, it is probable that the contests about boundaries of
power between the particular [i.e., state] governments and the general
government and the *momentum* of the larger states in such contests
will produce a dissolution of the Union. This after all seems to be
the mostly likely result."[32] Even after the Constitution's ratification,
Hamilton knew that he and his fellow Federalists had their work cut
out for them if the new government were to succeed and endure.

CHAPTER 5

STRUGGLING TO
ADD ENERGY

T HROUGHOUT WASHINGTON'S PRESIDENCY, Hamilton
sought to bolster America's constitutional order in every way
that he knew how.[1] The helm of the Treasury Department,
which he occupied for more than five years, was an opportune perch
from which to do so. A number of factors combined to make this
the most important position within the cabinet, and Hamilton the
most powerful individual within the new government save Washington himself.[2] To begin with, the Constitution provided only the
vaguest of outlines of what the executive branch would look like, and
Hamilton immediately seized on the opportunity to help create one
from scratch, throwing all his enterprising spirit into building the
right institutions and setting the right precedents. Whereas Jefferson spent much of his time in New York and Philadelphia pining
for Monticello, Hamilton was right where he wanted to be, fighting
to establish a more vigorous federal authority. It also helped that
Washington trusted Hamilton so much, not just because they shared
many of the same political principles but also because Washington
was well aware of Hamilton's impressive administrative capacities and
wide-ranging policy expertise. Since their war days Washington had
been accustomed to relying on Hamilton to give orders and to write
letters and speeches on his behalf. Hamilton reprised some of these
roles within the cabinet, such that at times he was the eighteenth-
century equivalent of Washington's chief of staff, in addition to being
his treasury secretary.

Washington also granted more leeway to Hamilton than to his
other cabinet officers simply because of his own knowledge base:
Washington had the background in military and foreign affairs to be

in effect his own secretary of war and secretary of state, but he had far less experience with arcane financial matters. Moreover, the Treasury had a slightly different legal status than the other departments. Whereas the secretaries of war and state were responsible only to the president, the treasury secretary was also required to report directly to Congress, given the Constitution's stipulation that all bills for raising revenue must originate in the House of Representatives. As a result, Washington felt that intruding too much in Treasury affairs risked a breach of the separation of powers. For all these reasons, Henry Knox and Jefferson often served as mere advisors while Hamilton was more of a full-fledged administrator. Added to all this was the fact that the Treasury was easily the biggest of the departments: Hamilton soon had several dozen employees reporting to him, whereas the entire State Department consisted of five people. A multitude of customs inspectors were needed to oversee the collection of import duties, so the Treasury staff not only started out larger but also grew faster than those of the other departments, even in relative terms. A few dozen workers hardly seems like a sprawling bureaucracy from today's perspective, but it was enough to raise red flags among Republicans.

Finally, the head of the Treasury Department was bound to be a powerful position because the occupant of that office was responsible for tackling so many of the new government's most pressing problems. When Hamilton assumed his post, the nation's economy was sluggish, and its finances were in disarray: the states quarreled with one another over trade across their borders, there was no uniform national currency or reliable source of government revenue, American credit was exceptionally weak abroad, and both the federal and the state governments faced massive debts. Indeed, so oppressive were these debts that the interest on them alone was greater than the entire national revenue under the Confederation Congress. It would take a monumental effort to get the United States to the point of solvency, much less prosperity. Yet Hamilton's ambition was such that he regarded this formidable task as a mere stepping-stone on the path toward his even larger objectives: solidifying the union, consolidating authority in the federal government, and ultimately transforming the United States into a great nation.[3]

Hamilton wasted no time: after taking office in September 1789 he immediately set about developing a sweeping financial program. He delivered his Report on Public Credit in January 1790 and his Report on a National Bank by the close of that year. Two further reports—one on the creation of a mint and another on the promotion of manufacturing—followed in 1791. Each of the four reports was the length of a small book, and together they laid out an audacious state-building project that is difficult to imagine coming from any other pen. By seizing the reins so decisively, Hamilton helped to establish the tone for Washington's administration and to set much of the agenda for Congress in the new government's early years. Hamilton's program also helped to bring about America's first political parties and to turn his new colleague Jefferson and his recent collaborator Madison into implacable enemies.

Hamilton's program was modeled on Britain's financial system, which had enabled that relatively small island nation to become the world's greatest military and economic power. The idea was to establish a reliable source of government revenue and a stable currency, thereby restoring public credit. The ability to borrow more and at better rates would in turn allow the government to undertake grand projects, including the development of a robust military, without bankrupting itself. Hamilton realized that the best way to achieve these ends would be for the federal government to assume all public debts and to "fund" them by setting aside specific revenues—deriving from import duties and an excise tax on distilled spirits—for their future repayment on a specified timetable.

The assumption and funding of these debts would have three key advantages, as Hamilton saw it. First, these measures would reassure creditors, thereby enabling the government to borrow more, and more affordably. Second, government-issued bonds would serve as a stable, uniform currency until a national bank and mint could be established, which would facilitate trade and thereby reinvigorate the economy. Third, the assumption of the states' debts would help to consolidate power, both by shifting the creditors' allegiance from the states to the federal government and by ensuring that the states had less of a need

to raise revenue of their own. For all these reasons, Hamilton argued, the nation's debts could be transformed from a crushing burden into a "national blessing" if they were funded properly.[4] These advantages would all be redoubled by creation of a national bank, which would help to stabilize and expand public credit and the money supply, collect revenues and deposits, and make the required payments on the debt.[5]

From the outset, then, Hamilton's financial program was designed to further political as well as economic goals. What was at stake, in his view, was nothing less than the authority and reputation of the government of the United States, both at home and abroad—for what is credit, after all, but a signal of confidence in one's reliability? And it all worked like a charm: within a few years the economy was booming, tax revenues were up, the nation's debts were steadily being paid down, and Washington was bragging that "our public credit stands on that ground which three years ago it would have been considered as a species of madness to have foretold."[6]

The problem, of course, was that Hamilton's program also aroused fierce opposition that would continue to grow over the course of the decade and eventually, in the election of 1800, spell the doom of Hamilton's broader aspirations (at least in his own eyes). Jefferson, Madison, and their followers found it difficult even to count their objections to Hamilton's scheme: the assumption of state debts favored the North at the expense of the South, since a number of southern states had already paid off most of their wartime loans; the full funding of existing debts benefited greedy speculators, who also tended to be from the North; the creation of a national bank was unconstitutional, since there was no clause in the Constitution granting Congress the power to establish such an institution; the whole program smacked of Hamilton's notorious Anglophilia, and hence of monarchy; it was also an obvious power grab on the part of the federal government, which would come at the expense of the proper authority of the states; and, most broadly of all, it threatened to transform their country of simple, honorable farmers into one dominated by cities, industry, "stockjobbers," and corruption. In short, the emerging Republican party regarded Hamilton's blueprint as a betrayal of everything that the United States had fought for and achieved in the Revolution.

Though Hamilton's financial program inspired an opposition movement that would eventually wipe out his Federalist party, we should not overlook how much it accomplished in the meantime. Given the dire state of the nation's economy and the public finances when the Constitution was ratified, it is difficult to imagine the new government lasting through the decade, much less prospering as it did, without Hamilton's ingenious handiwork. Moreover, while the Republicans triumphed in 1800, Jefferson himself worried that his antagonist's vision would still win out in the end. Just shy of a year into his presidency he commented that "when this government was first established, it was possible to have set it a going on true principles. but the contracted, English, half-lettered ideas of Hamilton destroyed that hope in the bud. we can pay off his debt in 15 years: but we can never get rid of his financial system."[7]

As ambitious as Hamilton's financial program was, it would have never occurred to him to limit his campaign to empower the federal government to a single front. Another avenue of attack was constitutional interpretation. Soon after Hamilton proposed the idea of a national bank, Madison contended in the House of Representatives that the creation of such a bank was unnecessary and hence unconstitutional. Jefferson and Edmund Randolph both submitted written opinions to Washington making a similar case. As they all saw it, the federal government should be strictly limited to the powers specifically enumerated in the Constitution; anything beyond this would infringe on the states' authority and the people's liberty. And there was, of course, no provision in the document granting Congress the power to incorporate a bank. Seeking to convince Washington of the bank's constitutionality, Hamilton wrote an opinion of his own that would prove to be a classic brief for a liberal interpretation of the Constitution. Indeed, this essay has been called "perhaps the most brilliant and influential one-man effort in the long history of American constitutional law."[8]

Hamilton's argument rested on the notion of "implied powers": while it is true that the Constitution does not explicitly grant Congress the authority to establish a bank, it does explicitly grant Congress

the authority to collect taxes, pay debts, borrow money, regulate inter-state commerce, coin money, and—importantly—"to make all Laws which shall be necessary and proper for carrying into Execution" these enumerated powers. And a national bank, Hamilton argued, clearly fit into the latter category: it was a necessary and proper means for carrying out Congress's delegated ends. Jefferson had contended that the "necessary and proper" clause authorized only laws that were ab-solutely *essential* for carrying out specified congressional powers, such that the powers would be inoperative without them, but Hamilton countered that such a cramped reading "would be fatal to the just & indispensable authority of the United States."[9] After all, "the means by which national exigencies are to be provided for, national inconvenien-cies obviated, national prosperity promoted, are of such infinite variety, extent and complexity, that there must, of necessity, be great latitude of discretion in the selection & application of those means."[10] There was, in other words, simply no way that the framers of the Constitution could have anticipated every law and every program that would be needed in an indefinite and unpredictable future, so the government should have a good deal of discretion in choosing the proper means to its given ends. As one scholar writes, for Hamilton "the Constitution was more properly viewed as a grant of powers than as a catalogue of limitations. He searched in it almost always for encouragement rather than dissuasion, for ways to get things done rather than ways to keep things from being done."[11]

Hamilton's immediate audience, at least, was convinced: Wash-ington had initially been swayed by the arguments against the bank's constitutionality and seemed set to veto the bank bill, but after reading Hamilton's rebuttal he signed it into law instead. In fact, Hamilton's case for a liberal reading of the nation's fundamental charter has been so influential for so long—from John Marshall down to the present day—that his defense of the bank has almost certainly had a greater long-term impact than the bank itself had.

Once again, however, the heated Republican opposition to Ham-ilton's policies and arguments cast a pall over his achievements. His state of mind as Washington's first term neared its end was revealed in a memorable twenty-page letter that he wrote to Edward Carrington, a Virginia Federalist, in May 1792. At the outset of the letter he prom-

ised to "unbosom myself to you on the present state of political parties and views . . . agreable to the real and sincere impressions of my mind." When he took up his position at the Treasury Department, Hamilton told Carrington, he had expected to have the full support of Madison in the House of Representatives. The two had just collaborated on *The Federalist*, after all, and at the Constitutional Convention Madison had appeared to be almost as vehement a supporter of a strong national authority as Hamilton himself. Yet over the course of the government's first few years Hamilton became "unequivocally convinced" that "*Mr. Madison cooperating with Mr. Jefferson is at the head of a faction decidedly hostile to me and my administration, and actuated by views in my judgment subversive of the principles of good government and dangerous to the union, peace and happiness of the Country*" (Hamilton's emphasis). At this time it was still considered an insult to suggest that someone was a member of a faction, much less the head of one that endangered the union and America's peace and happiness. "These are strong expressions," Hamilton admitted, but "I have not lightly resolved to hazard them. They are the result of *serious alarm* in my mind for the public welfare." The Republicans' opposition to his financial program was so rabid and indiscriminate, in his view, that in order to subvert it they were willing "to risk rendering the Government itself odious."[12]

Nor were the Republicans the only force sapping the energy of the federal government, in Hamilton's eyes: the state governments too stood constantly opposed to its authority. "If the States were all the size of Connecticut, Maryland or New Jersey," he told Carrington, "I should decidedly regard the local Governments as both safe & useful. As the thing is now, however, I acknowledge the most serious apprehensions that the Government of the U States will not be able to maintain itself against their influence. . . . Hence a disposition on my part toward a liberal construction of the powers of the National Government and to erect every fence to guard it from depredations, which is, in my opinion, consistent with constitutional propriety."

The opposition from the Republicans and the state governments had not been enough to prevent Hamilton from implementing most of his financial program, but it was more than enough to sustain his worries about the long-term viability of the American regime. He

assured Carrington "with the utmost sincerity" that "I am *affectionately* attached to the Republican theory. I desire *above all things* to see the *equality* of political rights exclusive of all *hereditary* distinction firmly established by a practical demonstration of its being consistent with the order and happiness of society." Yet he also felt obliged to add "in candor" that "I am far from being without doubts. I consider its success as yet a problem. It is yet to be determined by experience whether it be consistent with that *stability* and *order* in Government which are essential to public strength & private security and happiness."[13]

Two further fronts in Hamilton's multipronged campaign to bolster the federal government, both of which came to the fore during Washington's second term, were foreign affairs and the military—never mind that his bailiwick was the Treasury and not the State or War Department. Hamilton's main foray into foreign affairs, at least while he remained part of the cabinet, came in defense of Washington's declaration of neutrality in the war between Britain and revolutionary France.[14] Hamilton had been an early and ardent critic of the French Revolution, and he was quick to connect the revolutionaries' utopian aspirations with the chaos that they had unleashed. Whereas many Republicans—harboring what Hamilton called "*a womanish attachment to France*"—wanted the United States to intercede on behalf of its recent ally, Hamilton agreed with Washington that it was in the nation's interests to stay out of the conflict so far as possible.[15] His greatest efforts, however, were directed not at a particular foreign policy but rather at defending Washington's prerogative to declare neutrality without the consent of Congress. He made his case in a series of essays under the pen name "Pacificus," to which Madison rather grudgingly replied at Jefferson's behest, writing as "Helvidius."[16] At stake in this debate was not just America's stance toward the European war but also the scope of executive power.

As in his opinion on the constitutionality of the national bank, Hamilton argued for a liberal reading of the Constitution, this time attributing the implied powers to the president.[17] Article II of the Constitution opens by stating that "the executive Power shall be vested in a President of the United States," and Hamilton read this clause less

as a designation of a title than as a general grant of power. In other words, as he saw it, all executive powers should be entrusted to the president except those that are explicitly denied to him or reserved for another branch elsewhere in the document; the subsequent discussion of presidential powers should be read simply as illustrating this general principle, not as prescribing limits on the president's actions. And while it is true that the Constitution grants Congress the sole authority to declare war, Hamilton insisted that it was the president's duty to preserve peace until war is declared, and Washington's neutrality proclamation was an obvious and legitimate means toward that end. Of course, the prospect of far-reaching, unilateral presidential power was anathema to Republicans, who associated it with the royal prerogatives that they had worked to overthrow during the Revolution. Though the partisan opposition to Hamilton and his vision continued to mount, the "Helvidius" essays were not Madison's strongest efforts, and the administration's position prevailed in the end.

Hamilton gained an even more unmitigated success in the Whiskey Rebellion, which he treated as an opportunity to augment and display the nation's capacity to enforce the laws. When the insurrection in western Pennsylvania turned violent in the summer of 1794, Hamilton quickly moved to sound the alarm. As had become his custom, he wrote a series of pseudonymous essays—this time using "Tully" as his alias—warning the public that the rebels were committing "treason against society, against liberty, against every thing that ought to be dear to a free, enlightened, and prudent people."[18] Hamilton also helped to convince Washington to call up a large force of militia and then joined the president in leading the westward expedition. Yet Hamilton seems never to have been truly worried that the rebellion posed much of a threat to the constitutional order. From Bedford, Pennsylvania, he wrote playfully to his sister-in-law: "I am thus far my dear Angelica on my way to attack and subdue the wicked insurgents of the West. But you are not to promise yourself that I shall have any trophies to lay at your feet. A large army has cooled the courage of those madmen & the only question seems now to be how to guard best against the return of the phrenzy." In fact, he was already confident that "the insurrection will do us a great deal of good and add to the solidity of every thing in this country."[19]

Like Washington, Hamilton felt vindicated by the insurrection's speedy and bloodless collapse: the kind of decisive demonstration of federal power that he always advocated had had its intended effect, and the government's reputation received a corresponding boost. He would have preferred for the federal government to have a standing army to wield in such situations rather than being forced to rely on the state militias, but that would be a project for another day.

In January 1795, Hamilton resigned his office. The reason was simple: he had a growing family to support, and he was broke. He had managed to make his position as treasury secretary a powerful one by taking every initiative that he could, but at this time cabinet appointments still provided little prestige and even less money. As Hamilton had carefully attended to the nation's finances his own had fallen into disarray, and he was forced to return to his law practice.[20] His accomplishments during his tenure were legion and had helped to establish and fortify the federal government in myriad ways. Indeed, his biographer Ron Chernow writes that "if Washington was the father of the country and Madison the father of the Constitution, then Alexander Hamilton was surely the father of the American government."[21] For all his triumphs, however, Hamilton remained frustrated. Jefferson, Madison, and their followers, suspicious of his every move, had continually whipped up popular opposition to his aspirations and prevented him from realizing the full extent of his vision—and that opposition would only be harder to surmount from outside the cabinet.

Just a few weeks after his resignation, Hamilton wrote to Rufus King, a senator from New York and a fellow Federalist: "I disclose to you without reserve the state of my mind. It is discontented and gloomy in the extreme. I consider the cause of good government as having been put to an issue & the verdict against it."[22] There were at least two immediate sources of this gloominess. The first concerned Hamilton's final effort as treasury secretary, a detailed plan to retire the remaining national debt over a period of thirty years. When some of his proposals met with reservations in Congress, Hamilton exploded: "The unnecessary capricious & abominable assassination

of the National honor by the rejection of the propositions respecting the unsubscribed debt in the House of Representatives haunts me every step I take, and afflicts me more than I can express. To see the character of the Government and the country so sported with, exposed to so indelible a blot puts my heart to the Torture."[23] As it happened, Hamilton's proposals were soon passed into law almost in their entirety, but clearly he still believed that the nation's prospects were hanging by a thread, such that the smallest misstep could send it hurtling into the abyss.

And there was a much bigger threat than any debt or financial measure looming on the horizon: the other immediate source of Hamilton's gloom came from Europe, where France's revolutionary armies were conquering more and more of the continent even as the Terror claimed more and more lives back in France. Hamilton feared that this growing menace could, with the Republicans' certain co-operation and support, cross the Atlantic. He wrote to an old friend from his college days, Robert Troup, that "there is at present a great crisis in the affairs of mankind which may in its consequences involve this country in a sense most affecting to every true friend to it." In Hamilton's inflamed mindset, even being subjected to a revolutionary tribunal or sent to the guillotine did not seem beyond the realm of possibility: "The game to be played may be a most important one," he told his friend. "It may be for nothing less than true liberty, property, order, religion and of course *heads*. I will try Troupe if possible to guard yours & mine."[24]

Some of Hamilton's anguish likely stemmed from the knowledge that he would no longer be there in Philadelphia to help guide the administration. As it turned out, however, his influence hardly diminished after he stepped down from his Treasury post. Washington and his cabinet officers—all of whom were Federalists by this point save Edmund Randolph, whose tenure as secretary of state would last only through the summer—continued to confide in Hamilton, to rely on him for advice, and even to request that he draft some of Washington's speeches (which he duly did).

The most significant political event in the remaining two years of Washington's presidency would prove to be the fallout over the Jay Treaty, and here too Hamilton played a central role. While he was

still in the cabinet he had helped to choose Jay as the administration's envoy and to draft his instructions, and even as a private citizen he became one of the leading defenders of the treaty after it was made public. Hamilton gave speeches, participated in public debates, organized petitions, and once again wrote dozens of anonymous essays on its behalf—all while keeping up his full-time legal practice. Such was his continued influence among Federalists in Congress that without his full-throated support the treaty may well have failed to reach the threshold for ratification.

The revolutionary atmosphere that surrounded the debate over the Jay Treaty did little to revive Hamilton's spirits. The opponents of the treaty regularly waved tricolor flags and even threatened violence if the government were to (as they saw it) side with Britain over France. On one occasion some hecklers threw stones at Hamilton when he attempted to defend the treaty; his partisan opponents were turning into the mob that he had always feared. According to a newspaper report, Hamilton declared at one meeting that "unless the treaty was ratified, we might expect a *foreign war* [i.e., with Britain], and if it is ratified we might expect a *civil war*."[25]

As he had so often, Hamilton used the debate over the treaty to champion a liberal reading of the Constitution and a wide scope for executive action. In the thirty-eighth and final installment of a series of essays under the title *The Defence*—ten of which had been written by Rufus King, the remainder by Hamilton—he insisted that the framers' intent, in the provision on the treaty-making power, was "to give to that power the most ample latitude to render it competent to all the stipulations, which the exigencies of National Affairs might require."[26] It was in the context of this blizzard of public commentary that Jefferson paid Hamilton the backhanded compliment of calling him "a colossus to the antirepublican party. Without numbers," Jefferson marveled to Madison, "he is an host [i.e., army or multitude] within himself. . . . We have had only midling performances to oppose to him. In truth, when he comes forward, there is nobody but yourself who can meet him."[27]

Hamilton was relieved when the administration squeaked out a pair of victories on behalf of the treaty—getting it narrowly ratified in the Senate and narrowly funded in the House—but the relief

did not last for long. He was one of the first to learn of Washington's unbendable determination to retire at the end of his second term, since Washington solicited his help in drafting what would become the Farewell Address. Hamilton was not exactly surprised by Washington's decision, but few events could have done more to erode Hamilton's influence or the likelihood of realizing his broader political vision. Though Washington was never Hamilton's dupe or pawn in the way that the Republican press often suggested, it is true that Hamilton could have never achieved even a fraction of what he did without Washington's sympathy and cooperation. As one scholar writes, Washington's departure from the presidency was, for Hamilton, "altogether too much like divesting himself of his armor and going defenseless among his enemies."[28] Washington's enormous prestige had also enabled Hamilton to fight more effectively for a strong executive branch: if a less widely trusted and admired individual had occupied the president's chair for those first eight years, then the public would surely have been even more wary of according him far-reaching power. Finally, without Washington's good judgment to guide and restrain him, Hamilton would—as events would soon prove—become more impetuous and even reckless in his words and actions, which only served to undermine his own cause.

All these liabilities would be redoubled by the fact that the incoming president, John Adams, despised Hamilton to his very core, and the president who would follow him, Thomas Jefferson, despised not just Hamilton himself but also virtually every principle that he espoused.

CHAPTER 6

THE FRAIL AND WORTHLESS FABRIC

O N THE SURFACE, Hamilton had quite a bit in common with President Adams. Both were Federalists, even if Adams was averse to being seen as a partisan; both harbored a healthy distrust of human nature and of utopian hopes about what was politically possible; and both believed that an excess of democracy would lead to anarchy or tyranny (or both). Yet there was also much that separated the two, which would prove to be fateful for their relationship. Adams hated banks and high finance almost as much as Jefferson and was troubled by much of Hamilton's financial program; for all his admiration of the British constitution and detestation of the French Revolution, Adams had no desire to cozy up to Britain in foreign affairs; and Adams was uncomfortable with the idea of a standing army, preferring to construct a defensive navy instead. Just as importantly, the overlaps in their personalities—both were headstrong, proud, and a bit volatile—bred contempt rather than harmony between the two. Adams would later describe Hamilton as "the most restless, impatient, artful indefatigable and unprincipled Intriguer in the United States, if not in the World."[1] During the next four years Hamilton would still have some influence within the cabinet, whose members Adams retained from the Washington administration, but none with the president himself. The result was predictable: the Federalist party that had remained united for eight years under the shelter of Washington's renown would soon unravel as Adams and his followers squared off against Hamilton and the "High Federalists," which would in turn pave the way for the ascendancy of Jefferson and the Republicans.

The dominant issue of Adams's presidency, particularly as far as Hamilton was concerned, was America's relationship with France.

The growing discord between the two nations in the wake of the Jay Treaty exacerbated the partisan divide within the United States and eventually culminated in the Quasi-War, America's first undeclared military conflict. From the outset Hamilton feared that the Republicans ("our Jacobins") would collaborate with the French if they were to come to blows and, above all, that the government and the military would prove too feeble to handle the threat. America's armed forces were, truth be told, in a dire state when Adams took office: the entire national army comprised fewer than four thousand troops, the navy was essentially nonexistent beyond a few ships under construction, and the fortifications along the Eastern Seaboard were severely decayed. Hamilton addressed the problem as he always did: by taking to the press.

Over the first few months of 1797, Hamilton published a series of six newspaper articles titled *The Warning* that sounded the alarm about the French menace and how unprepared the United States was to meet it. The first number opened by declaring that "there are appearances too strong not to excite apprehension that the affairs of this Country are drawing fast to an eventful crisis."[2] The following spring Hamilton added another seven articles titled *The Stand*, which contained even more overheated rhetoric. Here the first essay began with the announcement that "the enlightened friends of America never saw greater occasion of disquietude than at the present juncture." At a time when the "essential rights of the country are perseveringly violated, and its independence and liberty eventually threatened, by the most flagitious, despotic and vindictive government that ever disgraced the annals of mankind," Hamilton continued, "how great is the cause to lament . . . that distracted and inefficient councils, that a palsied and unconscious state of the public mind, afford too little assurance of measures adequate either to the urgency of the evils which are felt, or to the magnitude of the dangers which are in prospect."[3]

Even getting caught up in one of the first great sex scandals in American history did not dampen Hamilton's eagerness to highlight the country's political woes. As the result of a variety of backroom machinations, Hamilton was forced to publicly confess to having carried on a protracted adulterous affair with a woman named Maria Reynolds, and to having then paid extorted hush money to her husband to keep

it secret. The pamphlet in which he laid out the details of the tawdry affair opened not with a personal apology but with a political premonition: "The spirit of jacobinism," Hamilton warned, "threatens more extensive and complicated mischiefs to the world than have hitherto flowed from the three great scourges of mankind, WAR, PESTILENCE and FAMINE. To what point it will ultimately lead society, it is impossible for human foresight to pronounce; but there is just ground to apprehend that its progress may be marked with calamities of which the dreadful incidents of the French revolution afford a very faint image. Incessantly busied in undermining all the props of public security and private happiness, it seems to threaten the political and moral world with a complete overthrow."[4] (It was Jacobin scandalmongers, it seems, rather than his own unchecked libido, that somehow produced this whole mess.)

As with the Whiskey Rebellion, Hamilton hoped to convert the threat from France into an opportunity to strengthen the federal government and, in this case, to build a proper military—and he reckoned that he had a fair chance of succeeding. In the spring of 1797, in the midst of his philippics against French depredations, Hamilton privately acknowledged to Rufus King that "the conduct of France has been a very powerful medicine for the political disease of this Country. I think the Community improves in soundness."[5] This time, though, Hamilton would overplay his hand.

Hamilton's ambition to develop a respectable military force for the United States faced an obvious obstacle: the fear and odium that was commonly attached to the very notion of a standing army. Since their colonial days most Americans had regarded a large peacetime military as an instrument of tyranny and corruption; indeed, one of the key grievances against King George III in the Declaration of Independence was that he had kept a standing army in the colonies. A standing army, it was widely worried, would give the government a tool with which to enforce its will, even at the expense of trampling on the people's rights; it would serve as an open invitation to gratuitous wars, with all of the corresponding costs in blood and treasure; during peacetime it would breed vice as the idle soldiery engaged in

various forms of debauchery; and at the extreme it could overthrow the government and institute military rule. Citizen militias, in contrast, were seen as bulwarks of liberty and seminaries of virtue. Yet so intense was the climate of fear and resentment against the French in 1798, particularly in the wake of the XYZ Affair, that the Federalist-controlled Congress authorized a massive military expansion of a kind that would have been unthinkable even a year earlier. The existing army was to be immediately quadrupled in size by the raising of a "New Army" of some 12,500 troops, and Congress also approved the creation of a "Provisional Army" of another ten thousand men that could be activated by the president in the event of a war or imminent danger of invasion.

All this went well beyond what most Republicans wanted and even what President Adams thought warranted, but it fell far short of Hamilton's aspirations: he had called for a standing army of twenty thousand regulars along with a reserve of another thirty thousand. Still, he regarded Congress's act as a promising first step, and he resolved to make the most of it. Hamilton set about convincing Washington to serve as the nominal head of the new army and then getting himself appointed as Washington's second in command—a scheme that, we have seen, Washington was all too willing to support, even in the face of Adams's objections.

With Adams often away in Quincy, Washington mostly cloistered at Mount Vernon, and Secretary of War James McHenry compliant to his every wish, Hamilton was master of the scene. As the effective commander of this sizable new force, he felt as if his fondest dreams were finally beginning to come true. He was now in a position—even more than he had been as the powerful first treasury secretary—to play a grand role on the world stage and to bring the young nation along for the ride. Who could tell what was in store, particularly in this frenzied atmosphere? One day he might even get the chance to square off against Napoleon himself. Hamilton worked as tirelessly as ever to recruit, organize, equip, and train the new army. As always, he was painstaking and meticulous in his preparations, down to the color of the buttons on various uniforms and the proper length of a marching step for the infantry—a subject to which he devoted seemingly countless letters.

As time wore on and the imagined threat of a French invasion diminished, the public's ardor for war began to cool, but Hamilton's plans only grew more extravagant and alarming. In the wake of the declaration by the legislatures of Virginia and Kentucky that states had the right to unilaterally overrule federal laws—which Hamilton, like Washington, regarded as a formula for destroying the Constitution and the union—he toyed with the idea of using the army to subdue the opposition in the refractory states. To Theodore Sedgwick, then a senator from Massachusetts, he proposed that "when a clever force has been collected let them be drawn towards Virginia for which there is an obvious pretext—& then let measures be taken to act upon the laws & put Virginia to the Test of resistance."[6] And it is clear that the Virginia and Kentucky Resolutions *were* just a pretext for flexing the federal government's muscles, even in Hamilton's own mind. Just a few days later he wrote to Rufus King of these resolutions: "If well managed this affair will turn to good account. In my apprehension it is only disagreeable not formidable. The general progress of things continues in a right direction."[7]

By the autumn of 1799 Hamilton would go even further, suggesting that the bigger states (read: Virginia) might be broken up into smaller entities in order to assuage the threat that they posed to the federal government. "Great States will always feel a rivalship with the common head, will often be disposed to machinate against it, and in certain situations will be able to do it with decisive effect," he wrote to Senator Jonathan Dayton of New Jersey. "The subdivision of such states ought to be a cardinal point in the Federal policy." Hamilton may have proposed this harebrained scheme half in jest—he admitted that it would probably be "inexpedient & even dangerous" to attempt it at the present time—but it nonetheless reveals how skewed his political judgment could be when released from the constraints of Washington's guidance.[8]

Hamilton also harbored grandiose dreams about the possibility of territorial expansion. In the early months of 1799 he began to suggest, in a series of letters, that the United States should consider seizing East and West Florida and the Louisiana Territory from Spain in order to prevent them from falling into French hands, and he even fantasized about joining forces with the Venezuelan revolutionary

Francisco de Miranda to liberate South America from Spanish control in order to further enhance America's security within the Western Hemisphere. In June he insisted to McHenry that the quotas for the new army should be filled at a faster pace than they had been to that point, commenting that "besides eventual security against invasion, we ought certainly to look to the possession of the Floridas & Louisiana—and we ought to squint at South America."[9] More and more, Hamilton seemed intent on confirming the Republicans' abiding suspicion that he longed to be a modern-day Caesar.

When Adams declared his intention to send a new peace commission to France in February 1799, it quickly deflated both the justification and the public support for the new army. Hamilton continued to work feverishly on organizing his troops for many more months, but it should have been clear by that point that it would all be for naught. The army never managed to enlist even half of the authorized number of soldiers, and the new force was disbanded altogether in the early months of 1800. Hamilton was distraught, writing to his wife, Eliza, that "at the bottom of my soul there is more than usual gloom."[10] A perfectly good outbreak of war hysteria had been wantonly wasted thanks to Adams and the peace mongers. Hamilton returned to New York, his dreams in tatters. Over the succeeding months he grew more and more convinced that not just the nation's future but also its very survival depended on the outcome of the impending presidential election—and none of the options seemed palatable.

Hamilton eventually conceded that France's army would not be landing on America's shores any time soon, but he remained convinced that France's malignant revolutionary principles were already in their midst. When Adams ousted James McHenry from his position as secretary of war in May 1800, Hamilton advised McHenry that he must persist in keeping up his guard: "my friend we are not to be discouraged. Zeal and fortitude are more than ever necessary. A new and more dangerous *AEra* has commenced. Revolution and a new order of things are aroused in this quarter. Property Liberty and even life are at stake."[11] Abigail Adams records Hamilton as saying to another interlocutor around the same time that "for his part, he did

not expect his Head to remain four Years longer upon his Shoulders, unless it was at the Head of a Victorious Army."[12] And in a letter to John Jay he described "the Antifederal party" (i.e., the Republicans) as "a composition indeed of very incongruous materials but all tending to mischief—some of them to the overthrow of the Government by stripping it of its due energies others of them to a Revolution after the manner of Buonaparte. I speak from indubitable facts, not from conjectures & inferences."[13]

At the head of the "Antifederal party," of course, was Hamilton's old nemesis Thomas Jefferson, who stood a strong chance of becoming the nation's next president. Back in 1796, Hamilton had insisted that the most important objective was to ensure that Washington's successor "shall not be Jefferson. We have every thing to fear if this man comes in. . . . All personal and partial considerations must be discarded, and every thing must give way to the great object of excluding Jefferson."[14] Two years later, in the midst of the Quasi-War, he went so far as to claim that Jefferson was the author of "a systematic design to excuse France at all events . . . and to prepare the way for implicit subjection to her will. To be the pro-consul of a despotic Directory over the United States, degraded to the condition of a province, can alone be the criminal, the ignoble aim of so seditious, so prostitute a character."[15] This charge of outright treason, coming as it did in a pseudonymous newspaper essay, may have been a piece of deliberately exaggerated political rhetoric, but there is no question that Hamilton regarded the idea of a Jefferson presidency as truly dangerous for the nation.

As one might expect, then, Hamilton entered the election of 1800 ready to support any candidate who could, as he put it in a letter to Theodore Sedgwick, "possibly save us from the fangs of *Jefferson*."[16] The obvious course, in that case, would be to support Adams's reelection bid. Yet only a few days later Hamilton had decided that a continuation of the Adams presidency was unacceptable, telling Sedgwick that "my mind is made up. I will never more be responsible for [Adams] by my direct support—even though the consequence should be the election of *Jefferson*. If we must have an *enemy* at the head of the Government, let it be one whom we can oppose & for whom we are not responsible, who will not involve our party in the disgrace of

his foolish and bad measures. Under *Adams* as under *Jefferson* the government will sink. The party in the hands of whose chief it shall sink will sink with it and the advantage will all be on the side of his adversaries."[17] Essentially, Hamilton seems to have concluded that it would be better to have an open enemy rather than a concealed one at the head of the government, one who could serve as a scapegoat for the country's problems and whose election might serve to unite the increasingly fractious Federalist party in opposition to their longtime adversary.

Accordingly, in October Hamilton published a long essay—under his own name, no less—attacking the "public conduct and character" of President Adams. His aim was to show, as he put it at the outset, that Adams "does not possess the talents adapted to the *Administration* of Government, and that there are great and immense defects in his character, which unfit him for the office of Chief Magistrate."[18] Strangely, after dozens of pages of detailed and harsh denunciation, Hamilton concluded by suggesting that even though the government "might totter, if not fall, under [Adams's] future auspices," he had nevertheless "resolved not to advise the withholding from him a single vote."[19] This bizarre, abrupt, and yet halfhearted about-face seems to have been driven by a hope that the electors would not abandon Adams for Jefferson, but instead give the edge to Adams's running mate, Charles Cotesworth Pinckney of South Carolina, who might prove more pliant to Hamilton's wishes. Hamilton's publication of this open letter has been aptly described as "an extended tantrum in print" as well as "the most lunatic political act of his life."[20] His fellow Federalists were flabbergasted, and the Republicans were overjoyed. Hamilton's injured pride and congenital inability to compromise had fatally weakened the one figure who had a realistic chance of keeping Jefferson from the executive mansion.

When the vote in the electoral college ended in an accidental tie between Jefferson and his running mate Aaron Burr—since candidates for president and vice president were not yet listed or voted for separately at this point—the election was thrown into the Federalist-controlled House of Representatives. Some Federalists were inclined to plump for the mercurial Burr over their familiar foe, but Hamilton would have none of it. He told everyone who would listen that Burr

was "as unprincipled & dangerous a man as any country can boast; as true a *Cataline* as ever met in midnight conclave" and that "he is bankrupt beyond redemption except by the plunder of his country. His public principles have no other spring or aim than his own aggrandizement."[21] Jefferson was by far the more preferable of the two, Hamilton insisted, notwithstanding the fact that "his politics are tinctured with fanaticism, that he is too much in earnest in his democracy, that he has been a mischevous enemy to the principle measures of our past administration, that he is crafty & persevering in his objects, that he is not scrupulous about the means of success, nor very mindful of truth, and that he is a contemptible hypocrite." Jefferson may have had all the wrong principles, but at least he *had* principles: "there is no fair reason to suppose him capable of being corrupted, which is a security that he will not go beyond certain limits."[22] Hamilton's influence helped to sway some Federalists to Jefferson's side, and after a protracted deadlock Jefferson was eventually elected on the thirty-sixth ballot.

Ironically, then, Hamilton may have done more than any individual beyond Jefferson himself to elevate his great rival to the president's chair. By sabotaging the efforts of Adams and Burr, the only plausible alternatives, he paved the way for Jefferson's ascendancy. Yet, as his evaluation of Jefferson made clear, Hamilton remained convinced that his election might very well prove fatal to the nation. He seems to have believed, in essence, that *any* of the potential victors in the election of 1800 would likely lead to the downfall of the government. After having devoted so much energy, over so much of his career, to making the presidency so powerful, it was almost as if no one was fit to occupy the office other than the singular Washington (or perhaps, Hamilton might have added, himself).

Once Jefferson assumed the presidency and the Republicans took control of both houses of Congress in 1801, Hamilton's political influence sank to its nadir. He held no office, his party was out of power and in disarray, and even within the party many found it difficult to forgive his inexplicable attack on Adams in the midst of the election. Still in his midforties, he had become an outmoded relic. Hamilton resolved

to turn his energy to his law practice and to the construction of a country house on the northern end of Manhattan that he named "The Grange," but it was not in his nature to remain aloof from politics for long. If he had to go down, he would go down fighting.

Jefferson adopted a conciliatory tone in his Inaugural Address, famously proclaiming that "every difference of opinion is not a difference of principle" and that in the end "we are all republicans: we are all federalists."[23] Hamilton initially latched on to the speech as "a ray of hope," reading it as "virtually a candid retraction of past misapprehensions, and a pledge to the community that the new President will not lend himself to dangerous innovations, but in essential points will tread in the steps of his predecessors."[24] Jefferson's actions and policies as president were indeed often more moderate than some of his earlier rhetoric portended, but it was not long until Hamilton came to regard the Jefferson administration as a terrible fulfillment of his most dire prophecies. As early as August—just five months after Jefferson's inauguration—Hamilton's old friend Robert Troup informed Rufus King that "Hamilton is supremely disgusted with the state of our political affairs. . . . He entertains no doubt that [Jefferson and his party] will finally ruin our affairs and plunge us into serious commotions. Although he does not think this result will immediately take place, yet he predicts it is not so remote as many might imagine."[25]

Hamilton resumed his indefatigable essay writing in the wake of Jefferson's First Annual Message to Congress in December, pumping out a series of eighteen articles titled *The Examination* over the next four months. The articles were devoted to proving that Jefferson's message was, as Hamilton put it in the first number, "a performance which ought to alarm all who are anxious for the safety of our Government, for the respectability and welfare of our nation. It makes, or aims at making, a most prodigal sacrifice of constitutional energy, of sound principle, and of public interest, to the popularity of one man."[26] With regard to the military, the internal revenue, the judiciary, immigration, and the relationship between the federal government and the states, Hamilton went on to argue in the succeeding essays, Jefferson and his policies were systematically rendering the government and the country weaker. "This is more than the moderate opponents of Mr. Jefferson's elevation ever feared from his administration," he lamented,

and "much more than the most wrong-headed of his own sect dared to hope; it is infinitely more than any one who had read the fair professions in his Inaugural Speech could have suspected. Reflecting men must be dismayed at the prospect before us. If such rapid strides have been hazarded at the very gristle of his administration; what may be expected when it shall arrive to manhood?" Jefferson's presidency, Hamilton proclaimed, represented a betrayal of America's founding principles as well as its greatest hero: "In vain was the collected wisdom of America convened at Philadelphia. In vain were the anxious labours of a Washington bestowed."[27]

Hamilton's despair only increased in the early months of 1802, as the Republicans set about repealing the Judiciary Act of 1801. This act, passed by the Federalists in the waning days of the Adams administration, reorganized the federal judiciary and created a raft of new judgeships that Adams took it on himself to fill with what became known as the "midnight judges." The judiciary was the last bastion of Federalist power within the federal government during the early years of Jefferson's presidency, and the Republicans' response was to try to neuter this stronghold by dismantling the Judiciary Act. Hamilton reacted with horror: the Constitution guaranteed that federal judges would hold their offices during good behavior, and now the Republicans were blatantly violating that guarantee under the flimsy pretext that they were not removing the judges themselves from office, but merely eliminating the judgeships that they occupied. The Republicans' willingness to commit this "glaring violation of our national compact," Hamilton predicted in *The Examination* number 12, "frowns with malignant and deadly aspect upon our constitution. Probably before these remarks shall be read, that Constitution will be no more! It will be numbered among the numerous victims of Democratic phrenzy; and will have given another and an awful lesson to mankind—the prelude perhaps of calamities to this country, at the contemplation of which imagination shudders!" When such a flagrant violation of the separation of powers is countenanced, he concluded, "experience, sad experience warns us to dread every extremity—to be prepared for the worst catastrophe that can happen."[28]

It was in this context that Hamilton sat down on a leap day—February 29, 1802—to write a famous letter to Gouverneur Morris that

concisely encapsulates the deep sense of disillusionment that he had come to feel toward America and its political order. "Mine is an odd destiny," he mused. "Perhaps no man in the UStates has sacrificed or done more for the present Constitution than myself—and contrary to all my anticipations of its fate, as you know from the very begginning I am still labouring to prop the frail and worthless fabric. Yet I have the murmurs of its friends no less than the curses of its foes for my rewards. What can I do better than withdraw from the Scene? Every day proves to me more and more that this American world was not made for me."[29] For all his doubts about the new charter at the Philadelphia Convention, it is difficult to imagine the Hamilton of 1787 describing the Constitution as not just "frail" but also "worthless"; his confidence in the durability of the American regime had ebbed and flowed over time, often in line with his own political fortunes, but it was now at rock bottom. He had lived in the United States for three decades at this point and had done as much to shape its new government as any other individual, yet he still felt that he and his views were somehow out of place.

This letter to Morris is the best-known expression of Hamilton's late-life disenchantment, but similar sentiments and a similar tone run through the correspondence of his final years. Just over a month later Hamilton wrote to James Bayard, a member of the House of Representatives from Delaware, that the survival of republican government in America would require "foundations much firmer than have yet been devised" in the United States. Because of the underlying weaknesses of the political order, even the greatest successes of the Federalists had proven fleeting: "What will signify a vibration of power, if it cannot be used with confidence or energy, & must be again quickly restored to hands which will prostrate much faster than we shall be able to rear under so frail a system? Nothing will be done till the structure of our National Edifice shall be such as naturally to . . . keep in check demagogues & knaves in the disguise of Patriots."[30] In another letter to Bayard, written around the same time, Hamilton broached the idea of forming a "Christian Constitutional Society," a sort of network of clubs that would seek to play on people's religious impulses to attach them to the cause of order and vigorous government, or at least to alienate them from the "atheist"

Jefferson.[31] As Ron Chernow writes, Hamilton hoped that "this new society would promote Christianity, the Constitution, and the Federalist party, though not necessarily in that order of preference."[32] Nothing ever came of this half-baked proposal, which appears to have been confined to this single letter.

Pessimistic messages continued to flow from Hamilton's pen throughout the remainder of the year. In June he wrote to Rufus King: "Truly, My dear Sir, the prospects of our Country are not brilliant. The mass is far from sound. At headquarters a most visionary theory presides. Depend upon it this is the fact to a great extreme. No army, no navy, no *active* commerce . . . as little government as possible within—these are the pernicious dreams which as far and as fast as possible will be attempted to be realized. Mr. Jefferson is distressed at the codfish having latterly emigrated to the Southern Coast lest the people there should be tempted to catch them, and commerce of which we have already too much receive an accession. Be assured this is no pleasantry, but a very sober anecdote."[33] In December he inquired of Charles Cotesworth Pinckney: "Amidst the triumphant reign of Democracy, do you retain sufficient interest in public affairs to feel any curiosity about what is going on?" Hamilton himself retained just enough interest to lament Jefferson's continued popularity: "In my opinion the follies and vices of the Administration have as yet made no material impression to their disadvantage. On the contrary, I think the malady is rather progressive than upon the decline in our Northern Quarter. . . . Mankind are forever destined to be the dupes of bold & cunning imposture."[34]

Hamilton did not yet know that the next great threat to the American republic would come not from Jefferson but from his own party—and that that threat would also lead indirectly to his premature death.

———

In 1803, in the greatest triumph of his presidency, Jefferson acquired the vast Louisiana Territory from the French for the paltry sum of $15 million, thereby nearly doubling the territory of the United States in one fell swoop.[35] Hamilton was one of the few Federalists to applaud the move, aligned as it was with his vision of national greatness, though he refused to give Jefferson any credit for it beyond having allowed

Napoleon to drop the prize in his lap. Many Federalists, particularly in New England, were appalled by the Louisiana Purchase, fearing that the states that would be carved out of the new territory would be overwhelmingly agricultural, slaveholding, and Republican, thereby further diminishing the already-dwindling influence that commercial New England and the Federalist party wielded over national affairs. In 1804 a group of extremists led by Timothy Pickering—who was no minor figure, having served as secretary of state under both Washington and Adams, and now as a senator from Massachusetts—sought to lay the groundwork for the New England states to secede from the union. Realizing that the success of the projected northern confederacy would depend on getting New York on board, the so-called Essex Junto approached Hamilton in hopes of joining forces. Hamilton furiously refused to take any part in dismantling the republic, urging them "for God's sake, to cease these conversations and threatenings about a separation of the Union. It must hang together as long as it can be made to."[36]

Though we lack hard evidence, the Essex Junto appears to have had greater success with the ever-adaptable Aaron Burr, who knew that his days as Jefferson's vice president were numbered after he had refused to yield the presidency during the election impasse in 1801. Burr ran for governor of New York in 1804—seeking to exchange places with Governor George Clinton, who was Jefferson's new running mate—and many (including Hamilton) assumed that if Burr won then he would try to put the Junto's plan into action. Hamilton once again campaigned against him, repeatedly and publicly depicting him as the very personification of unscrupulous ambition. At a meeting of Federalists in Albany, Hamilton charged Burr with desiring "a dismemberment of the Union" so that he could be "the chief of the Northern portion—And placed at the head of the state of New York no man would be more likely to succeed." As he so often did, Hamilton drew a broader moral from this episode: "Every day shews more and more the much to be regretted tendency of Governments intirely popular to dissolution and disorder."[37]

Burr lost the race by a rather lopsided margin, which appeared to put an end to his political career. It is doubtful that the opinions of Hamilton, whose influence was greatly diminished by this point,

had much effect on the outcome, but Burr placed some of the blame on his shoulders, knowing that Hamilton had also stood against him in 1801. The Federalist secession plot was thus an important step on the path toward the famous "interview in Weehawken" that would take place in July of that year. The duel itself is an oft-told tale whose details need not be recounted here.[38] More relevant for our purposes is Hamilton's final letter, written the night before the fatal encounter. "I will here express but one sentiment," he told Theodore Sedgwick, "which is, that Dismemberment of our Empire will be a clear sacrifice of great positive advantages, without any counterballancing good; administering no relief to our real Disease; which is DEMOCRACY, the poison of which by a subdivision will only be the more concentrated in each part, and consequently the more virulent."[39] Few sentences better exemplify Hamilton's political worldview, combining as it does his deep dedication to the American republic along with his equally deep worries about its basis and future.

ADAMS

CHAPTER 7

SUCH SELFISHNESS
AND LITTLENESS

O F THE PROTAGONISTS of this book, John Adams's disillusionment was in many respects the most predictable—one
might even say overdetermined.[1] Simply as a matter of temperament he was notoriously irascible and curmudgeonly. He hated
the idea of political parties almost as much as Washington, and he
worried about the ills of democracy or populism almost as much as
Hamilton. Moreover, unlike Washington and Hamilton he lived well
into the nineteenth century, long enough to see his erstwhile political
opponents, the Republicans, gain ascendancy over the political scene
for two and half decades. But the overriding source of Adams's pessimism, the one that he returned to again and again over the course
of his career, was the lack of virtue among the American people, and
hence their unfitness for republican government.

Just as Jefferson had no equal among the founders in terms of the
encyclopedic breadth of his interests, Adams was unsurpassed in the
depth of his knowledge about politics, history, and law. No one in
that age of remarkably learned political leaders—not even Madison—
read as voraciously or ranged as widely as Adams in contemplating
the proper underpinnings of government.[2] One of the key insights
that Adams gleaned from his studies was that republican government
depended not just on the right institutions but also on the people's
character. Above all, no country could remain free for long unless its
citizens exhibited a sense of civic virtue, of patriotism, of duty—a willingness to put the public good ahead of their own. Adams concluded
as early as 1772 that "the Preservation of Liberty depends upon the
intellectual and moral Character of the People."[3] In 1775, just before
the war for independence got underway, he proclaimed that "liberty

can no more exist without virtue . . . than the body can live and move without a soul."[4] The next year he reiterated that "the only foundation of a free Constitution, is pure Virtue" and explained to Mercy Otis Warren—a historian and family friend—that "there must be a possitive Passion for the public good, the public Interest, Honour, Power, and Glory, established in the Minds of the People, or there can be no Republican Government, nor any real Liberty. And this public Passion must be Superiour to all private Passions. Men must be ready, they must pride themselves, and be happy to sacrifice their private Pleasures, Passions, and Interests, nay their private Friendships and dearest Connections, when they Stand in Competition with the Rights of society."[5]

To be sure, Adams's sensibility was too modern, liberal, and enlightened for him to have contemplated a return to the kind of severe republican virtue that is often associated with ancient Sparta. For all his emphasis on the necessity of sacrificing private interests to the public good, the wholesale subordination of the individual to the political community struck Adams as both unnecessary and repressive. He described the Spartan regime as "the most detestable in all Greece" precisely because it sought to "extinguish every . . . appetite, passion, and affection in human nature" beyond love of the fatherland.[6] The alleged "civil liberty" of Sparta, he declared, "was little better than that of a man chained in a dungeon."[7] Adams was as strong a believer in individual rights as any of the founders.

Yet Adams also believed that a good deal more self-sacrifice was required of republican citizens than of monarchial subjects. In order for self-government to work, the people must be willing to put the public first, at least much of the time, for otherwise politics would be little more than an insoluble clash of conflicting interests. Republics were therefore continually threatened by the forces of selfishness and ambition, luxury and avarice, partisanship and factionalism. That is why, Adams admitted, such regimes are inherently fragile: their "Principles are as easily destroyed, as human Nature is corrupted."[8] At the same time, he regarded the reliance of republics on civic virtue as a sign of their nobility. In fact, on the eve of independence he sought to demonstrate the superiority of republican government through a kind of syllogism: "As Politicks . . . is the Science of human Happiness, and

human Happiness is clearly best promoted by Virtue, what thorough Politician can hesitate, who has a new Government to build whether to prefer a Commonwealth or a Monarchy?"[9]

Truth be told, Adams's model republican citizen was less a Spartan warrior than himself. He boasted a long and tireless record of service to his country, beginning with opposition to the Stamp Act in 1765 and continuing through arduous stints as a member of the Continental Congress, a commissioner to France, a minister to the Dutch Republic, a negotiator of the Treaty of Paris, and a minister to Great Britain, all capped off by two terms as vice president and then one as president. In all Adams devoted the better part of three and a half decades to America's independence and government, much of that time separated from his home and family. In the process he racked up more than thirty thousand miles of travel by sea and land, including several storm-filled voyages across the Atlantic and an equally hazardous thousand-mile journey across the Pyrenees in winter. If his country's well-being had been less of an obligation, he always insisted—sometimes protesting a bit too much—he could have lived a comfortable farmer-lawyer's life back in Massachusetts. Yet his acute sense of duty would never have allowed it; in all that he said and did, it was inconceivable that he would put his personal interests above those of the nation. In retirement he declared, with typical immodesty, "I have great Satisfaction in believing, that I have done more Labour, run through more and greater dangers, and made greater Sacrifices, than any Man among my Contemporaries living or dead, in the Service of my Country."[10] For Adams, this was an acceptable, republican form of pride: pride in service and self-sacrifice.

There was a brief period in the late 1780s—right around the time of the Constitutional Convention, during which Adams was in London—when he toyed with the idea that a properly balanced political order might compensate for a lack of virtue in the people. In his massive *Defence of the Constitutions of Government of the United States*, which was written in 1786–87 in defense of (some of) the state constitutions, he took direct issue with Montesquieu's claim that democratic republics require a virtuous citizenry.[11] "It is not true, in fact," he pronounced in the third volume, "that any people ever existed who loved the public better than themselves, their private friends,

neighbors, &c.," and so "all projects of government, formed upon a supposition of continual vigilance, sagacity, and virtue . . . are cheats and delusions."[12] Yet even in this work he maintained that virtue "cannot be too much beloved, practised, or rewarded" and that "the best republics will be virtuous, and have been so."[13]

Whatever Adams might have thought in the late 1780s, the idea that a republic might do without virtue did not long survive contact with America's new constitutional order. In fact, during every subsequent administration we find him repeating the point. As Washington's vice president he warned Abigail—who was not just his wife but also his dearest friend and closest political confidante—that "when Ambition and Avarice, are predominant Passions and Virtue is lost Republican Governments are in danger."[14] As president he declared that "Avarice, Ambition Revenge or Galantry, would break the strongest Cords of our Constitution as a Whale goes through a Net. Our Constitution was made only for a moral and religious People. It is wholly inadequate to the government of any other."[15] During Jefferson's presidency he proclaimed that "without national Morality a Republican Government cannot be maintained."[16] Under Madison's administration he reiterated that "Religion and Virtue are the only Foundations . . . of Republicanism and of all free Government."[17] And with James Monroe in the executive mansion he remained convinced that "without Virtue, there can be no political Liberty."[18]

As certain as Adams was that a virtuous citizenry was necessary for republican government to survive for long, he was never entirely persuaded that the American people possessed the requisite sense of duty. Early in his political career, during the war for independence, Adams had his doubts that his fellow citizens would reliably put the country first, and by the 1780s he was quite certain that they would not. Disillusionment with the American experiment thus came much earlier for Adams than it did for the other protagonists of this book, before the Constitution was even a twinkle in the framers' eyes. And the worries that began to develop during the Revolution persisted, in one form or another, through the remainder of Adams's long career and equally long retirement—for five full decades, altogether. Though Adams's disappointment in what the United States became was not

necessarily any deeper than that of his fellow founders, he expressed it more often and emphatically than they did, particularly in his voluminous, bracingly candid, and wonderfully colorful correspondence. (For all his pessimism and irascibility, Adams was also much funnier than the other founders, with his sardonic wit surpassed only by that of Benjamin Franklin.) One could easily fill a large volume with Adams's acerbic remarks on the American character, but here a few short chapters will have to suffice.

———————

Historians have sometimes claimed that there was a dramatic shift in Adams's outlook during the 1780s—that during the Revolution he optimistically believed that republican institutions would themselves suffice to render the American people virtuous, but that by the end of his diplomatic tours in Europe he had grown deeply pessimistic about the people's capacity for self-government.[19] The first half of this formulation, however, is overstated somewhat. It is true that one finds more sanguine comments about America's future in Adams's correspondence from the 1770s than at any point thereafter, but even in the midst of the Revolution his bouts of optimism rarely lasted for long and were frequently interspersed with far bleaker assessments, sometimes within the very same letter. The development of Adams's thought over the course of the 1770s and 1780s represented less a dramatic reversal than a shift in emphasis—a slow fading of already-faint hopes rather than an abrupt repudiation of earlier views.

All the same, let us begin with Adams's early hopes for republican government, however guarded and full of caveats they may have been. During the Revolution he had several reasons for believing that the American people possessed—or might come to possess—the necessary civic virtue. First, Adams initially assumed that the people would be more inclined to pursue the common good once independence was achieved and real political power was in their own hands. How could the people not want what was best for the public—which is to say, themselves? Whereas "under a Monarchy they may be as vicious and foolish as they please," he postulated, "under a well regulated Commonwealth, the People must be wise virtuous and cannot be otherwise."[20] Indeed, in his 1775 *Novanglus* ("New Englander") essays,

Adams went so far as to declare that "a democratical despotism is a contradiction in terms."[21]

Adams also presumed that the circumstances of the United States would help to render the American people virtuous, at least for the next few generations: as citizens of a new nation they would possess the vigor and vitality of youth, and as inhabitants of a relatively unspoiled New World they would embody the industry and simplicity of the frontier. They would replicate "the high Sentiments of Romans, in the most prosperous and virtuous Times of that Common Wealth," as opposed to the selfishness, luxury, and dissipation that generally attended declining empires like eighteenth-century Britain, where "the people . . . were depraved, the parliament venal, and the ministry corrupt."[22]

The most fundamental reason for Adams's early hopes, however, was also the simplest: he was often struck by the devotion, courage, and patriotism that Americans of all stripes exhibited during the war for independence. The people regularly rallied to defend their liberties when they came under attack from the British, whether that meant foregoing creature comforts without complaint, leaving their homes for months on end to attend the Continental Congress like Adams himself, or offering their military service—even their lives—for the cause. It was hard *not* to believe in the virtue of the American people after hearing of shoeless soldiers training through the winter at Valley Forge, tracking blood in the snow. As one historian writes, in Adams's view "the whole Revolution was one grand exercise in virtuous conduct."[23]

This was one great advantage of the trials and tribulations of the war, in his view: it required people to sacrifice on behalf of a common, higher purpose. As Adams wrote to Abigail on July 3, 1776, the day after the Continental Congress voted for independence: "It may be the Will of Heaven that America shall suffer Calamities still more wasting and Distresses yet more dreadfull. If this is to be the Case, it will have this good Effect, at least: it will inspire Us with many Virtues, which We have not, and correct many Errors, Follies, and Vices, which threaten to disturb, dishonour, and destroy Us.—The Furnace of Affliction produces Refinement, in States as well as Individuals."[24] This forecast seemed to be confirmed by America's victory in the war.

Adams remarked in his diary several years after the peace had been concluded that "a Revolution of Government, successfully conducted and compleated, is the strongest Proof, that can be given, by a People of their Virtue and good Sense. An Interprize of so much difficulty can never be planned and carried on without Abilities, and a People without Principle cannot have confidence enough in each other."[25]

Adams did what he could to buttress the incipient sense of virtue within the young republic. When it came time to choose an official seal for the United States, for instance, he proposed "the Choice of Hercules": an engraving of the ancient hero poised between "Virtue pointing to her rugged Mountain . . . and perswading him to ascend," on the one side, and "Sloth, glancing at her flowery Paths of Pleasure, wantonly reclining on the Ground, displaying the Charms both of her Eloquence and Person, to seduce him into Vice," on the other. (Adams ultimately admitted that this was "too complicated . . . for a Seal or Medal, and . . . not original.")[26]

There was a similar emphasis on virtue in the Massachusetts constitution that Adams drafted in 1779. This charter remains the oldest written constitution that is still in effect anywhere in the world, and it proved to be one of the most influential documents of the entire revolutionary period, as its declaration of rights and tripartite structure—with a bicameral legislature, a single elected executive, and an appointed judiciary—served as a prototype for many other state constitutions as well as the US Constitution itself. The section that Adams himself held most dear, however, was one that remained unique to Massachusetts. Because "wisdom, and knowledge, as well as virtue, diffused generally among the body of the people, [are] necessary for the preservation of their rights and liberties," Adams wrote, "it shall be the duty of legislators and magistrates, in all future periods of this Commonwealth, to cherish the interests of literature and the sciences, and all seminaries of them . . . to countenance and inculcate the principles of humanity and general benevolence, public and private charity, industry and frugality, honesty and punctuality in their dealings, sincerity, good humour, and all social affections, and generous sentiments among the people."[27] With this paragraph, Adams embedded into his state's constitution his deep conviction that virtue and education were vital elements of a healthy republic.

Even in the midst of the Revolution, however, Adams harbored some rather serious misgivings about the virtue of his fellow citizens. His appraisal of their character seemed to change from day to day—sometimes even from paragraph to paragraph. At times it seemed to him that the American people possessed every admirable character trait and that they were destined to have the brightest future of any nation in history, while at others he felt sure that they were as selfish and corrupt as all prior peoples had been and that their feeble attempts at self-government would soon meet with the usual swift demise. As early as January 1776, after telling Mercy Otis Warren that it was almost axiomatic that in a republic "the People must be wise virtuous and cannot be otherwise," Adams immediately went on to cast doubt on that axiom: "But Madam there is one Difficulty, which I know not how to get over. Virtue and Simplicity of Manners, are indispensably necessary in a Republic, among all orders and Degrees of Men. But there is So much Rascallity, so much Venality and Corruption, so much Avarice and Ambition, such a Rage for Profit and Commerce among all Ranks and Degrees of Men even in America, that I sometimes doubt whether there is public Virtue enough to support a Republic."[28] A few months later he reiterated to her that "our dear Americans perhaps have as much [public spirit] as any Nation now existing, and New England perhaps has more than the rest of America. But I have seen all along my Life, Such Selfishness, and Littleness even in New England, that I sometimes tremble to think that, altho We are engaged in the best Cause that ever employed the Human Heart, yet the Prospect of success is doubtfull not for Want of Power or of Wisdom, but of Virtue."[29]

This more pessimistic side of Adams's outlook too had a number of sources. One was the suspicion that human beings are inherently creatures of passion—indeed, of selfish passion—and that republican institutions could not change that basic fact. "No People ever had a finer opportunity to settle Things upon the best Foundations" than his own generation, Adams remarked. "But yet I fear that human Nature will be found to be the Same in America as it has been in Europe."[30] He was also worried that Americans lacked the moral fiber

for republican government because of their long tutelage under British monarchy: "We, in America, are So contaminated, with the Selfish Principles of Monarchy . . . that We have no Idea, no Conception, no Imagination, no Dream, of the Passions and Principles, which Support Republics. What will become of Us? God knows."[31]

Adams's most basic reason for doubt, however, was simple empirical observation. When he looked around at the conduct of his fellow citizens he sometimes saw noble patriotism, but he just as often saw ignoble selfishness. In the autumn of 1776 he grumbled to Abigail that "there is too much Corruption, even in this infant Age of our Republic. Virtue is not in Fashion. Vice is not infamous."[32] Whenever Adams read or heard of Americans not living up to the high expectations that he had set for them—every time a merchant or artisan showed greater concern for making money than for the public good, every time a housewife evinced a weakness for luxury, every time a soldier demonstrated a lack of discipline or abandoned the army, every time an election was decided through intrigue or demagoguery rather than true merit—he was shocked and appalled all over again. "There is one Enemy, which to me is more formidable, than Famine, Pestilence and the sword," he remarked to William Gordon, a minister and chronicler of the Revolution; "I mean the Corruption which is prevalent in so many American Hearts, a Depravity that is more inconsistent with our Republican Governments, than Light is with Darkness."[33] Similarly, he commented to his cousin Zabdiel Adams that if a sense of virtue "cannot be inspired into our People, in a greater Measure, than they have it now, They may change their Rulers, and the forms of Government, but they will not obtain a lasting Liberty.— They will only exchange Tyrants and Tyrannies."[34]

It was this darker side of the American character that made Adams so anxious to set up the state governments as quickly as possible after the colonies declared their independence, and to structure them in the right way. It would not do simply to give the people "unbounded Power," he insisted, for "the People are extreamly addicted to Corruption and Venality, as well as the Great."[35] As he made clear in his influential 1776 pamphlet *Thoughts on Government* as well as the Massachusetts constitution itself, Adams thought it was crucial to separate the legislative, executive, and judicial functions into different

branches, and to institute effective checks and balances among those branches—but even that was not nearly enough on its own.[36] Adams also advocated things like government support for education, compulsory service in the militia, and sumptuary laws regulating the consumption of luxury goods, all in the name of warding off the vices to which Americans, like their European forebears, had shown themselves prone.[37]

Adams's pessimism about the virtue of the American people, and hence their ability to sustain a republican government, only grew deeper and more unqualified in the years leading up to the Constitutional Convention. He spent most of the decade from 1778 to 1788 abroad, serving as a diplomat in France, Britain, and the Netherlands. Whereas the years that Jefferson spent as minister to France (1784–89) reinforced his belief in the unique purity of America and its people, Adams's time away from the United States had the opposite effect. His stay in Europe enabled him to view his fellow citizens with a distance and perspective that he had previously lacked, and he came to realize that they were not all that fundamentally different from the inhabitants of the European monarchies. There was no one precipitating event that led to Adams's growing disillusionment; rather, it arose gradually through the accumulation of many small but telling signs.

One such sign—one that was particularly glaring to Adams, charged as he was with negotiating alliances, loans, and treaties with his various European counterparts—was that the American people frequently failed to meet their obligations to other countries and to act in a unified way in foreign affairs. The dire state of the nation's finances under the Confederation Congress prevented the United States from paying off its foreign debts in a timely manner, and Adams placed the blame on what he perceived to be the extravagance and lack of discipline among the American people. "If there is no common Authority, nor any common Sense to secure a revenue for the discharge of our engagements abroad for money," he wondered, "what is to become of our honor, our justice, our faith, our Credit, our universal, moral, political & commercial Character?"[38] Adams was also aghast at America's behavior with regard to the Treaty of Paris, which concluded the

war and secured the nation's independence. As the treaty was being negotiated he was shocked that a majority in the Confederation Congress seemed inclined to allow the French to dictate the terms of the accord, and after it was concluded he lamented the inability of the United States to compel Britain to live up to its obligations as well as its failure to fulfill its own end of the bargain.

Another sign of the nation's fading virtue, in Adams's eyes—one that hit still closer to home—was that the American people did not sufficiently appreciate all that he had done, and continued to do, on their behalf. During his years in Europe Adams felt increasingly mistreated and ignored by his fellow citizens back at home, and he took this as proof that Americans no longer properly valued their dutiful servants, and instead idolized lazy, dissolute flatterers like his fellow minister Benjamin Franklin. (The two did not exactly take to one another during their time in Paris.) There was a part of Adams that reveled in his lack of popularity, which he regarded as a sure sign of his own disinterested virtue; there could be no doubt about the purity of his public-spiritedness if he reaped little but the scorn of his contemporaries as his reward. However, another part of him worried about what this lack of respect said about the American people and the future of their republic. Such was the people's growing "selfishness, Vanity, flattery and Corruption," he remarked on the way home from his first stint in France, that "if these proceed much longer in their Career, it will not be worth the while of Men of Virtue, to make themselves miserable by continuing in the service. If they leave it . . . there will be an End of our virtuous Vision of a Kingdom of the just."[39]

More broadly, Adams bemoaned the thirst for luxury and material gain that he saw gripping his fellow Americans, particularly after the end of the war. Taking his cue from the dark reports that streamed in from his stateside correspondents, Adams concluded that republican simplicity, industry, and frugality were giving way to the kind of ostentatious display, dissipation, and avidity that were thought to be more characteristic of monarchial peoples. On his first arrival in Paris in 1778 he reported to Abigail that "the Delights of France are innumerable. The Politeness, the Elegance, the Softness, the Delicacy, is extreme. . . . The Richness, the Magnificence, and Splendor, is beyond all Description." Unsurprisingly, none of this was to his own taste:

"stern and hauty Republican as I am . . . I receive but little Pleasure in beholding all these Things, because I cannot but consider them as Bagatelles, introduced, by Time and Luxury in Exchange for the great Qualities and hardy manly Virtues of the human Heart. I cannot help suspecting that the more Elegance, the less Virtue in all Times and Countries." Yet the conclusion that he drew was not as complimentary toward his own homeland as one might have expected: "I fear that even my own dear Country wants the Power and Opportunity more than the Inclination, to be elegant, soft, and luxurious."[40] By 1785 he was in fact "fixed in the belief," as he informed Samuel Adams, "that our Countrymen have in them a more ungovernable passion for Luxury than any People upon earth."[41]

The increasingly commercial nature of American society rendered the people not only more corrupt, as Adams saw it, but also more divided. The growth of wealth pitted the rich against the poor, and the growth of trade and manufacturing pitted merchants and cities against farmers. Measured against Adams's decidedly idealized memory of an American populace standing in unison against British depredations during the war, the United States of the 1780s could not help but look less cohesive by comparison. One particularly pernicious source and sign of social division, he believed, was the institution in 1783 of the Society of the Cincinnati, a club—presided over first by Washington and then by Hamilton—for officers of the Continental Army and their descendants. This society, Adams complained to Elbridge Gerry, was "sowing the Seeds of all that European Courts wish to grow up among Us, vizt. of Vanity, Ambition, Corruption, Discord, & Sedition. . . . We are in the high Road to have no Virtues left." The kind of "artificial Inequalities of Decorations, Birth and Title, not accompanying public Trusts" that the Cincinnati was introducing to the American republic, he argued, were "those very Inequalities which have exterminated Virtue and Liberty and substituted Ambition and slavery in all Ages and Countries."[42]

All told, by the end of his long European sojourn Adams was convinced that "our Country men have never merited the Character of very exalted Virtue" and that "it is not to be expected that they should have grown much better."[43] In October 1787, just weeks before the first copy of the Constitution reached him in London, he predicted

to Jefferson: "you and I have been indefatigable Labourers, through our whole Lives for a Cause which will be thrown away in the next Generation, upon the Vanity and Foppery of Persons of whom We do not now know the Names perhaps."[44] By the time that he penned his magnum opus, then, Adams was certain that virtue alone could not sustain a republican government in America.

CHAPTER 8

HIS ROTUNDITY

ADAMS WROTE HIS *Defence of the Constitutions of Government of the United States* in 1786 and 1787 while in London, serving as the first American minister to Great Britain. The *Defence* has been described as "the only comprehensive description of American constitutionalism that the period produced" and even "the finest fruit of the American Enlightenment."[1] It is also a rather uneven, long-winded, convoluted work whose central message is frequently lost in a maze of analyses of regimes, philosophers, and historians from the ancient world to Adams's own day, spread across three volumes.[2] The immediate catalyst for the *Defence* seems to have been the opinion of many French and British intellectuals of the time that the kinds of checks and balances that were embedded in the American state constitutions were unnecessary or even pernicious—that political sovereignty should be lodged in a single legislative body whose duty it would be to enact the popular will, without any constraints. In response, Adams rose to the defense of balanced government in the form of a bicameral legislature and a single, independent executive. Despite the work's title, then, he did not endorse *all* the state constitutions—Pennsylvania's, for instance, included a unicameral legislature and a weak, plural executive—but rather those that he believed achieved the right kind of separation and balance, the foremost examples being those of New York, Maryland, and (of course) Massachusetts.

Underlying this immediate objective, however, there was a more fundamental motivation for all of Adams's study and writing: he was seeking to determine—for himself and his country—whether it was possible to compensate for a lack of virtue within a republic through the proper political structure. There was no question, now, of the American people being disinterested and public-spirited enough to

make republican government work without substantial checks on their power. Whereas in 1775 Adams had suggested that "a democratical despotism is a contradiction in terms," by this point he was convinced that an unbridled democracy could not be anything *other* than a despotism.[3] "We may appeal to every page of history we have hitherto turned over," he stated in the concluding volume of the *Defence*, "for proofs irrefragable, that the people, when they have been unchecked, have been as unjust, tyrannical, brutal, barbarous, and cruel, as any king or senate possessed of uncontrollable power. The majority has eternally, and without one exception, usurped over the rights of the minority."[4]

Nor did Adams now believe, as he had sometimes dared to hope in the 1770s, that Americans were fundamentally different from, let alone inherently superior to, other peoples. Whereas Jefferson and others continued to cling to the illusion of American exceptionalism, Adams declared flatly that "there is no special providence for Americans, and their nature is the same with that of others."[5] In the wake of the war for independence, for instance, his fellow Americans immediately "rushed headlong into a greater degree of luxury than ought to have crept in for a hundred years."[6] In fact, as Gordon Wood writes, in the *Defence* "Adams gave Americans as grim and as dark a picture of themselves as they have ever been offered."[7] Adams was well aware that such a portrait would not win him many admirers back in the United States, but he felt that it was vital to avoid flattering the people too much. When the first volume was published in January 1787 he wrote to James Warren—a friend and fellow patriot, and Mercy Otis's husband—that "Popularity was never my Mistress, nor was I ever, or shall I ever be a popular Man. This Book will make me unpopular. But one Thing I know a Man must be Sensible of the Errors of the People, and upon his Guard against them, and must run the risque of their Displeasure Sometimes, or he will never do them any good in the long run."[8]

How, then, might the United States be saved from the dismal fate of earlier republics? How might order and stability be maintained in a society wracked by selfishness and licentiousness? In the *Defence* Adams proposed that the key was to institutionalize, and thereby manage, the conflict among the different social orders—the one, the

few, and the many. In every society, he argued, including those of the American states, the populace would always be divided into the rich and the poor, gentlemen and commoners. And in a single legislative body, the former would always prevail: "The rich, the well-born, and the able, acquire an influence among the people that will soon be too much for simple honesty and plain sense, in a house of representatives." The solution was to separate the aspiring aristocrats and oligarchs from the rest of society and place them in a senate, where their ambition, wealth, and guile could do less harm. Adams described the establishment of such an upper chamber as being "to all honest and useful intents, an ostracism."[9] The passions of the people—more fundamentally decent perhaps, but also more turbulent and less informed—would in turn be confined to a lower chamber, and the two orders would be put in a position to check and balance one another. In order to maintain an equilibrium between them, Adams went on, it was also necessary to establish a single, independent executive—the republican equivalent of a monarch—with an absolute veto that could be used to resist the foolish or oppressive measures of either house of the legislature.[10]

Some of Adams's proposals in the *Defence* were a bit idiosyncratic—few of his fellow founders other than Hamilton, Gouverneur Morris, and James Wilson would have welcomed the idea of an executive with an absolute veto over legislation, for instance, and it was fanciful to assume that stationing the rich and wellborn in a senate would *limit* their influence—but the general blueprint was well within the mainstream of Federalist thinking at the time.[11] The more striking feature of the work was just how unequal its proposals seemed to the task at hand. If the American people were as thoroughly vicious as Adams now insisted they were, then it is difficult to see how a government of the kind that he outlined, no matter how well balanced, would produce the necessary order and stability, much less provide the degree of personal liberty and popular accountability that Americans so obviously craved. As Wood remarks, "Adams's constitutional remedy could scarcely have been more disproportionate to the severity of the social ills he described."[12] At least for the moment, however, Adams appeared to hold out some hope.

Adams's faith in the American experiment was also temporarily buoyed by the new Constitution. Throughout the 1780s he had been far less scornful of the Articles of Confederation than Washington and Hamilton had been. As late as his writing of the *Defence*, Adams appears to have believed that the proper response to America's political woes was to bolster the state constitutions rather than to overhaul the federal government. When he received a copy of the proposed national constitution from John Jay in the autumn of 1787, however, he greeted it warmly. On the whole, he told Jefferson in November, "it seems to be admirably calculated to preserve the Union, to increase affection, and to bring us all to the same mode of thinking."[13]

It would have been entirely out of character, of course, if Adams had failed to find some faults with the new charter—particularly since he had no direct hand in devising it. In fact, some of his objections were so substantial that he informed Jefferson that he found it "difficult to reconcile myself" to them. Though the Constitution's framers clearly sought to create a balanced political order, just as Adams had recommended on the state level in the *Defence*, he did not believe that they managed to strike quite the right balance. Above all, he thought that the presidency should have been made stronger and the Senate weaker. When Jefferson expressed concern about the powers of the executive, Adams replied that he was of the opposite opinion: "You are afraid of the one—I, of the few. . . . You are apprehensive of monarchy: I of Aristocracy. I would therefore have given more power to the President and less to the Senate." Adams argued that the president should have been accorded a stronger veto over legislation, for instance, as well as the authority to make appointments to the cabinet, the federal judiciary, and ambassadorships without Senate approval. And whereas Jefferson feared that "the President when once chosen, will be chosen again and again as long as he lives," since there was as yet no term limit on the president, Adams was entirely unperturbed by this possibility: "So much the better as it appears to me."[14]

One reason for Adams's apparent nonchalance on this score was that he had come to regard elections—especially elections for high

office—as moments of potential danger. "You are apprehensive of foreign Interference, Intrigue, Influence," he wrote to Jefferson. "So am I—But, as often as elections happen, the danger of foreign Influence recurs. the less frequently they happen the less danger. . . . Elections, my dear Sir, Elections to Offices which are great objects of ambition, I look at with terror—Experiments of this kind have been so often tryed, and so universally found productive of Horrors, that there is great Reason to dread them."[15] One issue on which Adams and Jefferson agreed was the desirability of a bill of rights of the kind that Adams had included in the Massachusetts constitution, though Adams admitted that he was "sensible of the Difficulty of framing one, in which all the States can agree."[16] Despite his reservations, however, Adams was firmly in favor of ratifying the new Constitution. In his response to Jay, which he knew would be widely quoted back in the United States, Adams remarked that "a Result of Accommodation and Compromise, cannot be supposed, perfectly to coincide with any Ones Ideas of Perfection. But as all the great Principles neccessary to Order, Liberty and Safety are respected in it, and Provision is made for Corrections and Amendments as they may be found neccessary, I confess I hope to hear of its adoption by all the States."[17]

The two-year period in which Adams wrote the *Defence* and first took stock of the Constitution marked the apogee of his belief that the proper political structure might enable republican government to succeed in the United States even without a virtuous citizenry. After the new government was launched, he quickly became much more pessimistic about that prospect.

Adams's experience as the nation's first vice president resembled the experience of many later vice presidents, which is to say that he found the office to be exceedingly frustrating. During his eight years in that role he exercised very little real political power and was rarely consulted by Washington or Hamilton about the administration's policies. His primary duty was to preside over the Senate, which meant that he was forced to sit through countless hours of tedious debate without the consolation of being able to chime in himself and share his hard-won wisdom with the legislators. On a personal level, Adams was elated to

be back in the United States and to see his family on a more regular basis, but his estimation of the new government plummeted soon after the Constitution went into effect. He concluded almost immediately, in fact, that it could not last for long in its current form. Scarcely a month after his inauguration as vice president, Adams wrote to Abigail from the temporary capital of New York to insist that "we must make this place our home, and think no more of Braintree, for four years,"but then quickly qualified that timeline: "I Said four Years, upon the supposition that the Government should support itself so long."[18] Within another year he was already asserting that he could "think of no Remedy" for the political ills afflicting the nation "but another *Convention*."[19]

A number of events and circumstances contributed to Adams's rapid return to a state of disillusionment. One was simply his continued belief that the constitutional scheme was improperly balanced. In July 1789 he warned Roger Sherman that the roles given to Congress in declaring war, approving treaties, and confirming executive appointments, along with the ability to override a veto, all combined to place too many limits on the president's power. These limitations, he wrote, "will be the destruction of this Constitution, and involve us in Anarchy, if not amended.... The Legislative Power in our Constitution, is greater than the Executive. it will therefore encroach— because both Aristocratical and democratical Passions"—which he saw as represented in the Senate and the House of Representatives, respectively—"are insatiable." He remained particularly concerned about the Senate, remarking that "the Aristocratical Power is greater than either the Monarchical or Democratical" and that it "will therefore Swallow up the other two."[20]

Adams also came to worry, like Hamilton, that the power and stature of the state governments might prove too much for the federal government. As the new constitutional order was being established he began to sense that "we are in great danger" since "the Superiority, the Sovereignty of the national Govt" was "not in fact secured" by the Constitution, even if it had been "in words ascertained."[21] By 1791 he fretted that "the Rivalry between the state Governments and the national Government, is growing daily more active and ardent. Thirteen strong Men embracing thirteen Pillars at once, and bowing themselves in concert, will easily pull down a frail Edifice."[22]

Adams was further dismayed by much of Hamilton's financial program. While he was not opposed to all trade and manufacturing in the way that Jefferson sometimes appeared to be, Adams viewed luxury and avarice as signs of corruption, and he regarded banks and paper money as little better than frauds perpetrated on ordinary Americans. As for Hamilton's plan for the debt, Adams maintained that "the funding system is the hair shirt which our sinful country must wear as a propitiation for her past dishonesty" since it was "the bad morals of the people" that had brought on their immense indebtedness.[23] Nor did Adams grow reconciled to the financial program over time. Near the end of the decade, as president, he still insisted that "there is not a democrat in the world, who affects more horror than I really feel, at the prospect of that frightful system of debts and taxes, into which imperious necessity seems to be precipitating us."[24]

Another cause of Adams's despair was the rise of partisanship within the new government. Like Washington, Adams regarded political parties as sources of domestic conflict, instability, and corruption, as well as avenues for foreign influence. Whereas Washington was satisfied that the federal government remained reasonably free of faction for its first few years, however, Adams predicted as early as the summer of 1789, in the midst of Congress's very first session, that "we shall very soon have parties formed," one of which "will support the President and his Measures and Ministers—the other will oppose them."[25] The following year he told Benjamin Rush that "awful Experience has concurred with Reading and Reflection to convince me that Americans are more rapidly disposed to *Corruption* in Elections, than I thought they were fourteen years ago"—that is, when he wrote *Thoughts on Government*. "I lament the deplorable Condition of my Country, which seems to be under such a Fatality that the People can agree upon nothing."[26] (By corruption in elections, Adams meant that private and party interests prevailed in voters' minds above the national interest.) In 1791 Adams declared to Jefferson that "those unbridled Rivalries which have already appeared, are the most melancholly and alarming Symptoms that I have ever seen in this Country."[27] By the election year of 1792—which is when Washington's long-term disillusionment first began to set in—Adams had long since made up his mind: "If ambition and avarice are not as strong in this Coun-

try, as in others, my observations have been inaccurate. If intrigues and manuvres in Elections have not been practised, and are not now practising, I have been misinformed; and if the people are not every day deceived by artifice and falsehood, I have no understanding."[28]

Still another reason for Adams's loss of faith was the influence of the French Revolution on American affairs. Adams was, along with Hamilton, among the earliest critics of the sweeping changes in France. Adams told his son Charles in 1794 that "majorities, banishing, confiscating, massacring guillotening Minorities, has been the whole History of the French Revolution, which I had told them would be the Case in three long Volumes before they began [i.e., in the *Defence*]— But they would not believe me."[29] Like Washington and Hamilton, Adams was appalled by the undiminished enthusiasm that many Republicans showed for the revolution even after it turned violent. With the Republicans' welcome of Citizen Genêt in 1793, support of the Democratic Societies in 1794, and opposition to the Jay Treaty in 1795, it seemed that every year demonstrated their continued susceptibility to "the French delirium."[30] By 1795 Adams went so far as to envision a "general and total . . . destruction" in Europe: "If all Religions and Governments all Arts and sciences are destroyed the Trees will grow up, Cities will moulde into common Earth, and, a few human Beings may be left naked to chase the Wild Beasts with Bows, and arrows." He held out some hope that "Religion and Learning will find an Asylum in America," but he feared that "too many of our fellow Citizens are carried away in the dirty Torrent of dissolving Europe."[31]

In response to these worries about the fate of America's constitutional order, Adams began to advocate measures that led many of his contemporaries to believe that he had renounced republicanism altogether. One was his suggestion that a degree of splendor and ceremony should be introduced into the new government, particularly the presidency. Adams advised Washington that he should conduct himself in a formal manner and keep a "large and ample" household in the executive mansion, including a retinue of "Chamberlains, Aids de Camp, Secretaries, Masters of Ceremonies &c."[32] He also proposed in the Senate that Washington should be addressed by a suitably majestic

title—something along the lines of "His Highness, the President of the United States of America, and Protector of Their Liberties."[33] Perhaps unsurprisingly, Adams was mocked for all of this: his detractors dubbed him "the Duke of Braintree" and "His Rotundity." Many, including Jefferson, concluded that Adams had spent altogether too much time at Versailles and the Court of St. James's and that he had grown infatuated with the trappings of monarchy. Such accusations were doubly ironic, given both Adams's middling background—he was never nearly as rich, or as aristocratic in his lifestyle, as Jefferson was—and his stern republican disposition. (Recall Adams's distaste for the excessive politeness, elegance, and magnificence that he encountered in Paris.)

It was the absence of republican virtue in the United States that led Adams to advocate introducing all these allegedly monarchial trappings.[34] Because the people could not be counted on to respect the government or its officers out of a spirit of patriotism, he thought, it was necessary to find an alternative means of invoking the proper sense of dignity. Titles and ceremonies might be mere frivolities in and of themselves, but they often succeeded in capturing the people's imagination and eliciting their esteem. "As far as I can judge," Adams explained to Benjamin Rush, "there is as much Vice, Folly, and more Infidelity, Idleness Luxury and Dissipation, in any of our great Towns, in Proportion to Numbers, as in London.—But the question should be what would be, the degree of profligacy in London, if there were no titles? and I Seriously believe it would be much greater than it is.—Nay I don't believe it would be possible to support any government at all, among such multitudes without Distinctions of Rank and the Titles that mark them."[35]

Similarly, Adams believed that titles and ceremonies would help to induce the most capable individuals to serve in public office. Because Americans could not be counted on to serve their country out of a sense of duty, it was necessary to lure them to do so through the promise of being honored and admired. "Has the national Govt at this moment, attractions enough to make a seat in it, an object of desire, to the Men of greatest Fortune, Talents, Birth, or Virtue?" he asked William Tudor, a wealthy Boston lawyer. "You will not babble to me about Patriotism, Zeal, Enthusiasm, Love of Property, and Country,

at this time of day. . . . I see nothing since I arrived from Europe, but one universal and ungovernable rage for the Loaves and Fishes. The Corruption of Ambition and Avarice, has more universal possession of the Souls of the Gentlemen of this Country, than of the Nobility of any Country in Europe—But the new Govt has no Objects of Ambition or Avarice, sufficient to satiate the appetites that crave." The solution seemed clear: "If the People would give Titles or marks of Distinction, this would go a great way."[36]

Adams's supposed apostasy from republicanism was also evident in his repeated predictions, during the new government's early years, that America would eventually be forced to introduce elements of hereditary succession into its political order. The nation's elections routinely produced so much instability and partisanship, he believed, that one day the people would find it safer simply to do away with them, at least for the presidency and the Senate. The current form of government would continue to exist, he conjectured, "till Intrigue and Corruption, Factions and Seditions shall appear in [the nation's] Elections to Such a degree as to render hereditary Institutions, a Remedy against a greater Evil."[37] Adams never advocated the immediate introduction of hereditary succession into American politics, but he did believe that it might be necessary in the relatively near future. To Rush he wrote that "I am clear that America must resort to [hereditary rule] as an Asylum against Discord Seditions and Civil War, and that at no very distant period of time. I shall not live to See it—but you may."[38] Given that Rush was forty-three at the time—all of twelve years Adams's junior—it appears that Adams foresaw all this happening within the next few decades.

As might be expected, Adams's talk of replacing elections with hereditary succession prompted further charges of monarchism, but he insisted that he remained "as much a Republican as I was in 1775," when he led the charge toward independence. It was, he swore, not with longing but with regret that he envisaged the introduction of hereditary rule into America's political order, for it signaled the utter failure of his earlier republican hopes. Once again, it was the lack of virtue in the American people that made self-government so difficult. Still, Adams found it unfortunate that virtually all his contemporaries treated aristocracy and monarchy with such utter contempt. It was

"impolitick," he felt, to entertain "prejudices against Institutions which must be kept in view as the Hope of our Posterity." While America was "not ripe for" hereditary rule just yet, "our ship must ultimately land on that shore or be cast away."[39]

Most of Adams's predictions about the inevitability of hereditary rule came in private correspondence, but he did make one such comment in a very public forum. Between April 1790 and April 1791 he published a series of thirty-two essays called *Discourses on Davila* in John Fenno's Federalist-leaning *Gazette of the United States*. He would later describe these discourses as the fourth volume of his *Defence*, but whereas the *Defence* had focused especially on the dangers of aristocracy and the need to "ostracize" would-be aristocrats in a senate, the *Davila* essays—inspired at least in part by the growing tempest in France—concentrated even more on the dangers of excessive democracy. In the final installment, which was printed in Fenno's *Gazette* but not included in the later compilation of the discourses, Adams noted that most societies throughout history had concluded that "hereditary succession was attended with fewer evils than frequent elections." Speaking for himself, he then remarked that "this is the true answer, and the only one, as I believe."[40] This comment, coming from the vice president of the United States, provoked a storm of controversy; even Hamilton was disgusted by the artlessness that lay behind Adams's candor, which he worried might taint the Federalist cause.

Adams's open doubts about the continued viability of republican government in America would be used against him in the 1796 election, when he was depicted by the Republican press as an unabashed monarchist who hoped to assume the presidency and then institute hereditary rule in order to pave the way for his son, John Quincy. These unfair charges were not enough to prevail against his status as the "colossus of independence" and Washington's vice president, however, and so His Rotundity duly ascended to the president's chair in March 1797.[41]

Amid the excitement of his inauguration, Adams conveniently forgot—or perhaps papered over—some of his misgivings about America's constitutional order. Indeed, in his Inaugural Address he offered a full-throated endorsement of that order, describing the Constitution

as "a result of good heads, prompted by good hearts," proclaiming that "the operation of it has equalled the most sanguine Expectations of its Friends," and insisting that he had come to feel "an habitual Attachment to it, and Veneration for it. What other form of Government indeed can so well deserve our Esteem and love?" Adams did offer his listeners a few warnings. The nation's liberty would be endangered, he intoned, "if any thing partial or extraneous Should infect the Purity of our free, fair, virtuous and independent Elections." He also expressed a desire to promote "Knowledge, Virtue and Religion among all Classes of the People . . . as the only means of preserving our Constitution from its natural Enemies the Spirit of Sophistry, the Spirit of Party, the Spirit of Intrigue, the profligacy of Corruption and the Pestilence of foreign Influence, which is the Angel of destruction to elective Governments."[42] For the most part, though, the address rang a note of hope rather than one of gloom.

It was not long before Adams's worries resurfaced in full force. Just two weeks later he lamented to Abigail: "From the Situation, where I now am, I see a Scene of Ambition, beyond all my former suspicions or Imaginations. . . . Jealousies & Rivalries have been my Theme and Checks and Ballances as their Antidotes till I am ashamed to repeat the Words: but they never Stared me in the face in such horrid forms as at present. I see how the Thing is going. at the next Election England will sett up Jay or Hamilton and France Jefferson and all the Corruption of Poland will be introduced."[43] In another two months he would tell Elbridge Gerry that "the Want of *Principle*, in so many of our Citizens . . . is awfully ominous to our elective Government. . . . The Avarice and Ambition which you and I have witnessed for these thirty years, is too deeply rooted in the hearts and Education and Examples of our People ever to be eradicated, and it will make of all our Elections only a species of lucrative Speculation, and consequently Scenes of Turbulence Corruption and Confusion of which foreign nations will avail them Selves in the future as the French did in the last."[44] It is doubtful that any other American president has been as pessimistic about the entire political system at the very outset of his administration.

Adams was bound to face a challenging presidency. Anyone who attempted to replace the irreplaceable Washington would have had

his work cut out for him in terms of earning the people's respect and trust, and it did not help that Adams's public demeanor was often pugnacious and irritable where Washington's had been stately and stolid. Whereas Washington was elected unanimously twice, Adams prevailed over Jefferson in the electoral college by only three votes, seventy-one to sixty-eight. The narrowness of the victory attested to the deep partisan divide that had turned American politics into a powder keg by this point. In many policy areas Adams was opposed not only by the Republicans, but also by a substantial segment of his own party that remained loyal to Hamilton. This quandary was heightened by the fact that the latter group included most of Adams's own cabinet, which he unwisely retained in its entirety from Washington's administration.

Adams aimed to be the kind of independent executive that he had championed in his political writings, but he had little but his theories to draw on, as he was almost entirely without executive experience: he had never been a governor, a military leader, or even a cabinet officer, and as vice president he had generally been sidelined within the Washington administration. As his presidency wore on, he relinquished some of the little control that he had over the nation's affairs by spending more and more time back in Massachusetts, which was interpreted by his opponents as a cowardly flight from his troubles in the capital. All the while, Adams's every move was scrutinized for signs of his purported monarchism.

Looming over all these domestic liabilities was the threat of war with the colossus that was France; the growing tensions between the United States and its former ally was easily the dominant issue of Adams's presidency. With a meager army and no navy to speak of when he assumed office, the United States appeared to be exceptionally vulnerable to a French invasion, and French privateers preyed on American ships at will in the Atlantic and the West Indies. Much to the Republicans' chagrin, Adams supported the strengthening of the nation's armed forces, particularly the navy, to meet the threat. Yet he also sensed, as Washington had before him, that the nation was far too young and fragile to become mired in a European war, so he was much more determined than were Hamilton and his followers to resolve the impasse diplomatically.

Adams's self-control was tested in the wake of the XYZ Affair, when his defiance in the face of the outrages committed against America's diplomats made him wildly popular for the one and only time of his life. As public acclamations and songs of praise rained down on him from all corners of the country in the summer of 1798, Adams committed the greatest blunder of his presidency. Though he later swore that the Alien and Sedition Acts were the work of extremists in Congress—that he had never really desired such laws and accepted them only with regret—they nevertheless bore his signature. (Abigail, by contrast, supported these measures as fervently as any High Federalist.)

The crisis continued to grow deeper throughout the remainder of the year. The Quasi-War, which Adams called "the half War with France," proceeded unabated on the high seas, and the Republican opposition mounted a counterattack against the Alien and Sedition Acts in the form of the Virginia and Kentucky Resolutions.[45] Like Washington and Hamilton, Adams grew more and more convinced that the Republicans would collaborate with the French if the two countries were to come to blows, and he began to hear ominous rumors of militias arming themselves in Virginia in preparation for resisting the federal government. Meanwhile Hamilton, perhaps the individual in the world whom Adams trusted the least, was hatching his extravagant plans for the New Army. As Adams saw it, the very fabric of American society was being torn apart by a pair of hostile factions that were each prostrate before a foreign power and willing to put their own political ambitions ahead of the nation's well-being. His response, as a virtuous American patriot, was to save the country by sacrificing himself.

Adams stunned the nation in February 1799 by announcing that he planned to send a new peace mission to France, despite the insulting treatment that had been shown to the last set of American diplomats. He made the decision unilaterally, surprising even Abigail. Adams's bold move single-handedly alleviated the most serious foreign crisis that the nation had faced since securing its independence. It also outraged his fellow Federalists, many of whom were hungry for war.

They turned on Adams so thoroughly and violently that he started receiving death threats from supporters of his own party. After protracted negotiations, the peace mission eventually proved successful, though the news of the treaty did not reach the United States until after the election of 1800 was over. In the meantime, the irreparable divide within the Federalist party all but assured that Adams could not win reelection.

It would have been in Adams's political self-interest to escalate tensions with France, or even go to war, in order to align his party squarely behind him, but he was willing to risk his presidency in order to avoid what he knew would have been a calamitous mistake for the country. This was the kind of virtue that he always believed was so necessary, but so lamentably absent, in American politics. He could not have been prouder. Adams later proclaimed that "I will defend my Missions to France as long as I have an Eye to direct my hand or a finger to hold my pen. They were the most disinterested And meritorious Actions of my Life. I reflect upon them with So much satisfaction that I desire No other Inscription on my Grave Stone than 'Here lies John Adams who took upon himself the Responsability of the Peace with France in the Year 1800.'"[46]

The election of 1800 was perhaps the ugliest, most vicious presidential contest in American history.[47] Malicious slanders and bald-faced lies abounded on both sides. In the end Adams performed surprisingly well, all things considered. He lost by only eight votes in the electoral college, seventy-three to sixty-five, even after Hamilton, one of the leading members of his party, published a diatribe against him. If a few hundred votes had gone the other way in New York City, in fact, he would have won reelection. Of course, Adams took little solace in that fact. He tried to put on a brave face in public—even to glory in his defeat as proof of his integrity and independence—but it was clear that he was crushed. In spite of all that he had done for the country, it had turned on him. Whereas Washington had been able to leave office voluntarily, with his dignity intact, he was being forced out in humiliating fashion.

Adams took his loss especially hard because he saw it as confirmation that there was no longer room for someone like himself—someone who was willing to sacrifice himself or his party for the good

of the nation—in American public life. In some respects, he knew, his successor would be inheriting the presidency at an auspicious moment. "I Shall leave the State with its Coffers full, and the fair prospect of peace with all the World Smiling in its face, its Commerce flourishing, its Navy glorious, its Agriculture uncommonly productive and lucrative," he boasted.[48] Yet the peace and prosperity that America enjoyed was overshadowed by the degeneracy of its politics. A month before he left office, Adams wrote that "clouds black and gloomy hang over this country threatning a fierce tempest, arising merely from party conflicts at a time when the internal and external prosperity of it ... are the most pleasing and promising, that we ever beheld."[49] A few days later he predicted that "we shall be tossed ... in the tempestuous sea of liberty for years to come & where the bark can land but in a political convulsion I cannot see."[50] As always, the principal cause of the gloom and the tempests, in his eyes, was the absence of virtue in the American people: "Downright corruption has spread & increased in America more than I had any knowledge or suspicion of. Even parties themselves have no common principle of union that can long bind them together—notwithstanding at times & for short periods, they show an astonishing unanimity."[51]

Adams left the capital before dawn on the day of Jefferson's inauguration, leaving no messages and delivering no Farewell Address. He simply went back to Quincy to brood.

CHAPTER 9

THE BRIGHTEST OR THE BLACKEST PAGE

A DAMS'S RETIREMENT LASTED for more than twenty-five years—longer than that of any other American president until the twentieth century.[1] In all that time the farthest that he traveled from his home in Quincy was to Cambridge, around ten miles away. Adams also assumed very few public roles after he left the presidency. For the first four years or so, in fact, he stayed almost entirely out of the public eye and corresponded little with anyone beyond a tight circle of family and friends. After so many decades immersed in the whirlwind of high politics, he now devoted his days to his family and his farm. He characterized this self-imposed solitude as making up for lost time—savoring the everyday joys of domestic life that public service had denied him for so many years—but surely there was more than a little element of licking his wounds to be found in it, as well.

By all appearances, Adams was less preoccupied with politics and current events during Jefferson's first term than at any prior period in his adult life. Judging from the comparatively few comments that survive from these years, however, it is clear that Adams had grown no more optimistic about the character of the American people since leaving office. To François Adriaan van der Kemp, a Dutch patriot whom he had met in the Netherlands and with whom he kept up a warm correspondence, particularly after van der Kemp emigrated to the United States in 1788, he wrote that "the Virtue and good Sense of Americans, which I own I once had some dependence on, and which have been trumpetted with more extravagance by others, are become a byword."[2] In 1802 Adams groused to his daughter Nabby, "You speak of 'moderate people on both sides'—If you know of any

such, I congratulate you on your felicity. All that I know of that description are of no more consequence than if there were none.... I mourn over the accumulated disgraces we are bringing on ourselves: but I can do nothing."[3]

During this period Adams's attitude toward his successor was largely negative, though not despairing. Near the end of 1804, when it was clear that Jefferson would win reelection handily, Adams declared to John Quincy that "public affairs at present do not affect me So unpleasantly as you imagine. I regret the daring freedoms which have been practised on the constitution: I regret the Tryumph of Ambition over public Virtue: I regret the impudent front of Vice and Crime, which Shews itself So openly. But the general Conduct of public affairs is not to me So very terrible." Adams found fault with some of Jefferson's actions—the dismissal of so many Federalist officers, the repeal of the Judiciary Act of 1801 (the one that created the so-called midnight judges), the neglect of the navy—but on the whole he felt that Jefferson's ascendancy had not produced the radical revolution that the Federalists had feared and Jefferson had promised. In his view, their differences were mostly matters of style: whereas Adams had delivered his annual messages to Congress as speeches, Jefferson preferred to send them in writing; whereas Adams had held large, formal receptions, Jefferson preferred smaller, more intimate dinners. These changes were, Adams insisted, "mere Trifles, which give me neither pleasure nor pain."[4] Still, by 1808, as Jefferson's second term neared its end, Adams judged that "Mr Jefferson has reason to reflect upon himself. How he will get rid of his Remorse in his Retirement I know not. He must know that he leaves the government infinitely worse than he found it and that from his own Error or Ignorance."[5]

In February 1805, Adams reopened his correspondence with the Philadelphia physician and social reformer Benjamin Rush, a move that signaled his readiness to engage with the broader world once more. The two had been close friends during the Revolution, but some distance had grown between them in the 1790s as a result of Rush's support for Jefferson and the Republicans. "It seemeth unto me that you and I ought not to die without saying good-bye or bidding each other Adieu," Adams now wrote to his old friend. "Let me put a few questions to your conscience for I know you have one. Is the present

State of the Nation Republican enough? Is virtue the principle of our Government? Is honor? Or is ambition and avarice adulation, baseness, covetousness, the thirst of riches, indifference concerning the means of rising and enriching, the contempt of principle, the Spirit of party and of faction, the motive and the principle that governs? These are Serious and dangerous questions; but serious men ought not to flinch from dangerous questions."[6] Thus began one of the most spirited, frank, and downright entertaining exchanges of letters that is to be found in any of the founders' papers.[7] Though Adams's later correspondence with Jefferson is more famous today, it was in his letters to Rush that he felt most free to give voice to his innermost thoughts and feelings, releasing them in a torrent of vivid prose that Rush in turn both stimulated and matched. Their exchange served as one of Adams's chief preoccupations and outlets until Rush's death in 1813.

The Adams-Rush correspondence ranged over a vast array of subjects, but the ones that recurred most frequently were the character of the American people and the future of the American regime. Rush was at least as pessimistic on these scores as Adams, which spurred Adams to express his cynicism even more colorfully and candidly to him than he did to others. "Oh my country," Adams exclaimed to Rush in September 1806, "how I mourn over thy follies and Vices, thine ignorance and imbecillity, Thy contempt of Wisdom and Virtue and overweening Admiration of fools and Knaves!" These ills were, he suggested, "the never failing effects of democracy. I once thought our Constitution was quasi a mixed Government, but they have now made it, to all intents and purposes, in Virtue, Spirit and effect a democracy. We are left without resources but in our prayers and tears."[8] In December of the following year he remarked that "instead of the most enlightened people, I fear we Americans shall soon have the character of the silliest people under Heaven."[9] The next June he lamented the nation's inability to find a remedy for the "Universal Gangrene of Avarice" and the corruption that was "coming in like a flood."[10]

To be sure, Adams was never one to renounce his country altogether. When Rush pressed him whether America was still "worthy of the Patriotism of honest Men," Adams immediately responded that it was "as worthy as any other Country. Our People are like other People. Our Obligations to our Country never cease but with our Lives. We

ought to do all We can. Instead of being Frenchmen or Englishmen; Federalists or Jacobins, We ought to be Americans." His sense of duty to the nation—the whole nation, not just a favored part of it— remained as strong as ever. Still, Adams's view of that nation was by this point almost inexpressibly bleak. In the very next paragraph he described the United States as "an Aristocracy of Wealth, without any Check but a Democracy of Licentiousness" and predicted that "the eternal Intrigues of our monied and Landed and *Slaved* Aristocracy, are and will be our ruin."[11] (Adams was never a particularly outspoken critic of slavery, but he sometimes accentuated his aversion to the institution in his exchanges with the abolitionist Rush.)

In 1807 Adams told another correspondent that he had "no desire to be considered a prophet of ill" and that he was now confident that "the Federal Union . . . will last longer than we shall live." Yet this confidence rested in large part on his expectation that he would not be around much longer. As the nation "is rising with astonishing rapidity in population and oppulence, and proportionally sinking in Luxury, Sloth and Vice," he continued, "what Revolutions, what Wars, foreign or civil, what forms of government, or what divisions these causes may produce in one hundred, fifty, or even in twenty years, I leave to that wisdom, which is alone competent to foresee and determine. If we imitate the vices and follies of all the Nations, who have gone before us, we have no right nor reason to expect or hope to be exempted from such calamities as they brought upon themselves."[12]

Curiously, Adams's despondency over the nation's future did little to dampen his own spirits. Even as he complained endlessly about his fellow citizens' lack of virtue, his tone was often lighthearted, even playful. Aside from a slight tremor in his hands, his health remained remarkably strong well into his seventies. He continued his voluminous reading, tended to his farm and garden, went on long daily walks, rode horseback when he could, and enjoyed spending time with family and friends and visitors, almost always keeping the house full. In 1815 Adams wrote to John Quincy, "I assure you in the Sincerity of a Father, the last fourteen years"—that is, the period since he left the presidency—"have been the happiest of my Life."[13]

In contrast to Washington, who became an increasingly strident partisan in his old age, Adams grew more critical of the Federalist party over the course of his retirement, particularly during Madison's presidency. While Adams regretted many of the measures that the Republicans adopted, he now believed that even more damage would have been done under the auspices of Hamilton and the High Federalists. For all the Republicans' "crude and visionary notions of Government," he claimed, life under their reign was "better, than following the Fools who were intriguing to plunge Us into an Alliance with England an endless War with all the rest of the World and wild Expeditions to South America and Saint Domingo; and what was worse than all the rest, a civil War, which . . . would be the consequence of the Measures the heads of that Party wished to pursue."[14] (Notice the detached reference to "that Party": at times Adams spoke as if he were not even a Federalist.) Adams also found the continued veneration of his illustrious predecessor to be a bit excessive. Whereas during the Revolution he had celebrated Washington's character as "the greatest our Country ever produced," now Adams fretted that "the Feasts and Funerals in Honour of Washington Hamilton and [Fisher] Ames are mere hypocritical Pageantry to keep in Credit, Banks Funding Systems and other Aristocratical Speculation. It is as corrupt a System as that by which Saints were canonized and Cardinals Popes and whole hierarchical Systems created."[15]

As this last comment suggests, Adams continued to fume about the financial program that Hamilton had instituted and that subsequent administrations—including Adams's own—had found it necessary to retain and even extend. "The funding System and the Banking Systems Seem to threaten a total Destruction of all Distinctions between Virtue and Vice," Adams complained in 1809.[16] These systems were, as he saw it, engines of aristocracy and corruption, at once oppressing and defrauding the common people. They would surely prove fatal to republican government: "Commerce has in all times made wild Work with Elections," he told Rush in 1810, "but it never invented So artful a Scheme of Corruption for that purpose as our American Banks. I am almost as gloomy as Ames. At times I See nothing to prevent our Country both North and South America from becoming in another Century if not this, a Theatre for Gengizcans [i.e., Genghis

Khans] Mahoments Tamerlanes, Charlemagnes Napoleons, Burrs and Hamiltons."[17] Alas, little could be done to arrest the progress of "the Banking Infatuation": "You may as well Reason with a Hurricane."[18]

But the Federalists' greatest offense during this period, in Adams's view, lay in their repeated threats of secession, particularly in response to the Louisiana Purchase, the Embargo Act of 1807, and the War of 1812. New England had been the backbone of the continental union during the Revolution, at least as Adams saw it, but in the early nineteenth century it emerged as a wellspring of separatism. Adams believed that there were already "so many Seeds and Elements of division" within the nation that multiplying them was both foolish and dangerous.[19] When Josiah Quincy III, a member of Congress from Massachusetts, gave a speech hinting that a separation of New England from the other states might soon be necessary, Adams admonished him that the union was "the rock of our salvation and every reasonable measure for its preservation is expedient." A partition of the nation would, he was certain, bring with it serious "dangers to American Liberty . . . and a total loss of Independence for both Fragments, or all the fragments of the union."[20] Though the nation suffered from countless political ills, in Adams's view, its unity prevented still greater ones.

Adams's delightfully cranky letters to Rush proceeded apace through the early years of Madison's presidency. As the 1810 midterms got underway, Adams wrote that "our Electioneering Racers have Started for the Prize. Such a Whipping and Spurring and huzzaing! Oh What rare Sport it will be? Through thick and thin, through Mire and Dirt, through Bogs and Fens and Sloughs dashing and Splashing and crying out, the Devil take the hindmost. How long will it be possible that Honor, Truth or Virtue should be respected among a People who are engaged in Such a quick and perpetual Succession of Such profligate Collissions and Conflicts?"[21] The following year he took a broader view, waxing philosophical about his own impact and legacy: "Have I not been employed in Mischief all my days? Did not The American Revolution produce The French Revolution? and did not the French Revolution produce all the Calamities, and Desolations to the human Race and the whole Globe ever Since? I meant well however."[22]

After repeated prompting by Rush, Adams sent a short, friendly note to Jefferson on New Year's Day of 1812, which led to a reconciliation between these two giants of the Revolution after more than a decade of estrangement. Their regular epistolary exchange over the next fourteen years has been characterized as "the most remarkable correspondence in American political history" and indeed "perhaps the greatest work of early American letters."[23] After Rush died in 1813, Adams's letters to Jefferson came to serve as a sort of replacement outlet for his musings about America's past, present, and future. Adams was never quite as whimsical or as forthright with Jefferson as he had been with Rush, but he could not help but poke a bit of fun at Jefferson's inveterate optimism. "Let me now ask you, very Seriously my Friend," he proposed in one letter. "Where are now in 1813, the Perfection and perfectability of human Nature? Where is now, the progress of the human Mind? Where is the Amelioration of Society? Where the Augmentations of human Comforts? Where the diminutions of human Pains and Miseries? . . . When? Where? and how? is the present Chaos to be arranged into Order?"[24] At this point Jefferson still believed that a generally blissful future awaited the United States, but Adams was doubtful: "I dare not look beyond my Nose, into futurity. Our Money, Our Commerce, our Religion, our National and State Constitutions, even our Arts and Sciences, are So many Seed Plott's of Division Faction, Sedition and Rebellion. Every thing is transmuted into an Instrument of Electioneering."[25]

The War of 1812 brought a partial reprieve to Adams's habitual pessimism about the character of the American people.[26] The three-year conflict with Britain, which was sparked in large part by British violations of America's maritime rights, was regarded by many Americans as an effort to reclaim or reaffirm the nation's independence. Neither side managed to gain a sustained or decisive advantage, however, and the outcome of the war was essentially a draw, at least between the United States and Britain.[27] (For the native peoples in the western territories, it was an unmitigated disaster.) From the outset Adams deemed the war to be "just and necessary," and he persistently blamed the Madison administration for failing to prosecute it vigorously

enough.[28] What most delighted Adams, though, was the effect that the war had on the citizenry: among everyday Americans there was a sense of national unity, purpose, and patriotism that had not been seen since the days of the Revolution.

The only notable dissenters from this renewed sense of national spirit were the New England Federalists who opposed what they called "Mr. Madison's War," much to Adams's chagrin, chiefly because of the harm that it did to their own trading interests. When a few of the leading Federalists began to murmur about secession, Adams slyly suggested to Jefferson that they were merely following the path that had been trod by the Republicans fifteen years earlier in the Virginia and Kentucky Resolutions: "It is a mortification to me, to See how Servile Mimicks they are. Their Newspapers, Pamphlets, hand Bills, and their Legislative Proceedings, are copied from the Examples Sett them, especially by Virginia and Kentucky. I know not which Party has the most unblushing Front, the most lying Tongue, or the most impudent and insolent not to Say the most Seditious and rebellious Pen."[29]

Adams drew from the War of 1812 the disconcerting conclusion that occasional wars are indispensable for the inculcation of civic virtue and hence the long-term health of republican government. Just weeks after the war began, he was already telling Rush that "Wars at times are as necessary for the preservation and perfection, the prosperity, Liberty, happiness, Virtue, & independance of Nations as Gales of wind to the Salubrity of the Atmosphere, or the agitations of the Ocean to prevent its stagnation and putrefaction."[30] There is a definite echo here of Jefferson's famous claim that "a little rebellion now and then is a good thing, and as necessary in the political world as storms in the physical," as well as Adams's own hope during the Revolution that "the Furnace of Affliction" would help to purify the nation, ridding it of its softness and selfishness.[31] Back in 1799 Adams had bucked his party and sacrificed his presidency in order to avoid open war with France, in part because he worried that such a war would sow irreparable divisions among the American people, but now he welcomed the war with Britain as a means of unifying the country in opposition to a common enemy.

As the war dragged on, Adams became more and more convinced that a long span of peace and prosperity was a sure route to decadence

and corruption. In October 1814 he remarked to John Quincy that "human Nature cannot bear Prosperity. It invariably intoxicates Individuals and Nations. Adversity is the great Reformer.... Prosperity has thrown our dear America into an easy trance for 30 years. The dear delights of Riches and Luxury have drowned all her intellectual and physical Ennergies. But there are symptoms, that the Germ of Virtue is not destroyed. The Root of the matter is Still in us, and alive."[32] Adams's newfound optimism was far from total; just weeks later he moaned to another correspondent that "there is little Sense of national honour, and little real knowledge of national duty or interest."[33] Yet the war had inspired enough signs of virtue in the American populace to persuade Adams that while "We all regret or affect to regret War ... There never was a Republick; no nor any other People, under whatever Government, that could maintain their Independence, much less grow and prosper, without it."[34] Similar sentiments suffuse Adams's correspondence from these years, but clearly he was more than a little discomfited by his own conclusion: "What horrid Creatures we Men are," he mused, "that we cannot be virtuous without murdering one another."[35]

———————

Adams, the longest-lived of the major founders, would survive for another eleven years beyond the war. Now in his eighties, he still found great joy in everyday life. He suffered some devastating losses— his son Charles had died of alcoholism back in 1800, just before he left the presidency; his daughter Nabby succumbed to cancer in 1813; and Abigail herself passed away in 1818—but he delighted in the grandchildren and great-grandchildren that accumulated all around him. "You have no Idea of the prolific quality of the New England Adamses," he bragged to François Adriaan van der Kemp.[36] When Adams looked back on the life that he had led, he pronounced himself to be generally satisfied.

Adams's letters from these years focus much more on broad philosophical and religious questions and on history—particularly the history of the American Revolution—than on day-to-day politics or the nation's future. Judging from the comments that do survive, however, it appears that his long-standing disillusionment with the

American experiment underwent some moderation during the last decade of his life. At times Adams sounded positively upbeat in a way that he rarely had since the Revolution. In November 1815 he told one correspondent, "I contemplate with pleasure the rising Generation. As much Secluded as I am from the World I See a Succession of able and honourable Characters from Members of Congress down to Batchelors and Students in our Universities, who will take care of [America's] Liberties."[37] As Madison's second term neared its close, Adams judged that despite "a thousand Faults and blunders, his Administration has acquired more glory, and established more Union, than all his three Predecessors Washington Adams and Jefferson put together."[38] As James Monroe's presidency began, Adams remarked on the "profound tranquility" that appeared to have settled over the nation, which was "more United and Unanimous than ever."[39] A few years later he found gratification in the fact that he and his generation would be leaving the world better than they found it: science and literature were "greatly improved," persecution and bigotry were "some-what abated," and governments were at least "a little ameliorated." In all, he predicted, "our Country has brilliant and exhilerating prospects before it."[40]

Just as often, however, the old, sober Adams disposition reemerged, reminding him that the lessons of history and the darker side of human nature could not be escaped so easily. In November 1815, he commented to Jefferson that the eighteenth century, "notwithstanding all its Errors and Vices," had proven itself to be "the most honourable to human Nature," but he worried that the nineteenth century threatened to "extinguish all the Lights of its Predecessor."[41] The next year he added, "I fear there will be greater difficulties to preserve our Union, than You and I, our Fathers Brothers Friends Disciples and Sons have had to form it."[42] Less than a year into Monroe's first term, Adams declared to John Quincy: "If there is any Thing Serious in this World, the Selfishness of our Countrymen is not only Serious but melancholly, foreboding ravages of Ambition and Avarice which never were exceeded on this Selfish Globe. You have seen much of it. I have seen more. . . . The distemper in our Nation is so general, and so certainly incurable."[43] A few years later, Adams argued that there was not "in history one single example of a Nation throughly

Corrupted that was afterwards restored to Virtue—and without Virtue, there can be no political Liberty." And corruption, he thought, was more or less inevitable, even in a nation that started out virtuous: "Will you tell me," he asked Jefferson, "how to prevent riches from becoming the effects of temperance and industry—Will you tell me how to prevent riches from producing luxury—Will you tell me how to prevent luxury from producing effeminacy intoxication extravagance Vice and folly."[44]

Much as he had during the Revolution, then, Adams oscillated back and forth between hope and despair throughout this period. Sometimes his ambivalence was discernable within the span of a single paragraph: "My sanguine temperament has always endeavored to contemplate objects on the bright side," Adams wrote to John Jay in 1822. "Our prospects at present are magnificent beyond all example and beyond all comprehension—but this globe and as far as we can see this Universe, is a theatre of vicissitudes. If we peep into futurity . . . we may possibly discern objects of terror and make us start back with horror."[45] One explanation for the fluctuation in Adams's views—if indeed it demands an explanation—is that his occasional expressions of confidence in America's grand future were mostly a result of his contrarian nature. As Joseph Ellis rightly notes, Adams "rarely indulged in optimistic predictions except when presented with visitors or correspondents who, thinking he would agree, offered pessimistic estimates of the fate of the American republic. Then he would, as he put it, 'jump upon the great See-Saw' and balance the political equation. . . . His optimistic forecasts, in short, were almost always expressions of his oppositional disposition."[46] Another plausible explanation, which has been proposed by Gordon Wood, is that the partial abatement of Adams's pessimism in his final decade was, ironically, the result of its having lasted so long. It was precisely "Adams's cynicism and low expectations of human nature," Wood writes, that protected him from being overly "bewildered and frightened . . . by the new dynamic and popular world developing in the early nineteenth century."[47]

One event that unquestionably caused Adams a great deal of alarm—even if not quite the level of terror that Jefferson experienced—was the Missouri crisis. This episode will be a central focus of chapter 11

of this book; for now it suffices to say that Congress's consideration of Missouri's application for statehood beginning in 1819 led to a bitter and protracted conflict over the future of slavery in America. Adams never wavered in his belief that "Negro Slavery is an evil of Colossal Magnitude" and that it would be desirable for the nation to "totally abolish it," although he believed—like many other antislavery founders—that abolition should take place gradually and that the freed slaves should be colonized elsewhere.[48] Adams also pointedly refrained from taking any political steps toward ending the practice, or even making any public statements against it. As he told Jefferson, "I have been so terrified with this Phenomenon that I constantly said in former times to the Southern Gentleman, I cannot comprehend this object I must leave it to you, I will vote for forceing no measure against your judgements, what we are to see *God* knows and I leave it to him, and his agents in posterity."[49]

Like most northerners, Adams was utterly opposed to the idea of admitting Missouri to the union as a slave state, and he rightly saw that the disagreement over this question presaged an even deeper and broader sectional clash that loomed over the entire nation. In December 1819, he conveyed to Jefferson his hope that "the Missouri question . . . will follow the other waves under the Ship and do no harm." But Adams could not help but worry: "I know it is high treason to express a doubt of the perpetual duration of our vast American Empire," he continued, but he was sometimes "Cassandra enough" to believe that a conflict like this one might one day "rend this mighty Fabric in twain."[50] In the following weeks Adams told his daughter-in-law Louisa Catherine that "the Missouri question . . . hangs like a Cloud over my imagination" and that "I shudder when I think of the calamities which slavery is likely to produce in this country." "You would think me mad," he supposed, "if I were to describe my anticipations. If the gangrene is not stopped I can see nothing but insurrections of the blacks against the whites and massacres by the whites in their turn of the blacks . . . till at last the whites exasperated to madness shall be wicked enough to exterminate the negroes."[51] To another correspondent, Adams declared that if Congress were to reach the wrong decision on Missouri, it would "stamp our National Character and lay a foundation for Calamities, if not disunion."[52]

Whereas Jefferson would be preoccupied with the "Missouri question" for years to come, however, it appears to have dropped off of Adams's radar screen after the Missouri Compromise temporarily resolved the impasse in March 1820; there is almost no record of Adams's opinion on the settlement that Congress reached, much less the fate of slavery in its aftermath.

———————

In Adams's last few years, his remarkably durable health finally began to decline. He progressively lost his teeth, his ability to walk, and his eyesight. One obvious cause for cheer was the outcome of the 1824 presidential election, which installed at the head of the government the politician of this period whom Adams respected more than any other: his son, John Quincy.[53] When twenty-three-year-old Josiah Quincy IV called on Adams to congratulate him on his son's achievement, he found that Adams was "considerably affected by the fulfillment of his highest wishes." Yet Adams's cynicism remained firmly intact: Quincy records him as saying, "No man who ever held the office of President would congratulate a friend on obtaining it. He will make one man ungrateful and a hundred men his enemies for every office he can bestow."[54] To his grandson—John Quincy's son, also named John—Adams cautioned that his father's election was "not an event to excite vanity," but instead "ought to excite grave and solemn reflections." A dutiful patriot to the end, Adams counseled him to "reflect on the obligations this event imposes on us. Our joys ought to be no greater than the joys of the public."[55]

Adams and Jefferson were destined to die on the same day: July 4, 1826, the fiftieth anniversary of the adoption of the Declaration of Independence. Celebrations of the anniversary were planned across the nation, and the Declaration's three surviving signers—Adams, Jefferson, and Charles Carroll of Maryland—were invited to attend gatherings far and wide. The timing was in some ways ironic for Adams, for the festivities were commemorating a date whose significance he had long minimized. The fourth of July, 1776, was when the Second Continental Congress formally adopted the Declaration of Independence, but the Congress had approved a motion for independence two days earlier, leading Adams to conclude that July 2 would

be the day that would "be celebrated, by succeeding Generations, as the great anniversary Festival . . . with Pomp and Parade, with Shews, Games, Sports, Guns, Bells, Bonfires and Illuminations from one End of this Continent to the other."[56]

In fact, however, Adams believed that an even more decisive step had been taken back on May 15, 1776, when the Congress adopted a resolution that he had proposed that called on the states to form new, independent constitutions. Adams told Abigail that *this* move marked "the last Step, a compleat Seperation from [Britain], a total absolute Independence, not only of her Parliament but of her Crown."[57] It was important to Adams that the May 15 resolution was the nation's real declaration of independence not only because he rather than Jefferson was its author, but also because it demonstrated that the Revolution was fundamentally constructive in its orientation—that its chief purpose was to build new governments on new models rather than just to tear down old ones.[58] The Declaration of Independence itself was, in Adams's view, a mere ornamental appendage to the real work of the Revolution.

The nation was not of the same mind, however, and the Golden Jubilee was duly planned for July 4.[59] Adams was far too old and frail to attend even the festivities in Quincy, but he sent a poignant note expressing his regrets. With the entire nation memorializing an event with which he and Jefferson, more than anyone else, were identified, and with his own son occupying the president's chair, one might have expected Adams to take the opportunity to sound a note of triumph, or at least of pride. Instead, he described America's independence as "a Memorable epoch in the annals of the human race; destined, in future history, to form the brightest or the blackest page, according to the use or the abuse of those political institutions by which they shall, in time to come, be Shaped, by the *human mind*."[60]

Taken on its own, this statement nicely encapsulates Adams's late-life ambivalence: it was simply too soon to tell whether the American experiment would prove to be a glorious success or a miserable failure. In the context in which he delivered it, however—with his fellow citizens surely expecting a paean to the greatness of American democracy from one of its venerable founders, one that could be read aloud amid the fireworks and parades—Adams's statement reads more like a

reversion to his customary role of puncturing myths and summoning harsh truths. There was no inevitable destiny for America that was somehow written into history, he was suggesting. The project of self-government was still a fragile and precarious one, and threats would always surround it—so much so that if they were not adequately met then the American regime might eventually form the blackest page in human history. "Asked to pose for posterity," as Ellis remarks, Adams "chose to go out hurling it a challenge."[61] A half century of disillusionment, it turns out, is not so easily left behind.

JEFFERSON

WEATHERING
THE STORM

UNTIL THE FINAL decade of his life, Thomas Jefferson was consistently—one might even say relentlessly—optimistic about America's future.[1] He had a bottomless faith in the exceptional nature of the United States, and his zeal for democracy was unsurpassed among the major founders. Whereas Washington, Hamilton, and Adams tended to distrust the masses, Jefferson embraced them. He was confident that as long as the corrupting forces of luxury and privilege were held at bay, and as long as the people were properly educated, they would almost always prove to be wise and good.[2] Upon his return from France in 1790, Jefferson told his fellow citizens of Albemarle County, Virginia, that "the will of the majority, the Natural law of every society, is the only sure guardian of the rights of man. Perhaps even this may sometimes err. But it's errors are honest, solitary and short-lived.—Let us then, my dear friends, for ever bow down to the general reason of the society. We are safe with that, even in it's deviations, for it soon returns again to the right way."[3]

The fears of majority tyranny that are so prominent in the writings of the other founders—including Jefferson's closest political ally, James Madison—are all but absent from Jefferson's.[4] Occasionally he would grant, as he did in his First Inaugural Address, that "though the will of the majority is in all cases to prevail, that will, to be rightful, must be reasonable," and that "the minority possess their equal rights, which equal laws must protect." More often, though, Jefferson's stress was squarely on the desirability of enacting the people's will. Just two paragraphs later in the First Inaugural, he went on to identify "absolute acquiescence in the decisions of the majority" as one of "the essential principles of our government."[5] True, Jefferson believed that the

"natural aristocracy"—the few of true merit and virtue, as opposed to inherited wealth or birth—should lead the nation, but he also assumed that the many would instinctively choose and follow these exemplary leaders. It was the simple, sturdy yeomanry of America who were, he insisted time and again, the real backbone of the nation.

That this champion of popular self-rule was himself a rich, slave-holding aristocrat, born into a world of privilege and raised to occupy an elite position within Virginia's squirearchy—a "patriarch," as he sometimes called himself—is just one of the many paradoxes that marked the man, as historians have frequently noted. There was nothing common about Jefferson's lavish lifestyle or sophisticated tastes: during his time in Paris he shipped home eighty-six crates of French furniture, porcelain, silver, books, and paintings, along with 288 bottles of wine. Yet his fulsome odes to the wisdom of the common people have become a staple of American politics, from the stump speech to the civic holiday. More than Adams, Franklin, Hamilton, Madison, or even Washington, it is the democrat Jefferson who continues to serve as the country's national icon. Cutting icons down to size is a perennially popular activity, and Jefferson has frequently been taken to task for his hypocrisy, self-righteousness, naïveté, and deep-seated racism, but he has more often been celebrated for his eloquence, idealism, passion, and omnivorous intellect.[6] Gordon Wood writes that "despite persistent attempts to discredit his reputation, as long as there is a United States he will remain the supreme spokesman for the nation's noblest ideals and highest aspirations."[7]

As we will see in this chapter, Jefferson harbored a number of misgivings about the Constitution at the outset, just as Washington, Hamilton, and Adams did, and he expressed even deeper worries about the direction that the nation's politics took during the 1790s, above all due to the influence wielded by Hamilton. Through it all, however, he remained confident that time was on his side and that the American people would eventually set things right. And Jefferson believed that the people *did* set things right through what he immodestly called the "revolution of 1800," by which he meant his own elevation to the presidency. Moreover, the main source of the nation's woes, as Jefferson saw things—the stockjobbing, monocratic Federalists—were annihilated as a political force in the early years of

the nineteenth century. The Republican party that Jefferson founded came to dominate American politics for two and a half decades after his election, and he was succeeded in the nation's highest office first by his most trusted political partner, Madison, and then by his long-time acolyte James Monroe, for two terms each. It is in some respects unsurprising, therefore, that Jefferson retained a sense of hopefulness far longer than did his Federalist counterparts.

We will see in the next two chapters, however, that even Jefferson's inveterate optimism was not unbreakable.[8] In his final years, in fact, he too came to despair for America's future. Jefferson's late-life loss of heart was brought on by a number of factors, above all his anxiety about the growing divisions between the North and the South over slavery and his dismay about the centralization of political power. Disillusionment came later to Jefferson than to the other protagonists of this book, but it was every bit as intense and thoroughgoing when it did.

Like Adams, Jefferson was reasonably content with the government established by the Articles of Confederation and saw little need to radically overhaul it in the way that Washington, Hamilton, Madison, and many others felt was so urgently necessary. Whereas these latter figures were alarmed by Shays's Rebellion, seeing it as a harbinger of approaching anarchy, Jefferson breezily opined that "a little rebellion now and then is a good thing."[9] He was confident that the American governments—both federal and state—could weather such challenges above all because of their democratic nature. "Governments like ours, wherein the people are truly the mainspring ... are never to be despaired of," Jefferson assured the British philosopher Richard Price in 1785, since "when an evil becomes so glaring as to strike them generally, they arrouse themselves, and it is redressed."[10] The biggest change that Jefferson advocated making to the Confederation was to enable the Congress to conduct a more unified foreign policy. "My general plan," he often declared, "would be to make the states one as to every thing connected with foreign nations, and several as to every thing purely domestic." As late as August 1787, as the Constitutional Convention was nearing its end on the other side of the Atlantic, Jefferson reckoned

that even "with all the imperfections of our present government, it is without comparison the best existing or that ever did exist."[11]

When the constitution proposed by the convention reached Jefferson in Paris in November 1787, his initial reaction was almost entirely negative. Although he thought highly of many of the delegates who attended the convention—which he called "an assembly of demigods"—he found that "there are things in [the new constitution] which stagger all my dispositions to subscribe to what such an assembly has proposed."[12] In particular, he told Adams that the presidency, which did not yet include any kind of term limit, "seems a bad edition of a Polish king." At the time Poland elected its monarchs for life, and Jefferson thought that the American president would almost certainly "be reelected from 4. years to 4. years for life.... When one or two generations shall have proved that this is an office for life, it becomes on every succession worthy of intrigue, of bribery, of force, and even of foreign interference." All told, Jefferson regarded the charter as so deeply flawed that he felt the nation would be better off without it: "all the good of this new constitution might have been couched in three or four new articles to be added to the good, old, and venerable fabrick, which should have been preserved even as a religious relique."[13] (It is impossible to imagine Washington, Hamilton, or Madison describing the Articles of Confederation in such reverential tones.)

Over time, Jefferson's reservations softened. In December he wrote to Madison to outline the things that he liked about the proposed constitution—the separation of powers into three branches, the compromise whereby representation was based on population for the House of Representatives while each state was represented equally in the Senate, the exclusive right of Congress to levy taxes—as well as the things that he did not like, above all the president's perpetual eligibility for reelection and the lack of a bill of rights. "I own," he told his friend, "I am not a friend to a very energetic government. It is always oppressive."[14] The following summer, when Jefferson learned that New Hampshire had become the ninth state to ratify, thereby sending the Constitution into effect, he wrote, "I sincerely rejoice at the acceptance of our new constitution by nine states. It is a good canvas, on which some strokes only want retouching."[15] By March 1789, as the First Congress got underway, he insisted that while he was

"not a Federalist, because I never submitted the whole system of my opinions to the creed of any party of men whatever," he was "much farther from that of the Antifederalists."[16] In fact, he now pronounced that the Constitution was "unquestionably the wisest ever yet presented to men."[17] Later in his career, Jefferson would repeatedly deny that he had ever disapproved of the Constitution in the first place.

There are several explanations for this gradual yet stark reversal of opinion. Generally speaking, it would have been impolitic to voice too much displeasure with the Constitution once it had gone into effect and gained broad popular approval, particularly for someone who held high office within the government; by that point, such objections would have smacked of disloyalty. But Jefferson's eventual embrace of the Constitution was not just a matter of prudential calculation. After all, both of his main misgivings about the document were soon alleviated: the lack of a bill of rights was rectified by the adoption of the first ten amendments in 1791, and the president's perpetual eligibility for reelection was rectified (at least informally) by the example set by Washington, and then continued by Jefferson himself, of stepping down voluntarily after two terms.

With respect to the underlying basis of the government, Jefferson simply decided that his own principles were the "true" principles of the Constitution. Shortly before his election to the presidency, he proclaimed that "the Federal constitution according to it's obvious principles & those on which it was known to be received" by the American public embodied "all those principles which we [i.e., Republicans] have espoused and the federalists have opposed. . . . The true theory of our constitution is surely the wisest & best, that the states are independant as to every thing within themselves, & united as to every thing respecting foreign nations."[18] Like Hamilton, though coming from the opposite direction, Jefferson found it more convenient to read his own outlook into the Constitution than to convince his fellow citizens to fundamentally revise the nation's basic charter.

As we have seen, Jefferson spent most of Washington's presidency, including the years when he was a key member of the cabinet, struggling against the administration's policies. Indeed, his opposition to

Hamilton and his High Federalist minions ran so deep that it occasionally verged on the hysterical. In May 1792, while serving as secretary of state, Jefferson wrote to President Washington that the financial program developed by Hamilton—his fellow cabinet officer—had "furnished effectual means of corrupting ... a portion of the legislature" and that the "ultimate object" of this "corrupt squadron" was "to prepare the way for a change, from the present republican form of government, to that of a monarchy." The Hamiltonian faction so consistently and so drastically favored northern merchants and speculators at the expense of southern farmers, Jefferson warned, that they threatened the "incalculable evil [of] the breaking of the union into two or more parts."[19] That September he declared bluntly to Washington that Hamilton's entire system "flowed from principles adverse to liberty" and was deliberately "calculated to undermine and demolish the republic."[20]

Although Jefferson claimed to be opposed to political parties, he concluded that in such dire circumstances he would have to step forward and, along with his partner Madison, lead the forces of agrarian, republican virtue against the corrupt, stockjobbing monocrats. (More than any other founder, Jefferson routinely viewed the world in Manichean, black-and-white terms.) "Were parties here divided merely by a greediness for office, as in England, to take a part with either would be unworthy of a reasonable or moral man," he maintained, but when the conflicts over basic principle were "as substantial and as strongly pronounced as between the republicans and the Monocrats of our country I hold it as honorable to take a firm and decided part, and as immoral to pursue a middle line, as between the parties of Honest men, and Rogues, into which every country is divided."[21] Yet Jefferson also knew that he had to carry on much of his campaign surreptitiously, for Washington stood behind Hamilton's program, and openly challenging Washington would mean inevitable political suicide. "Such is the popularity of the President that the people will support him in whatever he will do," Jefferson realized, so he decided that the best strategy for the Republicans would be to "lie on their oars while he remains at the helm, and let the bark drift as his will and a superintending providence shall direct."[22]

Jefferson could afford to be patient, for underlying his expressions of alarm was an unswerving faith that the great majority of the

American people were at heart virtuous republicans—and indeed Jeffersonian Republicans—and that they would eventually set the country back on the right path. As Dumas Malone writes in the introduction to his classic, six-volume study of Jefferson, "there was no need for such an optimist to be in a hurry. He was confident that time was fighting for his ideas."[23]

Jefferson had a ready explanation for the ascendancy of the Federalists during this period: a sizable share of the populace had been temporarily swayed by the unparalleled prestige of Washington, and an equally sizable share of the legislature had been effectively bribed by Hamilton. Once these artificial props were removed, the Federalist edifice would crumble, and the natural Republican majority would take root. "It is happy for us," Jefferson told the Marquis de Lafayette in June 1792, that Hamilton and the advocates of monarchy were "preachers without followers, and that our people are firm and constant in their republican purity.... The voice of the people is beginning to make itself heard, and will probably cleanse their seats at the ensuing election."[24] A few days later he made a similar point to Thomas Paine, assuring him that the apparent dominance of the Federalists was "on the surface only. The bulk below is sound and pure."[25]

Jefferson's optimism was reinforced by the progress of the French Revolution, even after it turned bloody. In January 1793 he wrote to William Short, a friend and American diplomat then residing in Spain, that excepting a few high-placed officers within the government "this country is entirely republican, friends to the constitution, anxious to preserve it and to have it administered according to it's own republican principles.... The successes of republicanism in France have given the coup de grace to [the Federalists'] prospects, and I hope to their projects."[26] As Washington's second term neared its end, Jefferson remained sanguine that the "mass of weight and wealth on the good side is so great" that "we have only to awake and snap the Lilliputian cords with which [the Federalists] have been entangling us."[27]

Jefferson's confidence sometimes appeared to waver during Adams's presidency, but it generally returned after a time. In June 1798 he continued to assure his correspondents that "our present situation is not a natural one" and that with "a little patience ... we shall see the reign

of witches pass over, their spells dissolve, and the people recovering their true sight."[28] Soon afterward, however, Federalist hard-liners in Congress managed to pass the Alien and Sedition Acts, at which point Jefferson's patience quickly wore thin. He responded by penning a set of resolutions that were subsequently adopted by the legislature of Kentucky, though without his name attached. Jefferson's draft of the Kentucky Resolutions was so bold in its defense of states' rights that it appeared to many—even Madison—to imperil the union. Unless the Federalists' patently unconstitutional laws were "arrested at the threshold," Jefferson warned, they would "necessarily drive these states into revolution & blood."[29] A year later he wrote to Madison to propose a new set of resolutions that would threaten "to sever ourselves from that union we so much value, rather than give up the rights of self government which we have reserved, & in which alone we see liberty, safety & happiness."[30] Recall that when he wrote all these inflammatory words, Jefferson was the nation's vice president.

Yet Jefferson was far from despairing even as he issued these threats. In February 1799—just a few months after the Kentucky Resolutions and the more moderate, Madison-penned Virginia Resolutions were adopted, and despite the fact that the resolves had little appreciable effect on the national stage—Jefferson reckoned that "the spell is dissolving. the public mind is recovering from the delirium into which it had been thrown, and we may still believe with security that the great body of the American people must for ages yet be substantially republican."[31] The occasional fluctuations in Jefferson's optimism during the Adams administration were, in any case, temporary, just as he assumed (in his more hopeful moments) they would be. Any lingering doubts that Jefferson may have had about the brightness of America's future were entirely dispelled in 1800 by his own election to the presidency, which swept over him like a cool breeze on a muggy Virginia day.

———

Jefferson's assumption of the presidency in March 1801 marked the first transfer of that office from one party to another in American history, which was marred only by Adams's slinking away from the capital in the predawn hours so as to avoid having to attend the in-

auguration. In Jefferson's eyes, however, his election—along with the election of Republican majorities in both houses of Congress—was far more significant than that: he regarded this as the decisive proof that the American people *were* virtuous republicans at heart, just as he had always believed, as well as the moment when the American government was restored for good to its true principles.

It was actually a fairly close-run victory: Jefferson received seventy-three votes in the electoral college to Adams's sixty-five, and he ended up in an accidental tie with his ostensible running mate, Aaron Burr, leading to a protracted battle in the House of Representatives. The election could easily have gone the other way, particularly if Hamilton had not published his screed against Adams or if Burr had been less skillful in managing the elections on the Republicans' behalf in New York City. Adams would almost certainly have won if the electoral votes of the southern states had not been artificially inflated by their ability to count those whom they had enslaved as three-fifths of a person for purposes of representation.[32] There was also a fairly even partisan split within the Senate. Nevertheless, Jefferson took the outcome of the election as a clear mandate to implement the Republican program as well as confirmation that America's future was now safe. As he saw it, the Republicans' victory represented not the temporary triumph of a political party, but rather the permanent triumph of republican government, and indeed of liberty itself, in the United States. Jefferson later proclaimed that "the revolution of 1800 . . . was as real a revolution in the principles of our government as that of 76. was in it's form."[33] In other words, just as the American people had forever renounced the monarchial form of government when they declared themselves independent from Britain in 1776, twenty-four years later they forever renounced the monarchial principles of the Federalists by electing him president.[34]

Soon after his inauguration, Jefferson began sending letters to old friends and political allies, assuring them that the American Revolution had finally reached its successful conclusion. Most of these self-congratulatory missives were addressed to figures who had themselves played key roles in the Revolution; Jefferson seems to have thought that only they could appreciate the full, world-historical significance of what had just happened. On March 6, two days after

taking office, he told Robert Morris that while "the people were by art & industry, by alarm & resentment, wrought into a phrenzy . . . they never meant to throw off the principles of 1776." Now that the people had restored these good old principles, he continued, "I hope to see them again consolidated into a homogeneous mass, and the very name of party obliterated from among us."[35] That same day he wrote to John Dickinson that "the storm through which we have passed has been tremendous indeed." Though the Federalists had done their utmost to sink the ship of state over the course of the 1790s, "we shall put her on her republican tack, & she will now shew by the beauty of her motion the skill of her builders. . . . A just & solid republican government maintained here, will be a standing monument & example for the aim & imitation of the people of other countries."[36]

Jefferson continued to use the analogy of surviving a tempest and avoiding shipwreck with other correspondents. He told the Marquis de Lafayette that "the ship has weathered the storm," which "proves our vessel indestructible."[37] To Joseph Priestley he reiterated that "the storm is now subsiding & the horison becoming serene," adding that "we can no longer say there is nothing new under the sun. for this whole chapter in the history of man is new."[38] Jefferson remarked to James Warren that "it is pleasant for those who have just escaped threatened shipwreck, to hail one another when landed in unexpected safety. . . . I have seen with great grief yourself and so many other venerable patriots, retired & weeping in silence over the rapid subversion of those principles for the attainment of which you had sacrificed the ease & comforts of life. but I rejoice that you have lived to see us revindicate our rights."[39] Samuel Adams likewise received assurances that "the storm is over, and we are in port. . . . I hope we shall once more see harmony restored among our citizens, & an entire oblivion of past feuds."[40] Near the end of the month Jefferson finally discarded the ship-and-storm metaphor, writing to Elbridge Gerry that "we may now say that the U.S. from N.Y Southwardly are as unanimous in the principles of 76. as they were in 76. . . . Your part of the union"—that is, New England—"tho' as absolutely republican as ours, has drunk deeper of the delusion, & is therefore slower in recovering from it . . . but your people will rise again."[41] Jefferson was certainly not lacking for confidence as he embarked on his presidency.

Jefferson preached conciliation and harmony in his public speeches ("we are all republicans: we are all federalists"), but privately he vowed "to sink federalism into an abyss from which there shall be no resurrection for it."[42] It has long been debated how far Jefferson in fact departed from his Federalist predecessors in his conduct of the presidency.[43] We have seen that John Adams regarded most of Jefferson's reforms as matters of style rather than substance, so that the "revolution of 1800" was not nearly as transformative as Jefferson liked to believe. Adams's grandson, Henry Adams, famously claimed in his nine-volume *History of the United States during the Administrations of Thomas Jefferson and James Madison* that when in office Jefferson and the Republicans in effect out-Federalized the Federalists, expanding the scope of the federal government and executive authority through measures such as the Louisiana Purchase and the ill-fated Embargo Act of 1807. Recent scholarship has stressed, however, that Jefferson never advocated a weak executive, only one that was more democratically accountable than what the Federalists envisioned, so that his vigorous exercise of presidential powers did not run afoul of his broader principles.[44]

Although Jefferson and the Republicans found themselves obliged to retain much of Hamilton's financial system, including the national bank that they had so protested, they did manage to pare down the federal government in many areas, just as they had promised: they slashed taxes (including the hated excise on whiskey), began to pay down the national debt (despite the $15 million outlay on the Louisiana Territory), eliminated many government positions (and the Federalists who occupied them), shrank the military (particularly the navy, which would prove in the War of 1812 to have been a disastrous move), and allowed the Alien and Sedition Acts to lapse. Jefferson's first term has in fact been described as "one of the two or three most uniformly successful in American presidential history in achieving its stated objectives."[45] In accomplishing all this, it helped that Jefferson had inherited a nation that was increasingly prosperous and finally at peace with the European powers, thanks to the handiwork of Hamilton and Adams, respectively, and that the Federalist opposition was both weak and fatally divided.

Jefferson won reelection in a cakewalk—he prevailed over Charles Cotesworth Pinckney in the electoral college by the lopsided margin of 162 to 14—but his second term proved far more challenging than

the first. Jefferson was determined to keep the United States out of the Napoleonic Wars that raged across Europe after 1803, but both Britain and France routinely seized American sailors and plundered American cargo on the high seas and in European ports. The Republicans' aversion to foreign adventures and their drastic cuts to the navy meant that the country was unwilling and unable to retaliate militarily, so Jefferson decided to try to strike back through commercial warfare: the Embargo Act of 1807 essentially shuttered American ports to all international trade.[46] The results were catastrophic. National revenue came nearly to a standstill, since the Republicans' abolition of most internal taxes had left the federal government highly dependent on import duties; the economy went into a tailspin, particularly in the coastal cities of seafaring New England, which grew increasingly disaffected; smuggling abounded, prompting Jefferson to use the military to enforce the ban, which he frequently did in a high-handed fashion that would have made Hamilton smile; and the American market simply was not all that important to Britain or France, meaning that the embargo had little discernable effect on its intended targets. The embargo was aptly characterized by the historian Forrest McDonald as "a policy of pusillanimity and bungling, billed as a noble experiment in peaceful coercion."[47] Opposition soon mounted, and pressure from both parties forced a repeal of the measure in the waning days of Jefferson's presidency.

Although Jefferson's time in office concluded on a somewhat sour note, he left his post with undiminished confidence in America's future. He concluded his Eighth Annual Message to Congress by reiterating his faith that the American people's virtuous character and love of liberty were "a sure guarantee of the permanence of our republic," adding that he was happy to be taking with him to his retirement "a firm persuasion that Heaven has in store for our beloved country, long Ages to come of prosperity and happiness."[48] On his final day in office, he sang the praises of "this solitary republic of the world, the only monument of human rights, & the sole depository of the sacred fire of freedom & self-government."[49] Whereas Washington and Adams were both deeply embittered by the state of American politics by the end of their administrations, Jefferson departed the presidency with his idealism firmly intact.

Jefferson's optimism continued unabated for many more years—until near the end of Madison's second term. He was thrilled to return to Monticello, exchanging "the boisterous ocean of political passions" for "my family, my books, & farms," which he found far more congenial.[50] Like Adams, Jefferson rarely strayed far from home during his retirement; he never again set foot outside of Virginia. Enjoying reasonably good health and devoting himself to study, music, and agriculture, for a time he enjoyed the leisurely tranquility of which he had long dreamed. With his closest political partner in the president's chair and huge Republican majorities in both houses of Congress, Jefferson could rest assured that the country was in safe hands.

Like many Americans, Jefferson regarded the War of 1812 as a struggle to reaffirm the nation's independence from Britain. Both the war and the Madison administration's conduct of it had his unqualified support, though he lamented the fact that it soon became necessary to increase the size of both the military and the national debt. Jefferson was also sorry to see that the treaty that concluded the war did little to resolve the issue of British impressment of American sailors into the Royal Navy. Still, like Adams he rejoiced to see a groundswell of patriotism among his fellow citizens. As the war came to a close in February 1815, Jefferson wrote to the Marquis de Lafayette that "the cement of this union is in the heart blood of every American. I do not believe there is on earth a government established on so immovable a basis."[51]

Over the next decade, however, Jefferson would come to categorically reject the idea that the American government was so solidly based. On the contrary, he eventually concluded that the republic was almost certainly doomed. The most important source of this sea change had, in a sense, been lurking in the background from the very beginning.

CHAPTER 11

THE KNELL OF
THE UNION

FOR ALL THAT it accomplished in terms of creating a new nation based on liberal principles and proving that republican government could work on a large scale, the American founding was marred by not just one but two original sins: the widespread presence of black chattel slavery and the persistent betrayal and occasional slaughter of various American Indian tribes. The latter crime pricked the consciences of at least some of the founders, but it rarely led to deep doubts about the long-term viability of the American regime.[1] Given the facts on the ground, the westward expansion of white settlers was all but irresistible. Slavery was always a far more thorny problem for the founders. It was so vexing not just because it was such an immense moral evil—a point that struck nearly all of them as obvious—but also because it seemed to them so intractable, at least for the time being, and because the practice was concentrated so much more heavily in the South than in the North, thereby creating a major rift in the union in terms of practice and (eventually) principle.

Start with a few basic facts. When the nation declared its independence in 1776, slavery was legal and practiced in all thirteen states. By 1784, all the New England states plus Pennsylvania had either outlawed the institution altogether or at least enacted a gradual emancipation scheme, and they were joined by New York in 1799 and New Jersey in 1804. In addition, slavery was declared illegal in the entire Northwest Territory, which encompassed much of the present-day Midwest, in 1787. During this period there were also a surprisingly high number of individual manumissions in the South, particularly Virginia. Altogether this was, as Sean Wilentz notes, "the largest emancipation of its kind to that point in modern history."[2] By the

end of the eighteenth century the transatlantic market for tobacco was glutted, and it was widely believed that slave labor was so inefficient that it could not compete with free labor over the long run. Most Americans, North and South, recognized that it would be impossible to eradicate slavery in the immediate future, given how deeply it was woven into the fabric of southern society and how integral it was to the entire nation's economy, not to mention the protections that slaveholders were afforded by the Constitution. Nonetheless, many of the founders optimistically supposed that slavery was well on its way to dying a "natural death"—that the liberal and egalitarian forces that the Revolution had unleashed would eventually succeed in casting slavery from America's shores, just as they had cast out monarchy.

In retrospect this was, of course, a delusion, and a rather self-serving one at that: the founders could tell themselves that there was no need to devote too much effort to combatting an institution that was destined to be eliminated by history anyway. Far from dying out, slavery in fact underwent a boom—expanding demographically within the South and geographically to the West—after the invention of the cotton gin in 1793 helped to renew and indeed multiply its profitability. With slavery flourishing in the South even as it dwindled in the North, the nation was soon bisected by an indelible fissure that would only grow deeper over time. After 1820 the future of slavery became the central source of conflict in American politics, and in 1861 this conflict culminated in what remains the most destructive war in the nation's history. As exasperating as the issue was for the entire founding generation, no major founder had a more tortured relationship to slavery than Jefferson.[3]

———————

Though Jefferson was himself a major slaveholder who bought, sold, bred, punished, hunted down, and (in at least one case) slept with his chattel much as other plantation owners of the period did, early in his career he fought a reasonably forceful battle against the institution.[4] His first major move was to include a harsh denunciation of slavery in his draft of the Declaration of Independence. The final, climactic indictment in Jefferson's long list of grievances against King George III was that the king had "waged cruel war against human nature itself, violating it's most sacred rights of life & liberty in the persons

of a distant people who never offended him, captivating & carrying them into slavery in another hemisphere . . . determined to keep open a market where MEN should be bought & sold, he has prostituted his negative for suppressing every legislative attempt to prohibit or to restrain this execrable commerce."[5] In plainer terms, Jefferson was alleging that the king was responsible for the African slave trade and that he always vetoed the colonial legislatures' attempts to ban or tax it. It was patently absurd, of course, to blame the king for foisting slavery on innocent, liberty-loving Americans, and the entire passage was expunged from the Declaration by the Continental Congress in order to get the states from the Deep South to sign on. Still, Jefferson's attempt to include such language in the nation's founding document—"cruel war against human nature itself"; "a market where MEN should be bought & sold" (his capitals)—is noteworthy, particularly given that at this point slavery had persisted in America for more than a century and a half without serious challenge.

Over the next few years, Jefferson drew up two slightly different statutes that would have gradually abolished slavery in his home state of Virginia. The first, which he helped to devise in 1779, stipulated that all slaves born after the passing of the act would be granted freedom upon reaching adulthood and then colonized elsewhere, and the second, which he drafted in 1783, would have prohibited the further importation of slaves into the state and freed those born after December 31, 1800.[6] These efforts went no further than had Jefferson's efforts to pin American slavery on the British king, however. In fact, neither scheme was even introduced in the Virginia legislature, much less passed or implemented. One law that Jefferson and his colleagues did manage to enact around this time was a stricter slave code, instituting harsher punishments for slaves who attempted to escape or revolt. While slavery was deeply unjust and the enslaved should eventually be liberated, Jefferson seems to have reasoned, as long as they remained in bondage they could not be permitted to threaten the lives or livelihoods of slaveholders, or to hinder the war effort against Britain. A little rebellion now and then was a good thing, as long as it was not enslaved people who were doing the rebelling.

Jefferson's boldest practical move against slavery was a bill that he helped to draft for the Confederation Congress in 1784, which

would have applied to states formed from *any* of the nation's western territories, both north and south of the Ohio River. The bill provided that "after the year 1800 of the Christian era, there shall be neither slavery nor involuntary servitude in any of the said states, otherwise than in punishment of crimes, whereof the party shall have been duly convicted to have been personally guilty."[7] This remarkable proposal came within a single vote of passing. It is true that even if the plan had been adopted it would have effectively given slaveholders carte blanche to bring their chattel into the western territories for another sixteen years, at which point it might have proven impossible to eradicate slavery there in practice, whatever the law stipulated.[8] If the effort had been successful, however, it would have essentially nipped in the bud the chief source of conflict between the North and the South that ultimately culminated in the Civil War, namely the question of slavery's westward expansion. Though it narrowly miscarried, this was the most notable attempt that Jefferson ever made to combat slavery.

Jefferson also castigated slavery in the only book that he ever published, *Notes on the State of Virginia* (1787). He devoted an entire chapter to demonstrating that slavery was a great economic evil, insofar as it crippled industry and promoted indolence; a great social evil, insofar as it both degraded the enslaved and gave slaveholders and their children a taste for tyranny; a great political evil, insofar as it undermined the love of liberty that is so essential in a republican citizenry; and a great moral evil, insofar as it was an obvious violation of enslaved people's inalienable rights. "Indeed," Jefferson declared, "I tremble for my country when I reflect that God is just: that his justice cannot sleep for ever." He even envisioned the almighty turning the "wheel of fortune" so that one day it would be white people who were enslaved by black people, as retribution for the slaveholders' manifold sins against humanity.[9] For a slaveholder living in a slaveholding society, these were strong and courageous words. On reading the book, John Adams remarked that "the Passages upon Slavery, are worth Diamonds."[10] Similar antislavery sentiments are sprinkled throughout Jefferson's correspondence from this period, as when he exclaimed: "What a stupendous, what an incomprehensible machine is man! Who can endure toil, famine, stripes, imprisonment or death itself in vindication of his own liberty"—that is, during the Revolution and the

war against Britain—"and the next moment . . . inflict on his fellow men a bondage, one hour of which is fraught with more misery than ages of that which he rose in rebellion to oppose."[11]

Yet in both his book and his letters, Jefferson insisted that there was little for him and his contemporaries to do but wait. Partly, this was because he too assumed that slavery was already on the road to extinction. "Since the origin of the present revolution," he declared in *Notes on the State of Virginia*, "the spirit of the master is abating, that of the slave rising from the dust, his condition mollifying, the way I hope preparing, under the auspices of heaven, for a total emancipation."[12] In the letter quoted above, immediately after lamenting how "stupendous" and "incomprehensible" human beings can be, Jefferson went on to proclaim that "we must await with patience the workings of an overruling providence, and hope that that is preparing the deliverance of these our suffering brethren."[13] To Richard Price he added that the younger generation of Americans had "sucked in the principles of liberty as it were with their mother's milk, and it is to them I look with anxiety to turn the fate of this question. Be not therefore discouraged."[14]

Jefferson's apparent complacency was not just the result of misguided confidence, however: he actively *opposed* the pursuit of immediate emancipation, fearing that such an attempt would do more harm than good. The chief difficulty, as he saw it, was not how to actually free the throngs of enslaved people that pervaded the American South, but rather what to do with them once they were freed. The fate of the liberated slaves was so distressing to Jefferson for the simple reason that he was profoundly racist, even when judged by the standards of his time.[15] For all his recognition of slavery's evils, Jefferson believed that incorporating freed black people into the white population would be both impossible and undesirable—impossible because the two races could never live together on peaceful and equal terms, and undesirable because of the innate physical and mental inferiority of black people. Jefferson claimed to offer his views on racial inequality "with great diffidence" and "as a suspicion only," but he went to great lengths to muster pseudoscientific evidence to back them up and systematically discounted evidence that might have checked his prejudices.[16]

These passages of Jefferson's *Notes* make for excruciating reading today. Even Merrill Peterson, ordinarily a staunch defender of Jef-

ferson, conceded that they were "a product of frivolous and tortuous reasoning, of preconception, prejudice, ignorance, contradiction, and bewildering confusion of principles."[17] Jefferson was simply incapable of envisioning black people as citizens within the American republic. (Never mind that at the time free black people could vote and own land in both Pennsylvania and North Carolina—the states immediately to the north and south of Virginia.) As one of Jefferson's sharpest critics writes, "he trembled at the thought that God's 'justice cannot sleep for ever,' but he trembled more at the immediate prospect of free blacks in his community."[18] Hence, Jefferson argued that emancipation would be desirable only if it were accompanied by colonization: the liberated people must be resettled somewhere in Africa, or perhaps the Caribbean—anywhere that was sufficiently far away. (Never mind also that most enslaved people had no ties to these foreign lands and no desire to leave the only country that they had ever known.) And Jefferson recognized that colonization would not be a feasible option, either financially or logistically, for some time to come, until after the public had been persuaded to support such a gargantuan effort and a great deal of groundwork had been laid. All this is, again, why Jefferson categorically opposed the immediate abolition of slavery, despite his professed abhorrence of it.

It is also one reason why Jefferson granted freedom to only a handful of the hundreds of human beings whom he himself held in bondage: he insisted that it would be impractical and indeed immoral to free a large number of slaves unless it was part of a broader emancipation scheme that included colonization, for it would mean unleashing people who could not support themselves on a society that would not welcome them. There were, of course, other reasons for Jefferson's failure to personally renounce a practice that he knew to be deeply unjust. As one would expect, he depended on slave labor in order to maintain his lifestyle, and indeed to stay a step ahead of his creditors, since he had inherited considerable debts from his father-in-law and magnified them with his own profligate spending. Freeing his slaves would have also diminished Jefferson's social status and political electability in Virginia. And, more generally speaking, he believed—along with most of the other founders—that moving too far, too fast on this controversial issue would imperil the still-fragile

new nation. This conclusion might seem overly cautious coming from a self-described revolutionary, but early in his career Jefferson could at least tell himself that, whatever he did or failed to do back at Monticello, in his public statements and political proposals he was doing as much as one could responsibly do to oppose slavery, given the circumstances. Alas, his efforts to combat slavery—however qualified and ultimately futile—all but ceased after the 1780s.

Whereas Washington became increasingly uncomfortable with slavery as he aged, Jefferson appears to have grown more reconciled to it over time. To be sure, he still dutifully told his correspondents that it was an immoral institution, but he became decidedly more cautious about acting or speaking out against it, and his hopes for its eventual abolition receded ever further into the future and ever further into the back of his mind. In the 1790s Jefferson devoted most of his political energy to the fight against Hamilton and the Federalists, and it would have been difficult to muster the support that he needed for the Republican cause if he had alienated his fellow southerners by publicly denouncing the preeminent source of their wealth and power; a policy of silence and evasion on the slavery issue seemed far more prudent.

As president, Jefferson did support and sign a ban on the overseas slave trade that took effect on the first day permitted by the Constitution—January 1, 1808—but this was a relatively uncontroversial move that enjoyed a good deal of support even in the South. (By this point only South Carolina did not outlaw the overseas slave trade on the state level.) Jefferson failed to use his position in the nation's highest office or the enormous Republican majorities in both houses of Congress to make any other headway against slavery. On the contrary, he pointedly refused to seize the golden opportunity presented by the Louisiana Purchase to limit its spread. Whereas in 1784 Jefferson had proposed to exclude slavery from all of America's western territories, he raised no objections to its expansion into the vast tract of land that his administration acquired for the nation in 1803. In fact, when Congress voted in 1804 to prohibit both the international and the domestic slave trade into the Louisiana Territory, Jefferson opposed the latter part of the move, and Congress rescinded

it the following year. As it turned out, the first three states from the territory to enter the union—Louisiana (1812), Missouri (1821), and Arkansas (1836)—all did so as slave states, helping to further cement and extend the institution.

During the early years of his retirement, when he still enjoyed immense prestige, Jefferson continued his policy of calculated inaction. When younger colleagues pressed him to take a leadership role in the struggle against slavery as a sort of capstone to his distinguished career, he protested that this was "like bidding old Priam to buckle the armour of Hector. . . . This enterprise is for the young; for those who can follow it up, and bear it through to it's consummation. it shall have all my prayers, and these are the only weapons of an old man"—a particularly interesting formulation, given that Jefferson was not usually one to place much weight on the efficacy of prayer.[19] Always ready to shift the blame to the shoulders of others where slavery was concerned, he began to bemoan the sluggishness of "the rising generation, of which I once had sanguine hopes," and to admit that it now appeared exceedingly unlikely that abolition would come to pass "in my day."[20] By the end of his life Jefferson had grown even more pessimistic, accepting that the required "revolution in public opinion . . . is not to be expected in a day, or perhaps in an age," meekly adding only that "time, which outlives all things, will outlive this evil also."[21]

The chief source of Jefferson's eventual despair over the fate of the American republic, however, was not the lack of progress toward emancipation in the South, but rather the Missouri crisis of 1819–21. During these years Jefferson dove back into the national controversy over slavery that he had studiously avoided since the 1780s, but this time he embraced a distinctly reactionary position.

Political conflict over slavery had flared up on occasion during the first few decades after the ratification of the Constitution, but for the most part the issue was deliberately kept on the nation's back burner. As new states began to be carved out of the Louisiana Territory, however, it was difficult to avoid the question of whether they would join the union as slave states or free states. Most observers

recognized the gravity of this question: admitting more slave states would serve as an implicit endorsement of the institution and would allow it to become further entrenched, while confining slavery to its current limits would register the nation's disapproval of the practice and perhaps place it back on the road to the "natural" or nonviolent death that the founders had hoped for and expected. After all, if the free states were eventually to outnumber the slave states by a sufficiently large margin—such that they commanded two-thirds of both houses of Congress and three-quarters of the state legislatures—then they could simply pass a constitutional amendment outlawing slavery without the concurrence of a single slave state or slaveholder, and the South would almost certainly be incapable of seceding or winning a war at that point. Both sides, therefore, regarded slavery's westward expansion as the crucial issue that would decide the ultimate fate of the institution.

In 1819 the country was evenly split between eleven free states and eleven slave states, so a great deal appeared to hang in the balance when Missouri applied to Congress for statehood.[22] In February of that year James Tallmadge, a New York Republican, proposed an amendment to the Missouri statehood bill that would have prohibited the further importation of enslaved people into the state and imposed a system of gradual emancipation on the slaveholders who currently resided there. Southerners exploded with indignation: the (white) majority in Missouri had approved a constitution that permitted slavery, and proslavery members of Congress contended that the Tallmadge amendment would effectively deprive the state of its constitutionally guaranteed equality by allowing the federal government to overrule its decision. Northerners responded that the Constitution authorized Congress to regulate the slave trade after 1808 and to "make all needful Rules and Regulations" regarding the territories—not to mention that admitting Missouri as a slave state would give the South an advantage in the Senate at a time when it already enjoyed outsized influence in the House of Representatives and the electoral college thanks to the three-fifths clause.

After a series of protracted, bitter debates, in March 1820 Congress passed a compromise package that allowed Missouri to join the union as a slave state while also admitting Maine—which had up to

that point been a part of Massachusetts—as a free state in order to preserve the even balance within the Senate. The compromise further stipulated that slavery would be "forever prohibited" in the rest of the Louisiana Territory north of the 36°30′ latitude, which marked Missouri's southern border. (This latter element of the bargain was eventually repealed in the Kansas-Nebraska Act of 1854, the language about "forever" notwithstanding.) After some more wrangling about whether Missouri would be permitted to exclude free black people from its borders—a matter that was left ambiguous—it was finally granted statehood in August 1821.

In all, the South got more of what it wanted from the Missouri Compromise than did the North. The main principle for which the South had been contending—that new states must be treated just like existing states, so that Congress could not impose emancipation on an unwilling white majority—had prevailed; Maine and the 36°30′ restriction were granted to the North almost as consolation prizes. The votes for the measure in Congress came overwhelmingly from representatives and senators from slave states. Many northerners were startled by the near-unanimity with which the South had rejected the idea of gradual emancipation in Missouri. Up to that point even most slaveholders had agreed on the desirability of ending slavery one day, at least in principle and under the right conditions. Now they were fighting ferociously to expand the institution to a new land where it had not yet fully taken root and gradual abolition would not have been terribly difficult. True, most of those who opposed the Tallmadge amendment rested their case on constitutional grounds rather than proclaiming slavery to be a positive moral good, as John C. Calhoun and his ilk would do beginning in the late 1830s. Still, it was now clear that the majority of white southerners had quietly grown far more deeply committed to the perpetuation of slavery than they had appeared to be at the time of the founding.

Any hopes that the Missouri Compromise would produce sectional amity were exceedingly short-lived. The entire episode took place in the midst of what is often dubbed "the Era of Good Feelings," but there were few good feelings to be found in its wake. The northern and southern positions on slavery quickly hardened in Congress and around the nation, conflict over the issue came to dominate national

politics for the next four decades, and prospects for a peaceful resolution to the impasse grew increasingly dimmer—just as Jefferson had come to fear.

———————◆———————

Jefferson was, by all accounts, uncommonly obsessed with what he called "the Missouri question." Since retiring from the presidency he had largely refrained from writing or even reading much about current affairs, but letters on this subject poured forth from Monticello in the early 1820s, equal parts rage and despair. The source of Jefferson's frustration and despondency was not at all what one might have expected, given his stance on slavery back in the 1780s. The real problem, as he now saw it, was not the continued failure of the South to finally put slavery on the road to extinction, but rather the North's opposition to its expansion.

On the constitutional question, Jefferson lined himself up squarely behind the most extreme southern position: the right "to regulate the condition of the different descriptions of men composing a state" belonged exclusively to the state in question; Congress had no constitutional authority to dictate that a state—or even a territory that was soon to become a state—must eliminate slavery.[23] This stance cohered well with Jefferson's sweeping defense of states' rights in the Kentucky Resolutions, of course, but back in the 1790s his chief concerns had been Hamilton's financial program and the Alien and Sedition Acts—serious issues, certainly, but not matters of literal life and death. Now that slavery was the focus, Jefferson's prophecies turned even more apocalyptic. If Congress could impose a gradual emancipation scheme on Missouri as a condition of statehood, he reasoned, then it "may, and probably will next declare that the condition of all men within the US. shall be that of freedom[,] in which case all the whites South of the Patomak and Ohio must evacuate their states; and most fortunate those who can do it first."[24] In other words, Jefferson believed that the Tallmadge amendment was the opening wedge in a cunning northern plot to abolish slavery entirely without a colonization plan in place, and that the ultimate result of this project would be an all-out race war in the South. Jefferson wrote to John Adams that "the real question" for the states "afflicted with this unfortunate population, is,

Are our slaves to be presented with freedom and a dagger?"[25] He had now moved to the alarmist fringe of southern reaction.

Jefferson did not stop at defending Missouri's constitutional right to allow slavery within its borders if it so chose, however: he contended that Missouri *should* in fact allow slavery within its borders—that the unbridled expansion of this unjust institution was positively desirable. Whereas in 1784 he had proposed to ban slavery from the western territories in hopes of thereby placing it on the road to eventual extinction, Jefferson now espoused a theory known as "diffusion." The basic idea was that allowing slavery to expand into new territory would not lead to an increase in the number of enslaved people, only to their being more spread out, and that this would have a number of benefits. First, Jefferson hypothesized that "by spreading them over a larger surface, their happiness would be increased," apparently because slaves tended to be treated more harshly in areas where they were more highly concentrated, as in the large plantations of the Deep South. (Though Jefferson did not mention it explicitly, lower concentrations of enslaved people would also presumably reduce the number of slave revolts and provide more favorable conditions for continued white supremacy.)

Moreover, and more importantly, Jefferson argued that "the burthen of their [i.e., the slaves'] future liberation" would be "lightened by bringing a greater number of shoulders under it."[26] Essentially, he was suggesting that if there were more slaveholders, in more places, then the institution would be easier to eradicate, because each individual slaveholder would keep fewer people in bondage and so have less to lose from emancipation. Hence, Jefferson insisted to the Marquis de Lafayette that the real moral high ground belonged to the southerners who wanted to expand slavery rather than the northerners who wanted to prevent its spread: "permitting the slaves of the South to spread into the West . . . will dilute the evil every where and facilitate the means of getting finally rid of it, an event more anxiously wished by those on whom it presses than by the noisy pretenders to exclusive humanity."[27]

Everything about this theory was, of course, manifestly delusional. To be sure, Jefferson had some good company: James Madison and then-president James Monroe, among others, shared his conviction

that the diffusion of slavery would prove salutary. But it is a testament to humanity's powers of self-serving rationalization that these distinguished figures all managed to convince themselves that the demise of slavery could be brought about by giving it free rein. They were suggesting, in essence, that the problem could be solved by making it much *bigger*—more national rather than narrowly sectional in scope—as if the surest way to cure a fatal disease were to first allow it to spread throughout one's body. It is also difficult to square the diffusion theory with Jefferson's perennial insistence that emancipation must be accompanied by colonization. It is true that if more southern slaveholders moved their chattel to the West then there would be fewer free black people near him, in Virginia, if the day of liberation were actually to arrive—which may have been the point—but Missouri would seem to be a decidedly far-flung layover on a journey from Virginia to West Africa or Santo Domingo.

Jefferson nonetheless regarded the truth of the diffusion theory as so self-evident that he assumed that anyone who opposed the expansion of slavery—as, again, he himself had in the 1780s—must be acting in bad faith. He told correspondent after correspondent that "the Missouri question is a meer party trick" whose real object was political power.[28] His old enemies, the Federalists, had proven incapable of mustering a majority behind their monarchial principles after his election in 1800, Jefferson explained, so their descendants had changed tack and were now trying to gain office by dividing the nation geographically, pitting the more populous North against the South over the issue of slavery. "The Federalists compleatly put down, and despairing of ever rising again under the old division of whig and tory, devised a new one, of slave-holding, & non-slave-holding states, which . . . had a semblance of being Moral," he maintained. In fact "if there were any morality in the question, it is on the other side," given the myriad benefits of diffusion, but the North's underhanded tactics were well calculated "to throw dust into the eyes of the people and to fanaticise them."[29] He chided those who wanted to restrict the spread of slavery for "wasting Jeremiads on the miseries of slavery as if we were advocates for it," when in reality it was the northerners themselves who were exploiting the plight of the enslaved to further their own political ambitions.[30]

Jefferson had done almost nothing to combat slavery since the 1780s, but what he did during the Missouri crisis was much worse than nothing: he lent his powerful name to the forces seeking to expand slavery. He still considered himself to be an opponent of the institution, but by this point one might fairly say that with enemies like Jefferson, slavery hardly needed friends.

———

Easily the most famous expression of Jefferson's alarm over the Missouri crisis came in a letter that he wrote to John Holmes, a Republican from Maine, in April 1820. He had long since "ceased to read newspapers or pay any attention to public affairs, confident they were in good hands," Jefferson told Holmes, "but this mementous question, like a fire bell in the night, awakened and filled me with terror. I considered it at once as the knell of the Union. it is hushed indeed for the moment"—he was writing a month *after* Congress had passed the Missouri Compromise—"but this is a reprieve only, not a final sentence." In explaining why he saw the conflict over Missouri as the union's death knell, Jefferson all but prophesied the path to the Civil War: "a geographical line, coinciding with a marked principle, moral and political, once concieved and held up to the angry passions of men, will never be obliterated; and every new irritation will mark it deeper and deeper." Jefferson concluded the letter with an unforgettable expression of regret: "I am now to die in the belief that the useless sacrifice of themselves, by the generation of '76. to acquire self government and happiness to their country, is to be thrown away by the unwise and unworthy passions of their sons, and that my only consolation is to be that I live not to weep over it." The current generation was, Jefferson moaned, perpetrating an "act of suicide on themselves and of treason against the hopes of the world."[31] One would be hard pressed to compose a clearer, more forceful articulation of disillusionment than this, and it is all the more striking coming from the most perennially optimistic of the founders.

Some scholars have downplayed the significance of the Holmes letter, suggesting that Jefferson penned it mostly for tactical political reasons.[32] Holmes had, unlike most northerners, pushed for Missouri's admission to the union even without the Tallmadge amendment—largely in hopes of furthering Maine's own statehood ambitions—and

was now paying a political price for having done so. Jefferson wrote his bleak letter to Holmes, it has been supposed, so that Holmes could show it around and use it to justify his conduct. If the venerable Jefferson believed that the nation was on the very brink of collapse, after all, then surely Congress's compromise was worth supporting in order to avoid such a fate. And, indeed, Holmes did show Jefferson's letter around, and his political fortunes quickly revived: two months later he was elected to one of Maine's new Senate seats.

Yet the Holmes letter was far from the first or the last despairing statement about the Missouri crisis to come from Jefferson's pen. In fact, his letters from these years, not all of which were written to strategically significant figures such as Holmes, virtually overflow with similar sentiments, often couched in similar terms. Jefferson first sounded the alarm to John Adams in December 1819, writing that "from the battle of Bunker's hill to the treaty of Paris we never had so ominous a question. . . . I thank god that I shall not live to witness it's issue."[33] Two months later he likewise told Hugh Nelson, the representative from Jefferson's own House district in Virginia, that "the Missouri question . . . is the most portentous one which ever yet threatened our Union. in the gloomiest moment of the revolutionary war I never had any apprehensions equal to what I feel from this source."[34]

In the weeks after Congress passed its compromise package—which Jefferson might have been expected to welcome, given that the southern position that he had advocated had largely prevailed—his letters on the subject became, if anything, even more pessimistic. In March 1820, Jefferson reiterated to Nelson that the drawing "of a geographical line, which on an abstract principle is to become the line of separation of these states," would inevitably "render desperate the hope that man can ever enjoy the two blessings of peace & self-government. the question sleeps for the present, but is not dead."[35] He similarly told Mark Langdon Hill, another Mainer in favor of the compromise, that the "sleep of the Missouri question" would not last: "the idea of a geographical line, once suggested will brood in the minds of all those who prefer the gratification of their ungovernable passions to the peace and union of their country."[36]

On April 13—his seventy-seventh birthday—Jefferson laid out his worries in greater detail to William Short, a fellow Virginian whom

he regarded almost as an adopted son. Much of this letter closely anticipates the letter to Holmes, which he wrote just a week later: "Altho' I had laid down, as a law to my self, never to write, talk, or even think of politics, to know nothing of public affairs & therefore had ceased to read newspapers," Jefferson told Short, "yet the Missouri question arroused and filled me with alarm. . . . The coincidence of a marked principle, moral & political with a geographical line, once concieved, I feared would never more be obliterated from the mind; that it would be recurring on every occasion & renewing irritations, until it would kindle such mutual & mortal hatred, as to render separation preferable to eternal discord." Jefferson himself realized what a departure all this was from his habitual optimism, admitting that "I have been among the most sanguine in believing that our Union would be of long duration. I now doubt it much, and see the event at no great distance. . . . My only comfort & confidence is that I shall not live to see this: and I envy not the present generation the glory of throwing away the fruits of their fathers sacrifices of life & fortune, and of rendering desperate the experiment which was to decide ultimately whether man is capable of self government."[37]

One of the most extreme formulations of Jefferson's premonitions comes from a secondhand source: the diary of Isaac Briggs, a Maryland Quaker who visited Monticello in November 1820. Briggs quotes Jefferson as telling him, "I fear that much mischief has been done already, but if they carry matters to extremities again at the approaching session of Congress, nothing short of Almighty power can save us. The Union will be broken. All the horrors of civil war, embittered by local jealousies and mutual recriminations, will ensue. Bloodshed, rapine and cruelty will soon roam at large, will desolate our once happy land and turn the fruitful field into a howling wilderness. Out of such a state of things will naturally grow a war of extermination toward the African in our land." If the union were to be torn apart, Jefferson went on, "the predictions of our enemies will be fulfilled, in the estimation of the world, that we were not wise enough for self government. It would be said that the fullest and fairest experiment had been made—and had *failed*; and the chains of despotism would be rivetted more firmly than ever."[38]

Ominous remarks continued to pervade Jefferson's correspondence for many more months. In December he told Albert Gallatin, his

former treasury secretary and now the American minster to France, that "nothing has ever presented so threatening an aspect as what is called the Missouri question."[39] The following day he added to Richard Rush, the American minister to Britain and son of the founder Benjamin Rush, that "we are laboring hard under the portentous Missouri question. the preceding generation sacrificed themselves to establish their posterity in independent self-government, which their successors seem disposed to throw away for an abstract proposition. they have a right to do it, as we have to lament it."[40] In February he declared to James Breckenridge, a Virginia politician who was assisting Jefferson with the founding of the University of Virginia, that the division of the nation, though a mere "speck in our horizon" at the moment, would eventually "burst on us as a tornado."[41] To Spencer Roane, a fire-eating, prosouthern judge in Virginia, he wrote in March that "the Missouri question . . . is smeared over for the present: but it's geographical demarcation is indelible. what it is to become, I see not; and leave to those who will live to see it."[42] When Missouri was finally granted statehood in August 1821, Jefferson initially hoped that the controversy would be "lulled" by the resolution of the issue, but just days later he admitted, "whether the question it excited is dead, or only sleepeth, I do not know."[43] He subsequently returned to his initial conviction that the divide between the North and South could never be erased and that "a spark will revive it."[44]

Given the copiousness of Jefferson's expressions of anguish during these years, delivered to a wide variety of interlocutors, it seems evident that the Holmes letter was no anomaly: the great optimist had lost his faith in the American experiment. Jefferson had always taken great joy in peering into the nation's glorious future, but now he saw little in store but impending disunion and civil war, grisly racial combat, and a return of the hated Federalists from the dead. No wonder he was despondent: the Missouri crisis seemed to him to portend the realization of all his darkest, most deep-rooted fears. As he repeatedly noted, with more than a little self-pity, his only consolation was that he would not live long enough to weep over the destruction of his beloved republic.

CHAPTER 12

A CONSOLIDATION
OR DISSOLUTION OF
THE STATES

T HE MISSOURI CRISIS was far from the only source of Jefferson's gloom during his final decade. Although he enjoyed robust health well into his seventies, after a bout of illness in the autumn of 1818 he was never again free of physical discomfort. His debts continued to mount, and the threat of bankruptcy loomed over him constantly. In order to stave off financial ruin he was forced to sell off his superb library, which Congress purchased in 1815 after its original collection was destroyed by the British during the War of 1812. At several points Jefferson even feared that he would lose Monticello. He just barely managed to hang on to his prized estate, but the house and grounds soon fell into disrepair. Similar deterioration was visible throughout Virginia, which steadily lost economic and cultural ground to the more enterprising, industrious North and the growing, pioneering West. Once the nation's biggest, richest, most populous, and most politically dominant state, Virginia was gradually turning into a rural backwater whose land was largely depleted and whose main source of revenue was the selling of enslaved people to the Deep South and the West.[1] Given Jefferson's intense loyalty to his native state, this hit him particularly hard. Like many of his fellow planters and slaveholders, he responded by blaming the depraved, money-grubbing Yankees for all the nation's ills. It is only a slight exaggeration to say, as one scholar does, that by this point "he had become a bitter crank."[2]

In addition to these personal and local troubles, Jefferson also became increasingly disheartened by the nation's political order—and not just because of the sectional divisions that were laid bare by the

Missouri crisis. His other causes of concern were many and varied, but most of them revolved around his perception that, despite the continued, uncontested dominance of his own Republican party, political power was becoming far too centralized.[3]

———————

Jefferson's ardor for self-government, which was always considerable, increased still further as he aged. As he put it in the final year of Madison's presidency, "my most earnest wish is to see the republican element of popular controul pushed to the maximum of it's practicable exercise. I shall then believe that our government may be pure & perpetual."[4] Given that everyday Americans had little control over the decisions and actions of the federal government, Jefferson came to believe during his retirement—much as he had when he first read the Constitution back in 1787—that the government was insufficiently republican. In 1816 he offered a correspondent a rundown of each branch, pronouncing that the House of Representatives was "mainly republican," given its reasonably short terms of office; the Senate was "scarcely so, at all," because senators served such long terms and because at that time they were elected by the state legislatures rather than by the people themselves; the presidency was "more republican than the Senate," but only because of the informal and still-unsettled practice of retiring after two terms; and the judiciary was "independant of the Nation" and so entirely unrepublican. In all, Jefferson felt that "if . . . the controul of the people over the organs of their government be the measure of it's republicanism, and I confess I know no other measure," then it was difficult to avoid the conclusion that the American government contained "much less of republicanism, than ought to have been expected."[5]

Although Jefferson claimed to be "steadily for the support of the present constitution," he also advocated amending it in various ways to make the government more accountable to the popular will.[6] He never settled on a precise or consistent list of the constitutional changes that he deemed necessary, but at various times he pressed for instituting shorter Senate terms; formally limiting the number of terms that a president could serve; revising or scrapping the electoral college, so that the president would be elected more directly by the people;

finding some way to hold judges and justices more accountable to the people, since impeachment had turned out to be an empty threat; and guaranteeing that all congressional spending on internal improvements would be proportional to each state's "federal ratio," meaning its free population plus three-fifths of its enslaved population. With measures such as these, he proclaimed, he would "live in more confidence, and die in more hope."[7]

Even more striking is that Jefferson came to regard not just the federal government but also the state governments as overly centralized. In 1816 there was a movement within Virginia to hold a convention that would be charged with reforming or replacing the constitution that the state had adopted during the Revolution; such a convention never materialized during Jefferson's lifetime, but the idea had his firm support. He proposed to a number of correspondents that the state should institute a plan of radical decentralization. Each county, he suggested, should be divided up into smaller districts of no more than five or six square miles that he called "wards," each of which would take on as many of the duties of governance as possible. These miniature republics would be confided with, among other things, "the care of their poor, their roads, police, elections, the nomination of jurors, administration of justice in small cases, [and] elementary exercises of militia."[8]

Jefferson had included a similar idea in some of his educational proposals for Virginia back in the 1770s, but he returned to it with renewed fervor during his retirement. If something like his ward system were to be implemented, he declared in 1810, "I should consider it as the dawn of the salvation of the republic."[9] This in fact became something of a mantra for him: "As Cato . . . concluded every speech with the words 'Carthago delenda est' [Carthage must be destroyed]," he told a friend in 1816, "so do I every opinion with the injunction 'divide the counties into wards.'"[10] Such an arrangement would, in Jefferson's view, have a number of advantages: it would keep more power in the safe hands of the people themselves, rather than delegating it to a less trustworthy central authority; it would enable more people to become active participants in political affairs, thereby fostering a greater sense of patriotism among the citizenry; it would allow the larger political units—the counties, the states, and the nation itself—to focus on

their proper tasks, such as trade, defense, and foreign affairs; and it would provide an additional check on these larger units in the form of the wards.

Jefferson's ward system was, he admitted a bit sheepishly, reminiscent of the township governments that flourished in New England. He contrasted the small, vigorous townships of the Northeast with "the middle, Southern & Western states," with "their large & lubberly division into counties which can never be assembled."[11] It would not be quite right, then, to say that Jefferson was merely an advocate for states' rights, at least at this point in his career. He did believe that the states were important bulwarks against encroachments by the federal government, but he also believed that the states themselves were so consolidated, unwieldy, and overbearing that they needed to be broken up into much smaller units.[12] While America's political order has always been highly fragmented in comparison to those of other modern democracies, in Jefferson's view it was not decentralized nearly enough, even in the early nineteenth century.

Another cause of Jefferson's worries during this period was the ever-increasing role of commerce in American life. By this point he had more or less made his peace with small-scale, domestic manufacturing. He realized that Americans would remain forever dependent on Europe unless they were able to fabricate their own household goods, so he acknowledged that "we must now place the manufacturer by the side of the agriculturist."[13] He even set up a small nail manufactory at Monticello, with the labor performed by enslaved boys. Yet Jefferson remained steadfastly opposed to the production of goods in large, urban factories for export abroad. He regarded the kind of industrial society and economy that had by then become firmly entrenched in the North—and that he feared was gradually making its way southward and westward—as an inescapable source of luxury, inequality, dependence, and corruption. That Jefferson was able to sit in the ornate villa that he had built on his large plantation, surrounded by hundreds of enslaved laborers, and conclude with all sincerity that agriculture was the sure route to simplicity, equality, independence,

and virtue is yet another testament to his capacity for willful blindness and self-deception.

Jefferson was particularly aghast at the penchant that Americans, in both North and South, showed for banks, speculation, and paper money—the trappings of Hamilton's financial program that were still, decades later, bedeviling the republic. "Like a dropsical man calling out for water, water, our deluded citizens are clamoring for more banks, more banks," he lamented.[14] James Madison's rechartering of the national bank in 1816 was one of the few occasions on which Jefferson revealed disappointment in his successor. His letters frequently warned that "we are undone . . . if this banking mania be not suppressed" and that the banking system was "a blot left in all our constitutions, which, if not covered, will end in their destruction."[15]

The rechartered national bank was a key plank in the "American System," an economic plan that was backed by Henry Clay and others in the wake of the War of 1812. Other elements of the plan included a tariff designed to protect American industry and a system of federal subsidies for "internal improvements"—roads, canals, and other public works. Though Clay regarded the American System as an embodiment of Jeffersonian principles, Jefferson himself loathed everything about it.[16] In his view the bank encouraged wild speculation and risk taking, the tariff unduly favored manufacturing over farming, and the scheme of internal improvements was an unconstitutional power grab by Congress. Much to Jefferson's delight, Madison vetoed one effort at setting up a system of federally subsidized internal improvements, the Bonus Bill of 1817, but the idea would resurface with the presidencies of James Monroe and John Quincy Adams, leading to new depths of dejection and paranoia in the very last year of Jefferson's life.

In the meantime, however, an even bigger cause for concern for Jefferson was the federal judiciary, particularly the Supreme Court headed by Chief Justice John Marshall.[17] In the early 1820s—just after the Missouri crisis reached its temporary resolution—Jefferson eagerly backed a campaign to limit the powers of the federal courts. The leaders of the movement were a group of hard-line "Old Republicans" in

Virginia, including Spencer Roane, a longtime judge on the Virginia Supreme Court of Appeals; Thomas Ritchie, the editor of the passionately prosouthern *Richmond Enquirer* (which Jefferson admitted was the only newspaper that he read by this point); and John Taylor of Caroline, a writer and politician who was known for his zealous defense of states' rights.[18] The campaign was prompted by their dismay at some of the decisions that the Marshall Court had recently handed down, including *McCulloch v. Maryland* (1819), which established the supremacy of Congress over the state legislatures, and *Cohens v. Virginia* (1821), which established the supremacy of the Supreme Court over the state courts. Jefferson's alarm at the court's actions, which he saw as part of a devious ploy to concentrate ever more power in the federal government, ran as deep as anyone's.

On Christmas day of 1820, Jefferson wrote to Ritchie that the federal judiciary was a "subtle corps of sappers & miners constantly working underground to undermine the foundations of our confederated fabric. they are construing our constitution from a coordination of a general and special [i.e., state] governments to a general & supreme one alone. this will lay all things at their feet."[19] Piling metaphor upon metaphor, he made a similar point to Roane a few months later: "The great object of my fear is the federal judiciary. that body, like Gravity, ever acting, with noiseless foot, & unalarming advance, gaining ground step by step, and holding what it gains, is ingulphing insidiously the special governments into the jaws of that which feeds them."[20] Jefferson likewise told other correspondents that the justices were actively striving "to sap the independance of the states, to generalize first and then to monarchise the federal authority," and that "the foundations are already deeply laid, by their decisions, for the annihilation of constitutional state-rights, and the removal of every check, every counterpoise to the ingulphing power of which themselves are to make a sovereign part."[21]

The judiciary was widely regarded as the weakest and least dangerous of the three branches at the time of the founding, but Jefferson now believed that the Marshall Court—the last remnant of Federalist power within the federal government—was threatening to single-handedly reverse the sacred "revolution of 1800" by undoing all that he and his fellow Republicans had accomplished over the past two

decades. As one historian writes, "From the perspective of Monticello, the conspirators against 'true Republicanism' had merely shifted their headquarters from the office of the secretary of the treasury to the chambers of the Supreme Court, and Chief Justice John Marshall had grasped the torch of 'consolidationism' and 'monarchism' from the hand of the fallen Hamilton."[22]

Jefferson rejected the notion of judicial supremacy—the idea that the federal courts could unilaterally and definitively declare laws passed by Congress to be unconstitutional and hence void. In Jefferson's view, no one branch possessed the exclusive right to pronounce on the meaning of the Constitution; each had "an equal right to decide for itself what is the meaning of the constitution in the cases submitted to it's action"—as did the states. The notion of judicial supremacy would, in his view, render the judiciary the foremost of the three branches, in obvious contradiction to the framers' intent, by allowing it to invalidate the actions of the other two. Under this doctrine the Constitution would be "a mere thing of wax in the hands of the judiciary which they may twist and shape in to any form they please."[23] The ills of judicial supremacy were, in Jefferson's view, magnified still further by the *Cohens* decision—which he called "that insult to human reason"—since the right of the federal judiciary to authoritatively pronounce on the constitutionality of state laws gave an automatic priority to the federal government over the state governments.[24] The umpire was, in effect, playing on one of the teams.

In this context it is worth pausing to take note of one of Jefferson's frequently quoted statements. "Some men look at Constitutions with sanctimonious reverence, & deem them, like the ark of the covenant, too sacred to be touched," he remarked in a letter in 1816. "They ascribe to the men of the preceding age a wisdom more than human, and suppose what they did to be beyond amendment. I knew that age well: I belonged to it, and labored with it. it deserved well of it's country. it was very like the present, but without the experience of the present: and 40. years of experience in government is worth a century of book-reading." Jefferson went on to note that while he was "certainly not an advocate for frequent & untried changes in laws and constitutions," he was also convinced that "laws and institutions must go hand in hand with the progress of the human mind. . . . We might

as well require a man to wear still the coat which fitted him when a boy, as civilised society to remain ever under the regimen of their barbarous ancestors."[25] This passage accurately captures Jefferson's lack of reverence for the past and for long-standing laws and institutions, but it is often read as an implicit argument for the idea of a "living constitution"—that is, for keeping the Constitution abreast of the changing times through liberal judicial interpretation. Such a reading is grossly inaccurate: not only was Jefferson discussing the Virginia state constitution rather than the US Constitution in this letter; he was suggesting that it should be kept abreast of the changing times through formal amendment or a convention, rather than through judicial fiat. (His own ward system was chief among the reforms that he had in mind.) It was not Jefferson but his foe Hamilton who advocated a liberal reading of the nation's fundamental charter.

Jefferson found the idea of judicial supremacy—and the consequent turning of the Constitution into a thing of wax in the judiciary's hands—to be especially problematic given the lack of effective checks on the federal courts. The Constitution grants all federal judges—including, of course, Supreme Court justices—lifetime appointments "during good behavior," meaning that they are subject to impeachment, but Jefferson noted that judges were in fact impeached so seldom that this threat was "not even a scare-crow."[26] The framers had granted federal judges these lifetime appointments in order to preserve their independence both from the other branches and from the people themselves—since one of the courts' key functions, after all, is protecting the rights of individuals and minorities from the whims of the majority—but Jefferson considered this to be too great of a deviation from the republican principle of keeping government under the control of the people: "a judiciary independant of a king or Executive alone, is a good thing; but independance on the will of the nation is a solecism, at least in a republican government."[27] He accordingly proposed that federal judges should be appointed for set terms of four or six years, renewable by the joint concurrence of the president and Congress. Such a system would, he remarked, "bring their conduct, at regular periods, under revision and probation, and may keep them in equipoise between the general and special [i.e., state] governments."[28]

Jefferson's proposal went nowhere, of course, and he continued to worry about the threat posed by the judiciary throughout his few remaining years. As time wore on he grew more and more convinced that the Marshall Court's actions would soon necessitate radical constitutional reform or even a breakup of the union. "However strong the cord of compact may be, there is a point of tension at which it will break," he wrote in March 1825. "A few such doctrinal decisions, as barefaced as that of the Cohens, happening to bear immediately on two or three of the large states, may induce them to join in arresting the march of government, and . . . to modify [the Constitution] legitimately by the express consent of the parties themselves"—by which Jefferson meant the states—"and not by the usurpation of their created agents [i.e., the justices]. they imagine they can lead us into a consolidated government, while their road leads directly to its dissolution."[29] The stark choice between consolidation and dissolution was one that Jefferson would invoke many times in the year before his death.

When James Monroe embarked on his presidency in 1817, Jefferson assumed that partisanship had all but died out in the United States and that the nation's Republicanism was secure. "The federalists who were truly American, and their great mass was so, have separated from their brethren who were mere Anglomen, and are recieved with cordiality into the republican ranks," he told the Marquis de Lafayette two months after the inauguration. Rightly expecting that Monroe would serve two terms, just as he and Madison had, Jefferson went on to predict that "four and twenty years, which he will accomplish, of administration in republican forms and principles, will so consecrate them in the eyes of the people as to secure them against the danger of change. the evanition of party dissensions has harmonised intercourse, & sweetened society beyond imagination."[30] Aside from their temporary hold on the judiciary, he thought, the Federalists were done for.

By the middle of Monroe's second term, however, Jefferson judged that many of his fellow Republicans had become Federalists in all but name. The heresy that he ascribed to these apostates was not a Hamiltonian penchant for monarchy, but rather a propensity toward the centralization of power. "The papers tell you there are no parties now.

republicans and federalists forsooth are all amalgamated," Jefferson wrote to Lafayette in October 1822. "This, my friend, is not so. the same parties exist now which existed before." Even if no one claimed the name of Federalist any longer, there were still many leading figures in the government who advocated Federalist principles: "they see that monarchism is a hopeless wish in this country, and are rallying anew to the next best point, a consolidated government. they are therefore endeavoring to break down the barriers of the state rights, provided by the constitution against a consolidation."[31] He likewise told Albert Gallatin that the notion that parties were dead was nonsense: "do not believe a word of it. the same parties exist now as ever did." In Congress, he lamented, "you see many, calling themselves republicans, and preaching the rankest doctrines of the old federalists."[32]

The policies that Jefferson regarded as such rank Federalism seem, in retrospect, to be fairly innocuous. Many in Congress called for protective tariffs in the wake of the Panic of 1819, the first major economic downturn since the ratification of the Constitution, and they eventually succeeded in raising tariff rates slightly in 1824. Similarly, there was widespread support in Congress for federal subsidies for internal improvements. President Monroe agreed on the desirability of improving the nation's infrastructure, but for many years he opposed congressional legislation in support of public works on constitutional grounds. Soon after the Supreme Court ruled in *Gibbons v. Ogden* (1824) that Congress's constitutional power to "regulate Commerce . . . among the several States" included the authority to regulate navigation, however, Monroe—much to Jefferson's dismay—signed into law a pair of acts authorizing the president to conduct surveys for road and canal routes and to improve navigation on the Ohio and Mississippi Rivers. Both acts were, like the tariff raises of that same year, fairly modest in scope, but Jefferson regarded them as the first steps in an unassuming but concerted effort to subsume all political power into the federal government.

Even before any of these acts were passed, Jefferson found the support for them so worrisome that he began to wonder whether a breakup of the union might eventually be inevitable, or even desirable. In October 1822 he wrote to Justice William Johnson, whom he had nominated to the Supreme Court back in 1804, that "I scarcely know myself which is most to be deprecated, consolidation, or dissolution

of the states. the horrors of both are beyond the reach of human foresight."[33] To those who accused him of being overly alarmist in invoking the specter of disunion over a few rather minor transgressions of Republican orthodoxy, Jefferson retorted: "I answer by asking if a single state of the Union would have agreed to the constitution had it given all powers to the General government? . . . and if there is any reason to believe the states more disposed, now than then, to acquiesce in this general surrender of all their rights and powers to a Consolidated government, one and undivided?"[34]

Jefferson's worries were redoubled by John Quincy Adams's election to the presidency. The presidential election of 1824 was a messy, four-way race between Adams, Andrew Jackson, Henry Clay, and William Crawford of Georgia. Jackson won a plurality of votes in the electoral college, but since no candidate achieved a majority the decision was thrown into the House of Representatives, which ended up settling on Adams. Soon after the outcome was determined, Jefferson wrote to his old friend John Adams to offer warm congratulations on "the high gratific[atio]n which the issue of the late election must have afforded you," but his letters to other correspondents leave no doubt that Crawford had been his preferred candidate.[35] Jefferson wrote to Crawford himself that same day to confess that the election had "very much damped the confidence I had hitherto reposed in the discretion of my fellow citizens." The Supreme Court had long been in Federalist hands, he noted, and now there was a crypto-Federalist masquerading as a Republican heading to the executive mansion. Given the widespread support for tariffs and internal improvements, even Congress was no longer dependable: "a decided majority there seems to measure their powers only by what they may think, or pretend to think, for the general welfare of the States. all limitations therefore are prostrated, and the general welfare in name, but Consolidation in effect is now the principle of every department of the government."[36]

When the younger Adams laid out an ambitious program of internal improvements in his First Annual Message to Congress in December 1825—including not just a bevy of new roads and canals but also a national university, a naval academy, an astronomical observatory, and a new Department of the Interior to oversee all these projects—Jefferson was beside himself. He drafted a remonstrance

against this proposed program, titled "Solemn Declaration and Protest of the Commonwealth of Virginia," that he intended to submit to the Virginia legislature. Jefferson's proposal promised not to "raise the banner of disaffection, or of separation from [Virginia's] sister-states," but then proceeded to do precisely that: a rupture of the union would be "among the greatest calamities which could befall" the country, the document continued, "but not the greatest. there is yet one greater, submission to a government of unlimited powers. it is only when the hope of avoiding this shall become absolutely desperate, that further forbearance could not be indulged." In the meantime, Jefferson proclaimed on behalf of the state—much as he had back in the Kentucky Resolutions—that the federal government's actions were usurpations of state authority and hence "null and void, and never to be quoted as precedents of right."[37] Madison dissuaded Jefferson from submitting this screed to the legislature, but the fact that he composed it in the first place shows just how panicked he was. Even Dumas Malone, his highly forgiving biographer, recognized that by this point Jefferson's zeal for states' rights "bordered on fanaticism."[38]

As extreme as the "Solemn Declaration and Protest" was, Jefferson was even more frenzied in his private correspondence. Two days later he wrote a confidential letter to William Branch Giles, a former senator and soon-to-be governor of Virginia, to bemoan the strides that the federal government was taking toward centralization: "take together the decisions of the federal court, the doctrines of the President, and the misconstructions of the constitutional compact, acted on by the legislature," he insisted, "and it is but too evident that the three ruling branches . . . are in combination to strip . . . the States authorities of the powers reserved by them and to exercise themselves all functions foreign and domestic." Virginia should not resort to violence except as "the last resource," Jefferson told Giles, but he did not think that secession was at all out of the question. On the contrary, he declared that a separation of the states would be necessary "when the sole alternatives left are the dissolution of our union . . . or submission to a government without limitation of powers. between these two evils when we must make a choice, there can be no hesitation."[39]

Jefferson reached a similar conclusion—and issued a similar threat—in a letter that he wrote to William Gordon, a member of

the Virginia House of Delegates, on New Year's Day of 1826. "It is but too evident," he remarked, "that the branches of our foreign depart-ment of govmt, Exve, judiciary and legislative are in combination to usurp the powers of the domestic branch." (Note that Jefferson had resorted to identifying the federal government of the United States as the nation's "foreign department," whereas the state legislatures were the "domestic branch.") To Gordon too he insisted that they should not resort to arms—at least "not yet, nor until the evil, the only, greater one than separ[atio]n, shall be all but upon us, that of living under a government of discretion. between these alternatives there can be no hesitation."[40] Just a few years prior to this, we have seen, Jefferson had been unsure "which is most to be deprecated, consolidation, or disso-lution of the states," since "the horrors of both are beyond the reach of human foresight," but after Adams's annual message he had clearly made up his mind: dissolution was preferable to consolidation—and consolidation was nearly upon them.[41]

As might be expected, then, Jefferson was as despondent as ever about the nation's future in the early months of 1826. On January 9 he wrote to Claiborne Watts Gooch, who was now coeditor of the *Richmond Enquirer* along with Thomas Ritchie, to lament "all the evils which the present lowering aspect of our political horison so ominously portends." America's political order, he suggested, could hardly even be described as a free government at this point: "that, at some future day, which I hoped to be very distant, the free principles of our government might change, with the change of circumstances, was to be expected. but I certainly did not expect that they would not over-live the generation which established them." The most cheerful note that Jefferson was able to muster was to say that "altho' I have little hope that the torrent of consolidation can be withstood, I should not be for giving up the ship, without efforts to save her. she lived well thro' the first squall, and may weather the present one."[42] Little hope indeed.

———————

Strikingly, just five months later Jefferson would compose some of the most celebrated and optimistic lines ever to emerge from his pen. In the early months of 1826 he was increasingly infirm—he would turn

eighty-three in April—and was regularly taking laudanum to ease the debilitating pain from his inflamed prostate, but he was determined to live to see the fiftieth anniversary of the adoption of the Declaration of Independence on July 4. Like Adams, Jefferson was invited to attend celebrations of the Golden Jubilee far and wide but was far too frail to do so. He instead sat down on June 24 to write a self-consciously eloquent message about the significance of the anniversary to Roger Weightman, the mayor of Washington, DC, who was overseeing the festivities in the nation's capital. Jefferson painstakingly edited this letter, which he knew would be his final public statement.

After expressing his regrets at being unable to travel to Washington, Jefferson stepped back to reflect on the meaning and impact of the Declaration that the nation was celebrating:

> may it be to the world what I believe it will be, (to some parts sooner, to others later, but finally to all.) the Signal of arousing men to burst the chains, under which Monkish ignorance and superstition had persuaded them to bind themselves, and to assume the blessings & security of self government. . . . All eyes are opened, or opening to the rights of man. the general spread of the light of science has already laid open to every view the palpable truth that the mass of mankind has not been born, with saddles on their backs, nor a favored few booted and spurred, ready to ride them legitimately, by the grace of god. these are grounds of hope for others. for ourselves let the annual return of this day, for ever refresh our recollections of these rights and an undiminished devotion to them.[43]

Here was a classic statement of Jeffersonian optimism if ever there was one: the American Revolution not only had burst the chains of oppression and secured the blessings of self-government for this country—apparently for good—but had paved the way for the rest of the world to do so as well ("to some parts sooner, to others later, but finally to all"). The imagery about the masses not being born with saddles on their backs, nor the favored few with boots and spurs, was borrowed from a speech that one of Oliver Cromwell's soldiers had delivered from the scaffold almost a century and a half earlier, but this kind of appropriation and repurposing was considered unobjectionable

at the time.[44] We can perhaps also ignore for the moment the obvious applicability of this imagery to the enslaved people who labored and cared for Jefferson even as he wrote this message. This was as lyrical and uplifting of a vision as anything the founders ever penned, an unmistakable expression of faith in the American experiment.

For anyone who has read the prior decade of Jefferson's correspondence, however, it all rings rather hollow. He had spent the past ten years issuing countless dire warnings about the many imminent threats to the American republic: the government's lack of accountability to the popular will, the spread of industry and the rage for banks and financial speculation, the entrenched sectional divisions that the Missouri crisis had brought to light, the usurpations of the Supreme Court, the resurgence of Federalist principles under a different guise, the steady march of consolidation in all three branches of the federal government. Time and again Jefferson had prophesied the death knell of the union, lamented that the current generation was wantonly throwing away all that the founders had accomplished, and proclaimed that his only consolation was that he would not live to weep over the destruction of the republic.

How had Jefferson pivoted from bemoaning "the evils which the present lowering aspect of our political horison so ominously portends" and the downfall of "the free principles of our government" on January 9 to delivering an inspiring tribute to American democracy on June 24? It is impossible to say with any certainty, at a remove of almost two centuries, what motivated this abrupt reversal, but several possibilities spring to mind. The letter to Weightman may have represented a genuine, last-minute change of heart on Jefferson's part—a reversion to his more customary optimism, perhaps spurred by reflection on the jubilee. Or it may have represented a rather more calculated attempt to secure his own historical legacy, which he knew would be intimately bound up with his role in the Revolution and above all his authorship of the Declaration of Independence; the fiftieth anniversary of the adoption of his beloved Declaration is perhaps the single occasion on which Jefferson would have been most eager to ring a hopeful note. Or it may have represented simply a polite attempt to put on a good face for his fellow citizens who were eager to celebrate the republic at its half-century mark, along with those who

had founded it. Perhaps most likely is that the letter was prompted by some combination of these motives.

What is certain is that the letter to Weightman represented a stark departure from Jefferson's outlook during his final decade, rather than the culmination of it. Throughout his old age, the great optimist's faith in America's future had been emphatically riddled with doubts.

THE OTHER FOUNDERS

NO CHEERING
PROSPECT

WASHINGTON, HAMILTON, ADAMS, AND JEFFERSON were far from alone. Indeed, the great majority of the leading founders ended up disillusioned with what they had wrought. Start with the Anti-Federalists, many of whom are rightly regarded as founders, despite their opposition to the Constitution in 1787–88, because of the role that they played in the Revolution and the influence that they wielded in shaping the new government. A number of them, including George Mason and Patrick Henry, never made peace with the republic that America became, even after the addition of the Bill of Rights that they had demanded. They continued to believe that the national government had so much power and so little popular accountability that tyranny was more or less inevitable.[1] Others, including Samuel Adams and Elbridge Gerry, initially opposed the Constitution but soon came to support it, only to then become alarmed at the state of the republic later in life. Adams lamented that the people never lived up to the ideal of the "Christian Sparta" that he had long envisioned as America's destiny, while Gerry was convinced that party politics (particularly of the Federalist variety) posed a dire threat to the survival of the United States as a free, independent nation.[2]

Thomas Paine, whose pamphlet *Common Sense* helped to launch the Revolution, is difficult to categorize as a Federalist or Anti-Federalist, in part because he was no longer in America during the convention or the ratification debates. He had long recognized the need for a stronger national government, but he also vigorously disapproved of some features of the Constitution—he favored a plural executive, for instance. In any case, by the time of his return to the United States

in 1802, Paine was anathema to Federalists because of his association with the French Revolution, his friendship with Jefferson, and an open attack that he had launched on Washington back in 1796. Even many Republicans kept their distance because he persisted in aggressively criticizing Christianity in an age when Americans were increasingly pious. Paine initially lashed out, in a series of letters addressed "To the Citizens of the United States," at his Federalist critics and at the degree to which factionalism had infected America's body politic. After a year or so, however, he concluded that it was no use fighting for what was obviously a lost cause. He gradually slipped into an impoverished obscurity, drinking heavily and convinced that the radical promise of the American Revolution remained unfulfilled.[3]

Even many of the Constitution's staunchest supporters in 1787–88—in addition to those already discussed in this book—came to despair for the nation. The good doctor Benjamin Rush, even more than his friend and frequent correspondent John Adams, abandoned all hope for the American people and government in his later decades. As early as 1801, just months after Jefferson's inauguration—and despite his Republican politics—Rush concluded that the American experiment "will certainly fail. It has already disappointed the expectations of its most sanguine and ardent friends."[4] He told his children and everyone else who would listen that he had come to feel "shame for my zeal in the cause of our Country" during the Revolution and the ratification debates.[5] Indeed, he declared to Adams that "I . . . sometimes wish I could erase my name from the declaration of Independence." As for the Constitution, "I cannot meet with a man who loves it."[6] The year before he died Rush lamented that America had become "a bebanked, and a bewhiskied & a bedollared nation."[7]

The ever-colorful Gouverneur Morris, almost as much as James Madison, has a credible claim to the title "The Father of the Constitution." He spoke more frequently at the Constitutional Convention than any other delegate, and he actually drafted the majority of the document (including the famous preamble).[8] A Federalist to the core, he was dismayed by what he regarded as the South's political domination of the North during the Jefferson and Madison administrations. By the outbreak of the War of 1812, Morris was all but certain that the dismemberment of the union was imminent. "If peace be not im-

mediately made with England," he predicted, "the question on negro votes"—that is, the disproportionate power accorded to the southern states by their ability to count those whom they had enslaved as three-fifths of a person for purposes of representation—"must divide this Union." Nor did he assume that such a division would be an altogether bad thing. New England and New York could then leave it to the southerners to "exercise the privilege of strangling commerce, whipping Negroes, and bawling about the inborn inalienable rights of man."[9] Though the Constitution was constructed well at the outset, he believed, by that point it had been "so much perverted that it can hardly be restored to what it was."[10] When the war concluded the best that Morris could hope for was that "the peace may prevent a separation of the States, patch up our tattered Constitution, and perpetuate the blessings of a Jacobin administration."[11]

John Jay—coauthor of *The Federalist*, leading diplomat, and the first chief justice of the Supreme Court—had the longest retirement of any founder; he stepped down as governor of New York in 1801 and lived all the way until 1829. During this lengthy period he commented on national politics only occasionally, but those few comments suggest that his view of the American republic had darkened considerably. He lamented "the vices and violences of parties, and the corruptions which they generate and cherish," proclaiming that "*all* parties have their demagogues" and that "therefore (except now and then in particular instances) our affairs will commonly be managed by political intrigues."[12] Jay was aghast at those, like Morris, who flirted with the idea of secession, but he was enough of a Federalist to believe that "*pure* democracy, like *pure* rum, easily produces intoxication, and with it a thousand mad pranks and fooleries." As the nation became more democratic, he predicted, "this country, as well as others, will experience deep distress."[13]

James Monroe moderately opposed the adoption of the Constitution during the Virginia ratifying convention, but he quickly became a supporter and integral member of the new government—as a senator, minister to France and Great Britain, governor of Virginia, secretary of state, and president. Far more than his predecessors, Monroe entered the presidency at a time of international peace, economic prosperity, and broad political harmony. His fondest hope was to preside

over the ultimate demise of political conflict and partisanship, but "the Era of Good Feelings" did not last for long. Even during Monroe's first term the Missouri crisis shattered any sense of national unity, and the rancorous 1824 election to choose his successor confirmed—much to his dismay and bewilderment—that divisiveness would continue to be the rule rather than the exception of American politics. Most of Monroe's energy during his six-year retirement was devoted to trying to stave off personal financial disaster. He studiously sought to remain aloof from national politics during this time—it was beneath the dignity of an ex-president, he believed, to express an opinion on current affairs—but it is clear that the country did not even approximate the unified ideal that he had so long envisaged. On the few occasions when he broke his vow of silence, Monroe expressed "great concern & distress" at the growing enmity between North and South, noting that "whatever shakes our system, or menaces it, will create a despondence throughout the civilized world."[14]

Finally, John Marshall, the country's greatest chief justice, spent much of his long tenure on the Supreme Court (1801–35) fighting almost single-handedly against the forces of decentralization—with an impressive record of success. The court began to display less internal unity and to encounter more external resistance (including from Jefferson) during the last decade and a half of his tenure, but it was not until the nullification crisis of 1832–33 that Marshall's habitual optimism gave way to despair. Even as the prospect of nullification emerged on the national scene in 1830 Marshall remained hopeful, remarking that "the idea that a state may constitutionally nullify an act of Congress is so extravagant in itself, and so repugnant to the existence of Union between the States that I could with difficulty bring myself to believe it was serious[ly] entertained by any person."[15] Once it became clear that many in the South did in fact embrace this idea, Marshall lamented that "we are now gathering the bitter fruits of the tree ... planted by Mr. Jefferson, and so industriously and perseveringly cultivated by Virginia."[16] At this point he saw no way to avoid eventual secession and civil war, telling his friend and Supreme Court colleague Joseph Story, "I yield slowly and reluctantly to the conviction that our constitution cannot last. . . . The union has been prolonged thus far by miracles. I fear they cannot continue."[17]

Marshall died convinced that, politically speaking, "the future presents no cheering prospect."[18]

In all, then, the list of major founders who ended up disillusioned later in life is startling: John Adams, Samuel Adams, Elbridge Gerry, Alexander Hamilton, Patrick Henry, John Jay, Thomas Jefferson, John Marshall, George Mason, James Monroe, Gouverneur Morris, Thomas Paine, Benjamin Rush, George Washington. Aside from Benjamin Franklin, who died just as the new government was getting underway in 1790, the most conspicuous omission from this list—and the only other figure who can rival Washington, Hamilton, Adams, and Jefferson in terms of stature and influence—is of course James Madison.[19]

MADISON

CHAPTER 14

FAR FROM DESPONDING

DESPITE BEING A rather sickly hypochondriac, James Madison outlasted all the other founders, living until June 1836, almost through Andrew Jackson's second term as president.[1] (Aaron Burr survived Madison by a few months, but it is difficult to categorize Burr as a founder, given that he was not involved in politics in any serious way until after the Constitution's ratification.) Living as long as he did—a decade beyond even Adams and Jefferson—Madison saw much that the others did not: the rise of railroads (the Baltimore and Ohio began passenger service in 1830) and radical abolitionism (William Lloyd Garrison founded *The Liberator* in 1831), an ominous slave rebellion in his own backyard (the uprising inspired by Nat Turner in 1831) and an even more ominous constitutional crisis in which he became personally involved (the nullification crisis of 1832–33), and above all the populist, democratic revolution in American politics that Jackson's presidency (1829–37) both symbolized and galvanized. When Abraham Lincoln, in his Lyceum Address of 1838, referred to the founders as "a once hardy, brave, and patriotic, but now lamented and departed race of ancestors," Madison had only been "lamented and departed" for a year and a half.[2]

Through all this time and all these events—some of which seemed almost designed to inspire despair in someone with his eighteenth-century worldview—Madison remained relatively confident in the superiority and durability of the American republic. He did occasionally harbor some real worries and experience some palpable disappointments, as might be expected, but these concerns were never so deep and lasting as to lead to disillusionment with the political order as a whole or to despondency about its future. In this, Madison was

the proverbial exception that proves the rule among the founders. The obvious question is why he was such an outlier. Why did Madison remain largely optimistic about America's constitutional order when so many of his compatriots came to despair for the government and the nation?

One potential answer can be ruled out immediately. Given his familiar moniker "The Father of the Constitution," one might assume that Madison was sanguine for so long because he got what he wanted out of the Philadelphia Convention and remained satisfied with the result, but this was by no means the case. It is true that Madison played a pivotal role in the Constitution's design and ratification: he helped to set the agenda at the outset of the convention by formulating the Virginia Plan; he participated in the debates in Philadelphia more frequently than anyone but Gouverneur Morris and James Wilson; he wrote around a third of *The Federalist*, including the famous tenth paper; he led the forces in support of ratification at the critical Virginia convention in Richmond; and as the leading figure in the First Congress he contributed more than anyone else to the drafting and ratification of the Bill of Rights. Yet at first Madison deemed the Constitution to be radically defective.

Prior to the convention, Madison had thought as long and hard as anyone about the defects of the Articles of Confederation and the state constitutions. He drew on his vast historical research to help devise a constitutional blueprint that he hoped would ameliorate these problems, which became known as the Virginia Plan. Thanks to some deft politicking, this plan soon became the working model with which the delegates in Philadelphia began their deliberations, but many of the key planks were whittled away over the course of the summer. In order to bolster the authority of the federal government and to minimize that of the states, Madison had proposed, among other things, that representation in both houses of Congress should be based on a state's population—rather than granting the states equal representation, as the Articles had done—and that Congress should have a veto over state legislation. Indeed, Madison told Washington that "a negative [i.e., veto] *in all cases whatsoever* on the legislative acts of the States ... appears to me to be absolutely necessary, and to be the least possible encroachment on the State jurisdictions."[3] (That Mad-

ison would invoke and indeed emphasize the infamous phrase from the hated Declaratory Act of 1766, which proclaimed Parliament's right to legislate for the colonies "in all cases whatsoever," reveals the depth of his feelings on the subject.) Many of the delegates balked at the idea of such a strong national authority, however, and the federal veto was eventually dropped. Similarly, the states were granted equal representation in the Senate as part of the Connecticut Compromise and, to cap it off, the senators were to be elected by the state legislatures that Madison found so obnoxious. These were the most serious defeats that Madison sustained over the course of the convention, but they were far from the only ones. In fact, by one scholar's count, no fewer than forty of the seventy-one proposals that Madison moved, seconded, or unequivocally supported that summer in Philadelphia ended up losing.[4]

At the convention's close, Madison was profoundly disheartened. He wrote to Jefferson in September 1787 with the prediction that "the plan should it be adopted will neither effectually answer its national object nor prevent the local mischiefs which every where excite disgusts ag[ain]st the state governments."[5] In October he sent his friend another letter, this one more than seventeen manuscript pages long, detailing his dashed hopes.[6] The constitution that emerged from the convention left the central question of sovereignty up in the air, he lamented. The federal authority was stronger than the exceedingly weak one that had been created by the Articles of Confederation, but the threats posed by the state governments had been only curtailed, not eliminated altogether. It was a partial solution, rather than the complete and radical one that Madison believed to be necessary. As Jack Rakove writes, "save for the handful of delegates who later opposed its ratification, few members left Philadelphia in September more disappointed with the Constitution than the man history has called its 'Father.'"[7]

Like Hamilton, however, Madison soon set his reservations aside and got to work; reckoning that a partial solution was better than none at all, he jumped into the campaign to ratify the new charter with both feet. He also appears to have grown genuinely reconciled to the Constitution over time in a way that Hamilton never quite did. The radically centralizing Virginia Plan would have had no chance

of being ratified by enough states to go into effect, Madison came to realize, and the fudging of the sovereignty issue could end up being a source of dynamism rather than one of weakness in the new government. In fact, over the course of the 1790s Madison came to believe, with his partner Jefferson, not just that sovereignty should be divided between the federal government and the states after all, but that the federal government under the auspices of Washington, Hamilton, and Adams was continually encroaching on the states' rightful terrain.

Madison had worked in close cooperation with Hamilton on *The Federalist* and indeed throughout the ratification process in 1787–88.[8] At this time they appeared to be members of the same team, two of the leading proponents of the strongest practicable national authority. Almost immediately after the new government was launched, however, Madison came to regard nearly every step that Hamilton took—his wide-ranging financial program, his liberal reading of the Constitution, his desire for a military buildup, his advocacy of a wide scope for executive discretion in foreign affairs—as a glaring betrayal of the constitutional order that they had championed. Madison's disaffection with Hamilton began quite early, even before Jefferson returned from France in March 1790, but it was no doubt intensified by his close friend's presence in the capital after that point. Like Jefferson, Madison came to view Hamilton as a stockjobbing, monarchist Anglophile who had somehow managed to convince the most influential figure of the age—President Washington—to join in carrying out his subversive agenda. Madison worked hand in hand with Jefferson to found the Republican party in order to better oppose the administration's policies, with Madison leading the forces in Congress and Jefferson doing what he could within the cabinet. Although Madison was out of office for the entirety of Adams's presidency, he continued to attack the Federalist program—including the Quasi-War with France and the Alien and Sedition Acts—from his home at Montpelier during the latter part of the decade. (Madison hated Adams more fervently than Jefferson ever did.)

A tremendous amount of ink has been spilled in trying to explain—or explain away—Madison's abrupt conversion from being an

arch-Federalist in the 1780s to an arch-Republican in the 1790s. How did the ardent nationalist of the Constitutional Convention and *The Federalist*, the figure who feared tyrannical majorities within the state governments above all else and proposed a federal veto to check them, quite suddenly become an equally ardent advocate of states' rights and limited federal powers? Did Madison change his mind about some of the central issues of American politics, or did he merely shift his priorities in response to changing circumstances? Which was the "real" Madison?[9] Happily, for our purposes these thorny questions need not be resolved. Suffice it to say that Madison's attitude toward the nation's political order largely tracked Jefferson's for the next quarter century. Although Madison was alarmed by many of the Federalists' actions during the 1790s, he too expected that true Republican principles would win out in the end. After all, he wrote in 1792, "the mass of people in every part of the union, in every state, and of every occupation must at bottom be with [the Republicans], both in interest and sentiment."[10]

Madison was likewise convinced that true Republican principles *had* come out on top when Jefferson was elected president in 1800, and that they were fortified still further by his own election eight years later. Madison's presidency was not without its difficulties—the nation was distinctly unprepared for the War of 1812, and his administration was often rather bungling in its management of the conflict—but he nonetheless left office in 1817 as a hugely admired figure, and his secretary of state, James Monroe, won an easy victory to succeed him.[11] In his final message to Congress, Madison expressed his pride that the Constitution had managed "to bear the trials of adverse as well as prosperous circumstances" over the course of three decades and that it "contain[ed] in its combination of the federate and elective principles a reconcilement of public strength with individual liberty."[12]

Whereas Jefferson grew more and more disillusioned beginning around 1816, however, Madison remained mostly optimistic about the American experiment throughout Jefferson's gloomy final decade.[13] Madison was never the advocate that Jefferson was of radical decentralization or of ensuring that the government remained in close conformity to the popular will; his most famous and influential piece of writing, *Federalist* number 10, was in fact dedicated to showing

how to combat the tyranny of the majority—or what Madison called majority faction—within a republic, and the key to his solution was extending the sphere of governance. Hence, Madison was unperturbed by the allegedly "unrepublican" elements of the national and state governments that Jefferson found so problematic. Similarly, Madison was far less disturbed than Jefferson by the prospect of a commercialized, industrialized nation; recall that he himself rechartered the national bank in 1816. Nor was Madison nearly as alarmed by federal subsidies for internal improvements. It is true that he vetoed the Bonus Bill of 1817 on constitutional grounds, but after the election of John Quincy Adams eight years later he coolly told Jefferson, "I consider the question as to Canals &c as decided . . . because sanctioned by the Nation under the permanent influence of benefit to the major part of it."[14]

Madison was critical of some of the decisions handed down by the Marshall Court, particularly the "latitudinary mode of expounding the Constitution" that the court adopted in *McCulloch v. Maryland* (1819). Under the court's interpretation of the "necessary and proper" clause, he complained, "no practical limit can be assigned" to Congress's powers.[15] Yet Madison diverged from Jefferson and the hard-line "Old Republicans" in insisting that the Supreme Court was the proper arbiter of constitutional disputes between the federal government and the states. The court may have unjustifiably enlarged the federal government's powers in some recent cases, "but," he chided Jefferson in 1823, "the abuse of a trust does not disprove its existence."[16] Madison made light of the exaggerated fears of the hard-liners, telling Spencer Roane that "it is not probable that the Supreme Court would be long indulged in a career of usurpation opposed to the decided opinions & policy of the Legislature."[17] Chief Justice Marshall may have been frequently in the wrong, in other words, but he did not and indeed could not pose an existential threat to the republic.

Even the Missouri crisis failed to demoralize Madison. He agreed with Jefferson that, constitutionally speaking, Missouri should have the right to decide for itself whether to permit slavery within its borders, just as the other states did. He also agreed that, practically speaking, the expansion of slavery into new territory would serve to dilute the evil by improving the lot of the enslaved and hastening the day of their emancipation. Still further, he agreed that the pros-

pect of a marked difference of policy and principle that bisected the entire nation was disconcerting. "The tendency of what has passed and is passing, fills me with no slight anxiety," Madison remarked in November 1819, as the stalemate over the issue reached its apex.[18] Yet in stark contrast to Jefferson, Madison's worries were quelled by the compromise reached by Congress. By the following November, Madison was assuring the Marquis de Lafayette that the contest over Missouri was merely a transient problem, a "subject which ruffles the surface of public affairs," not a deep or long-term threat. "A Government like ours has so many safety-valves, giving vent to overheated passions," he insisted, "that it carries within itself a relief against the infirmities from which the best of human Institutions can not be exempt."[19]

Aside from one brief but notable interlude, Madison also remained sanguine about America's political order throughout the decade between Jefferson's death and his own. One might expect—and many of Madison's friends did expect—that he would have been appalled by Jackson's elevation to the presidency. It is difficult to imagine a starker contrast than that between the diminutive, shy, cautious, soberminded Madison, with his commitment to balance and stability and his fears of popular licentiousness, and the aggressive, freewheeling, quick-tempered general, whose instinct was always to inflame populist and partisan passions. While Madison did find much about Jackson distasteful, he appears to have greeted the rise of "Jacksonian democracy" with relative equanimity.[20] Nine months after Jackson's inauguration, he concluded his final public speech on a note of almost defiant optimism: "I never have despaired," he proclaimed, "notwithstanding all the threatening appearances we have passed through. I have now more than a hope, a consoling confidence that we shall at last find that our labours have not been in vain."[21] Madison even hosted Jackson for dinner at Montpelier in July 1832.

Madison disapproved of Jackson's capacious sense of executive power, but he regarded even this as a temporary transgression that would disappear along with his presidency. "The danger and even existence of the heresies which have grown up under the auspices of

[Jackson's] name, will expire with his natural or his official life, if not previously to either," Madison assured Edward Coles, his friend and former private secretary, in 1834. After all, "his popularity is evidently and rapidly sinking under the unpopularity of his doctrines," and "if the declension of his popular influence be such during his official life and with the *peculiar* hold he has on popular feelings, there is little reason to suppose that any succeeding President will attempt a like career."[22] If only.

One reason why Madison was so tolerant of Jackson's flaws was that Jackson stood firmly opposed to the South Carolina nullifiers, whom Madison regarded as a far greater threat to the union.[23] The nullification crisis of 1832–33 was in fact the closest that Madison ever came to outright despair.[24] The origins of the crisis lay in a tariff that was passed by Congress in 1828 in order to protect northern manufacturing, which southern detractors quickly dubbed "The Tariff of Abominations." Although Congress had enacted protective tariffs on a regular basis since its very first session, states'-rights advocates now began to argue that such legislation exceeded Congress's constitutionally delegated authority. The South Carolina "Exposition and Protest," which was written by Vice President John C. Calhoun but published anonymously by the state legislature, proclaimed that states had the right to unilaterally nullify federal laws that they deemed to be unconstitutional. This meant, in effect, that in order for federal legislation to survive it would have to be supported (or at least not actively opposed) by a majority in every state legislature. While the protective tariff was the nullifiers' immediate target, worries about the federal government meddling with slavery lurked in the near background of the debates.

In 1832 Congress passed, and Jackson signed, a law that reduced the tariff rates from the 1828 bill, but the new legislation did not go far enough for South Carolina, which held a formal convention to declare the tariff null and void within the state. Jackson threatened to send in federal troops to enforce the measure, but tensions cooled when Congress passed a compromise law in March 1833 that gradually reduced the tariff still further. The South Carolina convention reconvened and repealed its ordinance nullifying the tariff later that month, but in order to preserve its principles it issued a new ordi-

nance nullifying the bill that authorized Jackson to use military force against the state.

Madison believed firmly in the constitutionality—if not always the expediency—of protective tariffs, and he believed even more firmly that the doctrine of nullification was a recipe for minority rule or, more likely, disunion. Republican government simply could not subsist, he maintained, if each state had an effective veto over federal legislation. Such a doctrine would put "powder under the Constitution and Union, and a match in the hand of every party to blow them up at pleasure."[25] At best it would "convert the Federal Government into a mere League"—as it had been under the Articles of Confederation—"which would quickly throw the States back into a chaos, out of which not order, a second time, but lasting disorder of the worst kind, could not fail to grow."[26] Either prospect was, of course, disheartening indeed. Madison wrote to Nicholas Trist, a personal friend who also happened to be an advisor of President Jackson, that "the idea that a constitution which has been so fruitful of blessings, and a Union admitted to be the only Guardian of the peace, liberty and happiness of the people of the States comprising it, should be broken up and scattered to the winds, without greater than any existing causes, is more painful than words can express."[27]

Madison was also dismayed by that fact that the nullifiers invoked his own authority to bolster their case.[28] Calhoun and his followers presented themselves as following in the footsteps of the Virginia and Kentucky Resolutions that Madison and Jefferson, respectively, had drafted back in 1798. Madison was unaccustomed to issuing public statements by this point, but he felt compelled to wade into the controversy in order to set the nullifiers straight: the resolutions of 1798 were prompted by a far greater threat than South Carolina now faced—the repressive Alien and Sedition Acts rather than a mere tariff—and in any case the Virginia Resolutions by no means implied that a state could single-handedly nullify federal law. (Madison also fought to distance the nullifiers' position from Jefferson's more radical Kentucky Resolutions, but this was a more uphill battle.)[29] The nullifiers' opponents were thrilled by Madison's interventions in the debate—John Marshall rejoiced that Madison "is himself again. He avows the opinions of his best days"—but the nullifiers simply chalked them

up to the octogenarian's senility.[30] They would not accept Madison's word as the final interpretive authority on a document that he himself had written.

At perhaps his darkest moment, just before the compromise tariff was passed by Congress in March 1833, Madison went so far as to envision the nullifiers bringing about "a rupture of the Union—a Southern Confederacy, mutual enmity with the Northern—the most dreadful animosities and border wars springing from the case of Slaves—rival alliances abroad, standing armies at home to be supported by internal taxes—and Federal Governments with powers of a more consolidating and Monarchical tendency than the greatest jealousy has charged on the existing system."[31] At this point he appears to have been on the verge of full-blown disillusionment. Once the compromise was brokered and the standoff was averted, however, Madison's apprehensions were eased, even if not eliminated entirely. In April he wrote to Henry Clay, the chief architect of the compromise, remarking that the accord "has certainly had the effect of an Anodyne on the feverish excitement under which the public mind was laboring." The threat of nullification and secession was by no means eradicated by the compromise, Madison was sure, but he held out hope that the ills that would result from disunion were so obvious that "as the gulf is approached, the deluded will recoil from its horrors, and that the deluders, if not themselves sufficiently startled, will be abandoned & overwhelmed by their followers."[32]

As for the even larger problem lurking in the background of the nullification controversy, the persistence and indeed massive expansion of slavery, here too Madison was oddly, even foolishly, hopeful.[33] Like Jefferson, Madison regarded slavery as a self-evident evil but believed that its abolition must be accompanied by the colonization of the liberated slaves; he was in fact a founding member of the American Colonization Society in 1816 and became its ceremonial president in 1833. Although Madison was well aware of the political and financial obstacles that presently stood in the way of such a massive undertaking, he was "certain," he told the Marquis de Lafayette in 1830, "that Time 'the great Innovator' is not idle in its salutary preparations. . . . Outlets for the freed blacks are alone wanted for a rapid erasure of that blot from our Republican character."[34] The next year he likewise

remarked to the secretary of the Colonization Society that "many circumstances at the present moment seem to concur in brightening the prospects of the Society and cherishing the hope that the time will come when the dreadful calamity which has so long afflicted our Country and filled so many with despair will be gradually removed & by means consistent with justice, peace, and the general satisfaction: thus giving to our country the full enjoyment of the blessings of liberty and to the world the full benefit of its great example."[35]

Madison sketched several different emancipation-colonization plans at various points in his career, but the basic idea behind all of them was that some of the vast public lands in the West could be sold in order to subsidize the huge costs involved—compensating the slaveholders, transporting the liberated slaves to Africa or the Caribbean, and helping to get a society up and running there. As for amending the Constitution to grant the federal government the authority to do all this, Madison blithely assumed that "it can hardly be doubted that the requisite powers might readily be procured"— despite the fact that a constitutional amendment in the early 1830s would have required ratification by eighteen of the twenty-four states, presumably including all twelve free states and six of the twelve slave states.[36] In 1833 Madison admitted that on this issue "I may indulge too much my wishes & hopes, to be safe from error," but he was unwilling to despair: the day of peaceful liberation would surely one day come.[37] It was on the future of slavery, more than any other subject, that Madison appears in retrospect to have been driven by something like blind faith in the future.

Madison's letters and other writings from his very last years were, in stark contrast to those of the other founders, suffused with conspicuously optimistic observations about the American regime and its prospects.[38] In June 1834, Madison commented on "the security & prosperity" that the nation had "so long enjoyed" under the Constitution and "the bright prospects which it has opened on the Civilized world."[39] That December, in his final statement on nullification, he pronounced that America's constitutional order had "throughout a period of nearly half a Century" proven "successful beyond any of

the forms of Govts. ancient or modern, with which it may be compared; having as yet disclosed no defects which do not admit remedies, compatible with its vital principles and characteristic features."[40] In August of the following year he lamented "the extremes to which party excitements are liable" but then quickly moved on to note that "a sickly countenance occasionally is not inconsistant with the self healing capacity of a Constitution such as I hope ours is; and still less with the medical resources in the hands of a people such as I hope ours will prove to be."[41] That December he responded to an encouraging report from Secretary of the Treasury Levi Woodbury with the remark that "the exuberant prosperity of our Country is a happy illustration of the beneficent operation of its political Institutions."[42]

Madison announced in March 1836 that, however many ills the nation may face and however uncertain the future may be, "I am far ... from desponding, of the great political experiment in the hands of the American people." He then proceeded to explain why: "Much has already been gained in its favour, by the continued prosperity accompanying it through a period of so many years. Much may be expected from the progress & diffusion of political science in dissipating errors, opposed to the sound principles which harmonize different interests; from the Geographical, commercial & social ligaments, strengthened as they are by mechanical improvements, giving so much advantage to time over space, & above all, by the obvious & inevitable consequences of the wreck of an ark bearing as we have flattered ourselves the happiness of our Country & the hope of the World."[43] He concluded his very last letter, written just six days before his death, by proclaiming that of the "many good fruits" that America's constitutional order had produced, "no one has been a more rejoicing witness than myself."[44]

More evidence for Madison's sanguine outlook during this period comes from the record kept by Harriet Martineau, the famous English feminist and abolitionist, who visited Madison at Montpelier in February 1835. Martineau commented that "the finest of his characteristics appeared to me to be his inexhaustible faith—faith that a well-founded Commonwealth may ... be immortal; not only because the people, its constituency, never dies; but because the principles of justice in which such a Commonwealth originates never die out of the

people's heart and mind. This faith shone brightly through the whole of Mr. Madison's conversation." She did note that Madison spoke a great deal, sometimes dejectedly, about slavery, but even on this score she noted his confidence that colonization was both desirable and feasible—she herself found the idea preposterous—and quoted him as saying that he was "less in despair than formerly about slavery." In all, she concluded, "Madison reposed cheerfully, gaily, to the last, on his faith in the people's power of wise self-government."[45]

CHAPTER 15

GROUNDS FOR HOPE

THE QUESTION RECURS: what accounts for Madison's continued faith in the American experiment, not only through the 1790s, by the end of which Washington, Hamilton, and Adams had all grown disillusioned, and not only through Jefferson's despondent final decade, but also through much of the turbulent Jacksonian era? Any answer to such a question is necessarily a matter of speculation, but several factors taken together form a plausible explanation.

Madison's enduring confidence can be attributed, at least in part, simply to his temperament. This is not to say that he was an innate or unalloyed optimist; Jefferson was, for most of his life, much more likely than Madison to view the world through rose-tinted glasses, which made his disillusionment all the more painful and pronounced when it came. But Madison was far more even tempered than the passionate Jefferson, the fiery Hamilton, the irascible Adams, or even Washington, whose pent-up anger occasionally burst through the stoic facade that he generally showed to the world. Contemporaries consistently described Madison as composed, steady, and self-possessed. He remained almost maddeningly unperturbed even through the low points of his administration, when the Capitol building and the executive mansion were ransacked and put to the torch by British troops and rumblings of secession pervaded New England. Edward Coles, Madison's private secretary for most of his presidency, remarked that "nothing could excite or ruffle him" and that he never heard Madison "utter one petulant expression, or give way for one moment to passion or despondency."[1] We have seen that whereas Jefferson came unglued during the Missouri crisis, trembling at the "fire bell in the night" and weeping over "the knell of the Union," Madison declared at the height of the impasse merely that he felt

"no slight anxiety."[2] Madison's unflappable disposition no doubt contributed to his lack of despair.

Another factor, connected to the first, is that Madison had lower expectations than most of the other founders regarding what was politically possible, and he pointedly refused to let the perfect be the enemy of the good. When he set out to defend the Constitution in *The Federalist*, Madison remarked that "it is a matter both of wonder and regret, that those who raise so many objections against the new constitution, should never call to mind the defects of that which is to be exchanged for it"—that is, the Articles of Confederation. After all, he continued, "it is not necessary that the former should be perfect; it is sufficient that the latter is more imperfect. No man would refuse to give brass for silver or gold, because the latter had some alloy in it. No man would refuse to quit a shattered and tottering habitation, for a firm and commodious building, because the latter had not a porch to it; or because some of the rooms might be a little larger or smaller, or the ceiling a little higher or lower than his fancy would have planned them."[3] At the end of his life he was still appealing to "the monitory reflection that no Government of human device, & human administration can be perfect; that that which is the least imperfect is therefore the best Govt."[4]

It is true that most of the other founders had a pragmatic streak as well, but we can use the principal source of disillusionment for each of this book's protagonists to illustrate the especially sober nature of Madison's realism. To begin with, Madison was never as aghast at partisanship as Washington was. He occasionally paid the usual eighteenth-century lip service to the evils of party, but he readily accepted that, as he put it in *Federalist* number 10, "the latent causes of faction are . . . sown in the nature of man."[5] Rather than seeking in vain to avoid or eliminate factions, Madison advocated *multiplying* them so that it would be more difficult for any single faction to obtain a majority. In 1792 he penned an essay on the inevitability and indeed utility of parties in a free government, remarking that "if this is not the language of reason, it is that of republicanism."[6]

Similarly, Madison was never as insistent on civic virtue as Adams was. He did believe that in a republican government the people needed to honor and indeed venerate the Constitution and the laws, and to

be vigilant in defending their liberties. He declared at the Virginia ratifying convention that if there was "no virtue among us" then "we are in a wretched situation.... To suppose that any form of government will secure liberty or happiness without any virtue in the people, is a chimerical idea."[7] Yet Madison was well aware, as he famously put it in *Federalist* number 51, that men are not angels, and hence that constitutions must be designed under the assumption that most people, most of the time, will be self-interested and ambitious. The idea that people would consistently sacrifice their own good for that of the public struck Madison as a credulous fantasy.

Madison was likewise never as enamored of the idea of an energetic central authority as Hamilton was. In the 1780s he did fight alongside Hamilton to strengthen the federal government, and at times his essays in *The Federalist* could sound positively Hamiltonian, as when he declared that "energy in government is essential to that security against external and internal danger, and to that prompt and salutary execution of the laws, which enter into the very definition of good government."[8] Even in the 1780s, however, Madison's main aim was to empower the federal *Congress*—not the executive, which was Hamilton's special passion—to check the tyrannical majorities within the state legislatures. Madison recoiled at the quasi-monarchical view of presidential power that Hamilton championed, which was one reason for their dramatic split in the early 1790s. Madison aspired to a regime of ordered liberty, not all the machinery—a powerful executive, a large military, a sweeping financial program with its attendant bureaucracy—that Hamilton hoped would lead to national greatness.

On the other hand, Madison was never as dismayed by the prospect of "consolidation" as Jefferson was. This is one reason why Madison took the events of the 1820s, such as federal subsidies for internal improvements and the centralizing rulings of the Marshall Court, so much more in stride than Jefferson did. It is also one reason why his Virginia Resolutions were much more moderate than Jefferson's Kentucky Resolutions—Madison declared the Alien and Sedition Acts to be unconstitutional, but not null and void—and why he talked Jefferson out of submitting the "Solemn Declaration and Protest of the Commonwealth of Virginia," with its implicit threat of secession, to the state's legislature. Madison was far more pragmatic than Jef-

ferson about the possibility of centralized power occasionally doing some good, and he was far less idealistic about the benefits that would accrue from radical decentralization and perpetual adherence to the popular will.

In short, Madison simply expected less from politics than most of the other founders. He never supposed that his fellow citizens would consistently surmount partisanship or sacrifice their self-interest for the sake of the common good, nor did he long for the nation to achieve economic and military greatness on the international stage or for virtuous yeoman farmers to conduct the politics of their local ward—and this meant that he was less likely than the other founders to be disappointed in what America became.

Still another reason for Madison's late-life confidence in the durability of the American republic was precisely that, as "the last of the fathers," he had lived so long and seen so much in company with the nation that he had helped to found. His writings from this period frequently highlighted how long the constitutional order had lasted—nearly a half century by that point—and how many storms it had weathered. Madison appears to have reasoned that if the Constitution and the union had managed to survive 1798 (when the prevailing war hysteria led the government to clamp down harshly on civil liberties), 1814 (which saw much of the capital go up in flames), and 1819 (when the political world was shaken by the biggest confrontation yet over the nation's most divisive issue), then surely they could survive a president who played on people's passions a bit too much, or the citizens of one or two states who were overly exercised about a tariff. The longer the nation endured, the more durable it seemed.

Long experience had, moreover, persuaded Madison beyond a doubt that the American form of government was preferable to the alternatives—throughout history and around the world—and he sought to convince (or remind) his fellow citizens of that basic but crucial fact. We have already taken note of his public statement in 1834 that the nation's constitutional order had shown itself, through a course of five decades, to be "successful beyond any of the forms of Govts. ancient or modern, with which it may be compared." The

obvious lesson to be drawn from this fact, he went on to declare, was that the American people must work together to preserve and protect "the last hope of true liberty on the face of the Earth."[9] Madison similarly claimed just months before his death that "we owe it to ourselves and to the world, to watch, to cherish, and as far as possible to perfect" America's political system, "which aims at a better security against external danger, and internal disorder—a better provision for national strength and individual rights, than had been exemplified, under any previous form."[10]

A final explanation for Madison's singular hopefulness was that he was, in a sense, forced to return to the founding during his final years—even "to relive the 1780s," as one scholar puts it—which served to remind him of what an achievement the ratification of the Constitution had been, and of all the good that it had done.[11] This return to the founding was prompted by two different circumstances. First, as historian Drew McCoy has shown in a book that remains the best analysis of Madison's retirement years, Madison discerned some unmistakable parallels between the politics of the 1830s and those of the 1780s.[12] As he saw it, the South Carolina nullifiers, with their extreme notion of states' rights, were like modern-day Anti-Federalists seeking to rescind the Constitution and plunge the nation back into the tumult and disarray of the confederation period. Madison himself had drifted toward the states'-rights camp starting in the 1790s, but the threat of nullification brought him squarely back to his Federalist roots, reinforcing in his mind the indispensability of maintaining a strong union. "For in the event of a dissolution of the Union," he warned, "an impossibility of ever renewing it is brought home to every man by the difficulties encountered in establishing it. . . . The happy union of these States is a wonder: their Const[itutio]n a miracle: their example the hope of Liberty throughout the World. Woe to the agitation that wd. meditate the destruction of either."[13]

The other circumstance that prompted Madison's return to the founding during these years was the tremendous amount of time and energy that he devoted to organizing his papers, particularly his records of the Constitutional Convention. Madison's notes from the

convention debates were more detailed than those of any other delegate, but he refrained from publishing them during his lifetime, in keeping with the delegates' agreement at the outset of the convention that their deliberations would remain secret so that they would be able to express themselves as freely as possible. Starting in the 1820s, however, Madison began to prepare his notes for posthumous publication. He had several motives: once all the delegates were dead, he assumed, their vow of secrecy would no longer be binding; selling the publication rights would enable him to pay off his debts and provide for Dolley after his passing; in 1821 Robert Yates published a set of convention notes that Madison took to be inaccurate in many respects, and his own notes would help to set the record straight; and, most broadly, they would be a kind of gift to posterity, offering the reading public insight into the founders' mindset and intentions, and perhaps even inspiring some much-needed veneration for all that they had accomplished.[14]

Madison's work on his convention notes appears to have stirred in him not only a sense of nostalgia for bygone days, but also a renewed respect for the framers and the charter that they devised. Sometime during the 1830s, he began to compose—though never completed—a sort of narrative history of the rise of the Constitutional Convention, which he intended to use as the preface for the published version of his notes. He concluded this essay by expressing his "profound and solemn conviction" that "there never was an assembly of men, charged with a great and arduous trust, who were more pure in their motives, or more exclusively or anxiously devoted to the object committed to them, than were the members of the Federal Convention of 1787, to the object of devising and proposing a constitutional system which should best supply the defects of that which it was to replace, and best secure the permanent liberty and happiness of their country."[15] Madison clearly had far more appreciation for the convention and the Constitution at the end of his life than he had had in the summer and fall of 1787.

It was also sometime during the 1830s that Madison composed a brief piece headed "Advice to My Country," which he included in his papers to be found after his death. Although it is only four sentences long, he meant for this note to serve as his last political testament.

"As this advice, if it ever see the light will not do it till I am no more," Madison wrote, "it may be considered as issuing from the tomb where truth alone can be respected, and the happiness of man alone consulted." His final injunction to his fellow citizens was that they should preserve and protect the union: "The advice nearest to my heart and deepest in my convictions is that the Union of the States be cherished & perpetuated. Let the open enemy to it be regarded as a Pandora with her box opened; and the disguised one, as the Serpent creeping with his deadly wiles into Paradise."[16] It was a fitting epitaph for the one founder who retained his faith in the American experiment to the very end, well into the nineteenth century, when the fate of the nation seemed to many to be as uncertain as ever. Alas, Madison's advice was not made public until 1850, by which point the wily serpent had long since crept into the nation's republican paradise; only a decade later, the results of a presidential election would cause half of the country, including his home state, to renounce his beloved union.

A VERY GREAT
SECRET

"THE WISDOM, which our fathers taught us, is despised. And the liberty, with which you, and they made us free, is little else than a cloak for licentiousness," Josiah Quincy III lamented to John Adams in 1811. The son of one of Adams's friends from his revolutionary days, Quincy was at this point a member of the House of Representatives, though he would go on to become mayor of Boston and then president of Harvard. A staunch Federalist in an age of Republican dominance, Quincy had called for Jefferson's impeachment in the waning days of his second term, narrowly losing by a vote of 117 to 1. Now he was approaching Adams, the venerable elder statesman of his party and his state, for advice about how to combat the rising Republican tide. "I know not what fates await us," Quincy admitted, but he believed that the only way to avoid certain shipwreck was to adhere steadfastly to the founders' vision: "in the mysterious course pursuing, I can see no other way than to cast anchor upon long established principles and trust my own, and my country's fortune ... to their firmness."[1]

Adams had long yearned for his fellow citizens to properly recognize and honor the central role that he had played in the Revolution, so he easily could have taken Quincy's missive as an opportunity to bask in the glow of much-deserved adulation. "I ought not to object to your Reverence for your Fathers as you call them," he replied, "much less can I be displeased at your numbring me among them." Yet Adams was uncomfortable with the tendency of this new generation of Americans to look back at the founders as unerring heroes and unflinching patriots. Hence he decided to let Quincy in on what he called "a very great secret," confessing that "as far as I am capable of comparing the

Merit of the different Periods, I have no reason to believe that We were better than you are. We had as many poor Creatures and selfish Beings, in proportion among us as you have among you: nor were there then more enlightened Men . . . than there are now."[2]

Adams was far from the only figure of his generation to caution against regarding the founders as a band of demigods and their achievements as beyond criticism. We have already taken note of Jefferson's admonition that the founders' handiwork should not be regarded with "sanctimonious reverence" or treated "like the ark of the covenant, too sacred to be touched."[3] Similarly, Washington assured his nephew Bushrod just a few months after the Philadelphia Convention that "I do not conceive that we are more inspired—have more wisdom—or possess more virtue than those who will come after us."[4] Even Madison, who was more concerned than the other founders to assure popular veneration for the Constitution and those who framed it, proclaimed that it was "the glory of the people of America, that whilst they have paid a decent regard to the opinions of former times and other nations, they have not suffered a blind veneration for antiquity, for custom, or for names, to overrule the suggestions of their own good sense, the knowledge of their own situation, and the lessons of their own experience."[5] Uncritical reverence for the founders, then, runs squarely against their own counsel.

We would also do well to recall the founders' late-life despair about America's constitutional order when we are tempted, as we so often are, to assume that they had all the answers or that their intent must be obeyed in all things. Today Americans revere the Constitution almost to a person—despite having, in the great majority of cases, never actually read it. Its provisions are frequently accorded the kind of reflexive deference that is usually reserved for sacred texts, and outright criticism of the document is generally regarded as bordering on sacrilege. As we have seen, this is not at all how the founders themselves viewed the nation's fundamental charter—not in 1787, and certainly not (with the partial exception of Madison) at the end of their lives. On the contrary, they almost all considered it to be deeply flawed at the outset, and for most of them the Constitution's weaknesses—and the failings of the government and political culture that it produced—only became more glaring over time.

It is almost needless to say, moreover, that the founders' main causes for worry are still very much with us. The partisanship that so deeply disturbed Washington's later years has never been absent from American political life—not even during the so-called Era of Good Feelings—and it is currently on a marked upswing. It may be true that polarization is more pronounced among political elites than among everyday citizens, but it has proven more than sufficient to all but paralyze Congress, particularly during this age of relative parity between the parties.[6]

Likewise, the civic virtue that Adams believed to be indispensable in a republic is no more evident in today's America than it was in the nation's early decades. On the contrary, the dearth of civic engagement and community-mindedness is a perennial complaint, voter turnout lags far behind that of most other liberal democracies, and "the political ignorance of the American voter is," as one political scientist notes, "one of the best-documented features of contemporary politics."[7]

Most of the myriad sources of Jefferson's despair too have endured or even increased over time. Much as he feared, the sectional cleavage that was laid bare by the Missouri crisis did eventually tear the nation apart, producing the bloodiest war in American history, and the legacy of that war continues to divide the nation to this day. The "consolidation" that Jefferson found so problematic in the early nineteenth century has multiplied almost exponentially since that time, as political power has continued to flow away from state and local governments and toward the federal government. The Supreme Court still wields enormous influence over American political life; indeed, there is probably no other liberal democracy in the world in which the judiciary plays as great of a role in shaping public policy as it does in the United States. And, of course, America has never resembled the agrarian idyll of Jefferson's dreams, and today's breakneck capitalism and urbanization have surely eclipsed even his worst nightmares.

Hamilton's vision might seem to have fared far better, given his ambition to develop the nation's economic and military might through a strong federal government, particularly a powerful executive. Both the best-selling biography and the popular Broadway play about

Hamilton in fact depict him as the prophet of American capitalism, with the former claiming that during the founding era "he was the messenger from a future that we now inhabit" and that "today, we are indisputably the heirs to Hamilton's America."[8] There is a good deal of truth to this characterization. As we have seen, however, Hamilton considered America's constitutional order to be both overly popular and insufficiently vigorous or energetic, and it has only grown more democratic and sluggish over time. Hamilton would surely be aghast at the way in which elected officials feel compelled to pander so continually to the people, and he would just as surely lament that the federal government has been rendered impotent by gridlock and that it is so overwhelmingly difficult to pass major legislation.

There are, of course, many further ills besetting American politics today, some of relatively recent vintage—such as the mounting disregard in some quarters for the rule of law, the independence of the judiciary, the freedom of the press, safeguards against corruption, and the central importance of free and fair elections—and other ills more long-standing, such as gerrymandering, voter suppression, the enormous influence wielded by special interests, growing socioeconomic inequality combined with declining socioeconomic mobility, infringements on civil liberties in the name of national security, mass incarceration, and a hyperbolic and combative media environment. All told, it is perhaps unsurprising that survey after survey indicates that a solid majority of Americans are consistently dissatisfied with "the way things are going in the United States" and believe that the government and the country are "heading in the wrong direction."[9]

On the other hand, we might take a certain comfort, amid our worries about the state of American democracy, in the fact that the founders themselves voiced similar worries. Indeed, their anxieties ran far deeper than all but the most despairing assessments of contemporary America. The founders frequently predicted that the republic that they had established would not last beyond their own generation—that the union would soon be sundered, that a new constitutional convention would have be to called, or that the government would gradually lapse into a hereditary monarchy. Clearly, *that* level of pessimism now appears to have been unwarranted: the United States has not only survived as a constitutional democracy for well over two

centuries; it has become—and is likely to remain for the foreseeable future—the world's greatest economic and military power.[10] (Hamilton would be immensely pleased.) If Madison could find solace in the fact that America's constitutional order had managed to weather nearly a half century's worth of storms by the time he reached old age, perhaps we should be cheered to recall that it has now survived for more than two hundred and thirty years.

The Constitution is the oldest written charter of national government that remains in effect anywhere in the world, and it has rock-solid legitimacy among the American people. Although one often hears calls for modifying the system at the margins, no politician could hope to win election by criticizing the Constitution wholesale or demanding that it be fundamentally revamped. And the American form of government has long served as a model, to one degree or another, for other nations around the world as they have joined the ranks of liberal democratic governance. While there are good reasons to temper our often-excessive admiration for the founding, the Constitution, and the government that they produced, then, there are equally good reasons to refrain from following the founders into outright disillusionment.

Although the United States is often regarded as a land of hope and optimism, there is another, equally persistent strain of the American outlook that instead emphasizes peril and decay. One often hears that the America of old was a place of unparalleled freedom, virtue, and enlightenment, while the America of the present is, alas, carelessly abandoning the principles and practices that once made the nation so great. This viewpoint can be traced back not only to the early republic, as the letter from Josiah Quincy III that opened this epilogue suggests, but all the way to the Puritans: the jeremiads with which the ministers of seventeenth-century Plymouth and Boston harangued their congregations were suffused with complaints that the brand-new colonies were already in decline and warnings that the collapse of their society was imminent. The looming demise of American democracy has been announced countless times in the course of the nation's history, on each occasion with assurances that this time it really *is* the end of democracy as we know it. We are bombarded with similar pronouncements today.

Here too we might take a certain comfort in the fact that, however appalling the state of American politics might be at the moment, the political situation was even worse when the founders whom we so admire presided over the nation. Most obviously, we no longer countenance widespread chattel slavery or the routine dispossession and even massacre of indigenous tribes; on the contrary, basic civil and political liberties have never been extended to more people. We no longer face repeated, serious threats of secession and civil war. Political violence is far less common today; it is rare to see thousands of armed citizens marching on an army outpost in rebellion against a tax, or legislators brawling on the floor of the House of Representatives with canes and fire pokers. No contemporary election can compare with the presidential election of 1800—a contest between Jefferson and Adams, two of our most revered founders—in terms of sheer viciousness. Today's much-maligned "mainstream media" is in reality far more responsible and fact based than the newspapers of the 1790s. And so on. None of this is grounds for complacency, as today's political ills are both serious and pressing, but such a comparison may help us to summon a broader sense of perspective.

America's constitutional order has both virtues and shortcomings, and it always has. Our ultimate evaluation of that order will inevitably rest in large part on our basis for comparison. If we compare the United States to an idealized vision of what we believe democracy could be or should be, as the founders frequently did, then we are bound to be disappointed, as most of them were. But if, like Madison, we temper our expectations and remind ourselves that the illiberal and undemocratic alternatives have proven far worse, then we will be more inclined to count our blessings.

Moreover, the realization that many of our current political ills were also present at the founding of the nation may render us less apt to be surprised by these problems, or to assume that they will disappear any time soon. Too frequently we seem to expect that with the right tweak to our political system—eliminating the electoral college, ending the filibuster in the Senate, establishing fixed term limits for Supreme Court justices, reforming campaign finance laws, setting up independent redistricting commissions, instituting top-two

primaries or ranked-choice voting, promoting civic education—we might manage to fix all that ails us. While such reforms might help at the margins, the fact that many of today's problems have been with the nation since its inception suggests that they may be more systemic in nature than we often realize—but also that they are less likely to ultimately doom the republic than we often fear.

Still, the fact that a flawless utopia is beyond reach should not lead us to abandon all hope for improving America's constitutional order. It is noteworthy that the founders themselves, for all their late-life bitterness and disillusionment, never ceased to devote themselves to the American republic as long as they felt that they had something left to give. Washington served two vexing terms as president against his will, composed a Farewell Address to ensure that his worries and advice would be passed on to posterity, and even came out of retirement in his old age to head the resistance to the threat posed by France. Although Hamilton's reservations about the Constitution ran deeper than almost anyone's in 1787, he arguably worked harder than anyone to get it ratified. He did everything in his power to bolster the federal government throughout the 1790s, and even after Jefferson's election to the presidency, when Hamilton's hopes for the future were at their nadir, he continued his indefatigable efforts to mold public opinion through his essays. Adams grew disenchanted with the American republic much earlier than the other founders—at least by the mid-1780s—but, dutiful citizen that he was, he served his country for many more years as a diplomat in various European countries, in the thankless role of vice president, and as president. After he finally reached the pinnacle of power, he sacrificed his presidency in order to save the nation by sending a peace delegation to France in 1799. Even Jefferson, whose disillusionment came long after he had retired from public life, continued to write copious letters of advice—many of them, alas, wildly misguided—to the nation's lawmakers, administrators, and judges during his final decade, and he also devoted a great deal of energy to founding the University of Virginia in an effort to enrich the nation's future.[11] The founders' penchant for meeting deep disappointment with steadfast resolve is one that we would do well to emulate in the face our own political tribulations.

If this is indeed the lesson that we draw from the founders' disillusionment, then we must conclude that the sun that Franklin observed on the back of Washington's chair in Independence Hall was neither simply rising nor simply setting, but rather beckoning the nation onward toward the horizon, on a never-ending quest to perpetuate and improve the founders' creation.

NOTES

W HEN CITING LETTERS and other works by the book's protagonists, I have wherever possible used the authoritative
Papers project devoted to each figure. Where the relevant
volume has not yet been published, I have generally cited *Founders Online*, a wonderful website hosted by the National Archives that makes
the works of these figures (and those of Benjamin Franklin) freely
available in the form that they appear in their *Papers*, including "Early
Access" versions that often appear well in advance of their release in
print. Where this option too failed, I simply chose whichever version
of the text in question seemed the most reliable and comprehensive.
The notes use the following abbreviations for the more frequently
cited of these texts.

AFC   *Adams Family Correspondence*, ed. Lyman H. Butterfield
      et al., 13 vols. to date (Cambridge, MA: Harvard University
      Press, 1963–2017).

FO   *Founders Online*, http://founders.archives.gov.

PAH   *The Papers of Alexander Hamilton*, ed. Harold C. Syrett and
      Jacob Cooke, 27 vols. (New York: Columbia University
      Press, 1961–87).

PGWC *The Papers of George Washington: Confederation Series*, ed.
      W. W. Abbot, 6 vols. (Charlottesville: University Press of
      Virginia, 1992–97).

PGWP *The Papers of George Washington: Presidential Series*, ed.
      Dorothy Twohig et al., 19 vols. to date (Charlottesville:
      University Press of Virginia, 1987–2016).

PGWR *The Papers of George Washington: Retirement Series*, ed.
      W. W. Abbot, 4 vols. (Charlottesville: University Press of
      Virginia, 1998–99).

PJA   *The Papers of John Adams*, ed. Robert J. Taylor et al., 19 vols. to date (Cambridge, MA: Harvard University Press, 1977–2018).

PJM   *The Papers of James Madison*, ed. William T. Hutchinson et al., 17 vols. (Chicago: University of Chicago Press; Charlottesville: University Press of Virginia, 1962–91).

PJMR   *The Papers of James Madison: Retirement Series*, ed. David B. Mattern et al., 3 vols. to date (Charlottesville: University Press of Virginia, 2009–16).

PTJ   *The Papers of Thomas Jefferson*, ed. Julian P. Boyd et al., 43 vols. to date (Princeton, NJ: Princeton University Press, 1950–2017).

PTJR   *The Papers of Thomas Jefferson: Retirement Series*, ed. J. Jefferson Looney, 14 vols. to date (Princeton, NJ: Princeton University Press, 2004–17).

PROLOGUE. A RISING OR A SETTING SUN

1. Accounts of the convention's proceedings are legion, but see, among others, Richard Beeman, *Plain, Honest Men: The Making of the American Constitution* (New York: Random House, 2009); Carol Berkin, *A Brilliant Solution: Inventing the American Constitution* (Boston: Mariner Books, 2003); Christopher Collier and James Lincoln Collier, *Decision in Philadelphia: The Constitutional Convention of 1787* (New York: Ballantine Books, 1986); Michael J. Klarman, *The Framers' Coup: The Making of the United States Constitution* (Oxford: Oxford University Press, 2016); Clinton Rossiter, *1787: The Grand Convention* (New York: Macmillan, 1966); and David O. Stewart, *The Summer of 1787: The Men Who Invented the Constitution* (New York: Simon and Schuster, 2007).
2. On Franklin's role at the convention, see William G. Carr, *The Oldest Delegate: Franklin in the Constitutional Convention* (Newark: University of Delaware Press, 1990).
3. Gordon Lloyd, ed., *Debates in the Federal Convention of 1787 by James Madison, a Member* (Ashland, OH: Ashbrook Center, 2014), 546–47.
4. Although there were thirty-eight signers present that day, the Constitution has thirty-nine signatures, because George Read of Delaware signed on behalf of John Dickinson, who was absent owing to illness.
5. Lloyd, *Debates in the Federal Convention of 1787*, 564.

6. Gordon S. Wood, *The Radicalism of the American Revolution* (New York: Vintage, 1991), 365.

7. The anecdote was recorded by James McHenry, a delegate from Maryland. See Max Farrand, ed., *The Records of the Federal Convention of 1787* (New Haven, CT: Yale University Press, 1911), 3:85.

8. Alexander Hamilton, *Federalist*, no. 9 (21 November 1787), in PAH 4:333.

9. Lloyd, *Debates in the Federal Convention of 1787*, 146.

10. Alexander Hamilton, *Federalist*, no. 1 (27 October 1787), in PAH 4:301.

11. John Adams, *Defence of the Constitutions of Government of the United States of America*, vol. 1, in *The Works of John Adams*, ed. Charles Francis Adams (Boston: Charles C. Little and James Brown, 1851), 4:290.

12. George Washington, First Inaugural Address, 30 April 1789, in PGWP 2:175.

13. George Washington to Thomas Jefferson, 23 August 1792, in PGWP 11:30.

14. George Washington to Alexander White, 1 March 1798, in PGWR 2:113.

15. George Washington to James McHenry, 17 November 1799, in PGWR 4:410.

16. Alexander Hamilton, *Examination*, no. 9 (18 January 1802), in PAH 25:501.

17. Alexander Hamilton to Gouverneur Morris, 29 February 1802, in PAH 25:544.

18. Alexander Hamilton, Speech at a Meeting of Federalists in Albany, 10 February 1804, in PAH 26:189.

19. John Adams to Mercy Otis Warren, 8 January 1776, in PJA 3:398.

20. John Adams to Benjamin Rush, 19 September 1806, in FO.

21. John Adams to John Quincy Adams, 31 December 1817, in FO.

22. Thomas Jefferson to John Holmes, 22 April 1820, in FO.

23. Thomas Jefferson to Claiborne W. Gooch, 9 January 1826, in FO.

24. See, for instance, John R. Howe Jr., "Republican Thought and the Political Violence of the 1790s," *American Quarterly* 19.1 (Summer 1967), 147–65; and Marshall Smelser, "The Federalist Period as an Age of Passion," *American Quarterly* 10.4 (Winter 1958), 391–419. For four superb and complementary studies of the early republic, from the launch of the new government through the first decades of the nineteenth century, see Stanley Elkins and Eric McKitrick, *The Age of Federalism* (Oxford: Oxford University Press, 1993); Gordon S. Wood, *Empire of Liberty: A History of the Early Republic, 1789–1815* (Oxford: Oxford University Press, 2009); Sean Wilentz, *The Rise of American Democracy: Jefferson to Lincoln* (New York: W. W. Norton, 2005); and Daniel Walker Howe, *What Hath God Wrought: The Transformation of America, 1815–1848* (Oxford: Oxford University Press, 2007). Also helpful are John C. Miller, *The Federalist Era, 1789–1801* (New York: Harper and Brothers, 1960); and James Roger Sharp, *American Politics in the Early Republic: The New Nation in Crisis* (New Haven, CT: Yale University Press, 1993).

25. Joseph J. Ellis, *Founding Brothers: The Revolutionary Generation* (New York: Vintage, 2000), 16.

26. For a recent analysis of the government produced by the Articles of Confederation, see George William Van Cleve, *We Have Not a Government: The Articles of*

Confederation and the Road to the Constitution (Chicago: University of Chicago Press, 2017).

27. On the state ratification debates, see Michael Allen Gillespie and Michael Lienesch, eds., *Ratifying the Constitution* (Lawrence: University Press of Kansas, 1989); and Pauline Maier, *Ratification: The People Debate the Constitution, 1787–1788* (New York: Simon and Schuster, 2010).

28. Smelser, "Federalist Period as an Age of Passion," 396.

29. Lord Grenville to Robert Liston, 7 May 1800, quoted in Manning J. Dauer, *The Adams Federalists* (Baltimore: Johns Hopkins University Press, 1953), 241.

30. For works that set the American founding in its full global context, see Alan Taylor, *American Revolutions: A Continental History, 1750–1804* (New York: W. W. Norton, 2016); and Jay Winik, *The Great Upheaval: America and the Birth of the Modern World, 1788–1800* (New York: Harper Perennial, 2007).

31. David Hackett Fischer, *The Revolution of American Conservatism: The Federalist Party in the Era of Jeffersonian Democracy* (New York: Harper and Row, 1965), 182.

CHAPTER 1. THE DEMON OF PARTY SPIRIT

1. Washington's life is a story that has been told many times. The seven-volume biography by Douglas Southall Freeman (New York: Scribner, 1948–57) and the four-volume study by James Thomas Flexner (New York: Little, Brown, 1965–72) are both full of useful information. Among the best one-volume overviews are Ron Chernow, *Washington: A Life* (New York: Penguin, 2010); Joseph J. Ellis, *His Excellency: George Washington* (New York: Alfred A. Knopf, 2004); and John Rhodehamel, *George Washington: The Wonder of the Age* (New Haven, CT: Yale University Press, 2017). For a brief but helpful overview of Washington's political outlook, see Paul O. Carrese, "Liberty, Constitutionalism, and Moderation: George Washington's Harmonizing of Traditions," in *History of American Political Thought*, ed. Bryan-Paul Frost and Jeffrey Sikkenga (Lanham, MD: Lexington, 2003), 94–112.

2. As Forrest McDonald writes, there is "a dual mystery about the man: that the American people so trusted him and that historians have paid so little attention to the fact. Eighteenth-century Americans were a contentious lot, and their historians have been even more so; yet neither has found it especially surprising that a nation of independent and cantankerous people could have been unanimous on a question of such moment." Forrest McDonald, *The Presidency of George Washington* (Lawrence: University Press of Kansas, 1974), ix. Similarly, Peter Henriques remarks that "Americans in the eighteenth century were a divided and fractious people, but somehow George Washington—and he alone—was the one man who united all hearts." Peter R. Henriques, *Realistic Visionary: A Portrait of George Washington* (Charlottesville: University of Virginia Press, 2006), ix. Robert Faulkner likewise notes that "Washington's

unequivocal preeminence was the greatest political fact of the country's first twenty-one years." Robert Faulkner, "Washington and the Founding of Constitutional Democracy," in *Gladly to Learn and Gladly to Teach: Essays on Religion and Political Philosophy in Honor of Ernest L. Fortin, A.A.*, ed. Michael P. Foley and Douglas Kries (Lanham, MD: Lexington, 2002), 223.

3. This famous line comes from a eulogy for Washington that was commissioned by Congress and written by Henry "Light-Horse Harry" Lee (the father of Robert E. Lee), though actually delivered to Congress by John Marshall. See Chernow, *Washington*, 811.

4. On Washington and partisanship, see John Avlon, *Washington's Farewell: The Founding Father's Warning to Future Generations* (New York: Simon and Schuster, 2017), 111–29; Glenn A. Phelps, "George Washington and the Paradox of Party," *Presidential Studies Quarterly* 19.4 (Fall 1989), 733–45; and Rosemarie Zagarri, "George Washington and the Emergence of Party Politics in the New Nation," in *A Companion to George Washington*, ed. Edward G. Lengel (Oxford: Wiley-Blackwell, 2012), 490–505.

5. George Washington to Arthur Fenner, 4 June 1790, in PGWP 5:470.

6. George Washington to Joseph Hopkinson, 27 May 1798, in PGWR 2:300.

7. See Phelps, "George Washington and the Paradox of Party."

8. John Adams to Sylvanus Bourne, 20 August 1789, in FO. Stuart Leibiger rightly notes that "far from being a majestic figurehead presiding over powerful appointees who took the lead in decision making, Washington, guided by his own strong constitutional vision, always maintained control of his administration. He may have collected advice extensively, reached decisions deliberately, and employed ghostwriters regularly, but he always remained in charge, governed thoughtfully, and often cloaked his instrumentality." Stuart Leibiger, *Founding Friendship: George Washington, James Madison, and the Creation of the American Republic* (Charlottesville: University Press of Virginia, 1999), 10.

9. Rhodehamel, *George Washington: The Wonder of the Age*, 234.

10. On the idea of presidents remaining above party and for a case that Washington fits this description, see Ralph Ketcham, *Presidents above Party: The First American Presidency, 1789–1829* (Chapel Hill: University of North Carolina Press, 1984). For a case that Washington was a fairly thoroughgoing partisan Federalist, see John E. Ferling, *The First of Men: A Life of George Washington* (Oxford: Oxford University Press, 1988).

11. E. E. Schattschneider, *Party Government* (New York: Rinehart, 1942), 1. See also, for instance, John H. Aldrich, *Why Parties? A Second Look* (Chicago: University of Chicago Press, 2011); Russell Muirhead, *The Promise of Party in a Polarized Age* (Cambridge, MA: Harvard University Press, 2014); and Nancy L. Rosenblum, *On the Side of the Angels: An Appreciation of Parties and Partisanship* (Princeton, NJ: Princeton University Press, 2008).

12. On Washington as a modern-day Cincinnatus, see Gary Wills, *Cincinnatus: George Washington and the Enlightenment* (New York: Doubleday, 1984).

13. George Washington to Thomas Johnson, 12 November 1786, in PGWC 4:360.

14. George Washington to Alexander Hamilton, 10 July 1787, in PGWC 5:257.

15. For a discussion of what in the Constitution likely pleased and displeased Washington, see Glenn A. Phelps, *George Washington and American Constitutionalism* (Lawrence: University Press of Kansas, 1993), 112–16.

16. James Madison to Edward Everett, 3 June 1827, in FO.

17. Everett Somerville Brown, ed., *William Plumer's Memorandum of Proceedings in the United States Senate, 1803–1807* (New York: Macmillan, 1923), 518.

18. George Washington to Benjamin Harrison, 24 September 1787, in PGWC 5:339.

19. George Washington to David Humphreys, 10 October 1787, in PGWC 5:365.

20. George Washington to Marquis de Lafayette, 7 February 1788, in PGWC 6:95.

21. As Stephen Kurtz writes, "There was very little doubt that only Washington . . . could fill the office of first President. His election was unanimous, and if ever the general will existed or was exercised by a political body it was in the choice of Washington to launch this experiment." Stephen G. Kurtz, *The Presidency of John Adams: The Collapse of Federalism, 1795–1800* (Philadelphia: University of Pennsylvania Press, 1957), 7.

22. James Monroe to Thomas Jefferson, 12 July 1788, in PTJ 13:352.

23. George Washington to Marquis de Lafayette, 29 January 1789, in PGWP 1:262–63.

24. George Washington to Henry Knox, 1 April 1789, in PGWP 2:2.

25. Peter Henriques goes so far as to say that "if no president entered office with more personal prestige and affection than George Washington, only Abraham Lincoln and Franklin Roosevelt faced comparable crises." Henriques, *Realistic Visionary*, 136.

26. George Washington, First Inaugural Address, 30 April 1789, in PGWP 2:175.

27. On Washington's presidency, see David S. Heidler and Jeanne T. Heidler, *Washington's Circle: The Creation of the President* (New York: Random House, 2015); F. McDonald, *Presidency of George Washington*; and Jack D. Warren Jr., *The Presidency of George Washington* (Mount Vernon, VA: Mount Vernon Ladies' Association, 2000).

28. On Washington's creation of the presidential cabinet, see Lindsay M. Chervinksy, *The Cabinet: George Washington and the Creation of an American Institution* (Cambridge, MA: Belknap Press of Harvard University Press, 2020).

29. On the Washington-Madison relationship, at this period and throughout their lives, see Leibiger, *Founding Friendship*.

30. George Washington to Marquis de Lafayette, 3 June 1790, in PGWP 5:468.

31. George Washington to Gouverneur Morris, 13 October 1789, in PGWP 4:176.

32. George Washington to Catharine Macaulay Graham, 9 January 1790, in PGWP 4:553.

33. George Washington to David Stuart, 15 June 1790, in PGWP 5:524–25.

34. As Jack Rakove notes, "painstaking historical detective work has established [that] the deal making that allowed the assumption plan to pass the House

in exchange for a decision to build a capital on the Potomac did not occur solely because Jefferson, on or about June 20, invited a despondent Hamilton and a wary Madison to a conciliatory dinner at his new lodgings at 57 Maiden Lane. Some kind of bargain between Virginia and Pennsylvania, the nation's most populous states, was already afoot, under which the government would temporarily return to Philadelphia while work on a Potomac site began. But dinner chez Jefferson significantly advanced the negotiations." Jack Rakove, *Revolutionaries: A New History of the Invention of America* (Boston: Houghton Mifflin Harcourt, 2010), 426. See also Ellis, *Founding Brothers*, chap. 2.

35. George Washington to La Luzerne, 10 August 1790, in PGWP 6:229.
36. George Washington to Thomas Paine, 10 August 1790, in PGWP 6:230.
37. George Washington to David Humphreys, 16 March 1791, in PGWP 7:583–84.
38. George Washington to Catharine Macaulay Graham, 19 July 1791, in PGWP 8:357.
39. George Washington to David Humphreys, 20 July 1791, in PGWP 8:359.
40. George Washington to Marquis de Lafayette, 28 July 1791, in PGWP 8:379.
41. George Washington to la Luzerne, 10 September 1791, in PGWP 8:518.
42. On the growing rift between Washington and Jefferson, see Thomas Fleming, *The Great Divide: The Conflict between Washington and Jefferson That Defined a Nation* (Boston: Da Capo, 2015).
43. Gordon S. Wood, *Friends Divided: John Adams and Thomas Jefferson* (New York: Penguin, 2017), 309. See also Marcus Daniel, *Scandal and Civility: Journalism and the Birth of American Democracy* (Oxford: Oxford University Press, 2009); and Jeffrey L. Pasley, *"The Tyranny of Printers": Newspaper Politics in the Early American Republic* (Charlottesville: University of Virginia Press, 2001).
44. Alexander Hamilton to George Washington, 30 July 1792, in PAH 12:137; and Thomas Jefferson to George Washington, 23 May 1792, in PTJ 23:539.
45. George Washington to James Madison, 20 May 1792, in PGWP 10:401.
46. Tobias Lear to George Washington, 5 August 1792, in PGWP 10:624.
47. George Washington to Thomas Jefferson, 23 August 1792, in PGWP 11:30.
48. George Washington to Alexander Hamilton, 26 August 1792, in PGWP 11:38–39.
49. George Washington to Edmund Randolph, 26 August 1792, in PGWP 11:45–46.
50. Alexander Hamilton to George Washington, 9 September 1792, in PAH 12:348.
51. Thomas Jefferson to George Washington, 9 September 1792, in PTJ 24:358.

CHAPTER 2. FAREWELL TO ALL THAT

1. Thomas Jefferson to Walter Jones, 5 March 1810, in PTJR 2:272. For the most detailed study of the clashes between Hamilton and Jefferson during their time in Washington's cabinet, see Carson Holloway, *Hamilton versus Jefferson in the Washington Administration: Completing the Founding or Betraying the Founding?* (Cambridge: Cambridge University Press, 2015). See also Lance

Banning, *Conceived in Liberty: The Struggle to Define the New Republic, 1789–1793* (Lanham, MD: Rowman and Littlefield, 2004); and John Ferling, *Jefferson and Hamilton: The Rivalry That Forged a Nation* (New York: Bloomsbury, 2013).

2. Thomas Jefferson to Thomas Paine, 19 June 1792, in PTJ 20:312.

3. Thomas Jefferson to George Mason, 4 February 1791, in PTJ 19:241.

4. It is noteworthy that the final volume of James Flexner's magisterial four-volume biography of Washington, which focuses on his second term and retirement, is subtitled "Anguish and Farewell." See James Thomas Flexner, *George Washington: Anguish and Farewell (1793–1799)* (New York: Little, Brown, 1972).

5. George Washington to Henry Lee, 21 July 1793, in PGWP 13:261.

6. George Washington to Edmund Pendleton, 23 September 1793, in PGWP 14:124.

7. On the Genêt affair, see Harry Ammon, *The Genet Mission* (New York: W. W. Norton, 1973).

8. John Adams to Thomas Jefferson, 20 June 1813, in PTJR 6:254.

9. On the Whiskey Rebellion, see William Hogeland, *The Whiskey Rebellion: George Washington, Alexander Hamilton, and the Frontier Rebels Who Challenged America's Newfound Sovereignty* (New York: Simon and Schuster, 2006); and Thomas P. Slaughter, *The Whiskey Rebellion: Frontier Epilogue to the American Revolution* (Oxford: Oxford University Press, 1986).

10. George Washington to Charles Mynn Thruston, 10 August 1794, in PGWP 16:547–48.

11. George Washington to Edmund Pendleton, 22 January 1795, in PGWP 17:425.

12. Ibid., 17:426.

13. On the Democratic Societies, see Eugene Perry Link, *Democratic-Republican Societies, 1790–1800* (New York: Columbia University Press, 1972).

14. See Nicholas P. Cole, "George Washington and Republican Government: The Political Thought of George Washington," in *Companion to George Washington*, ed. Lengel, 443–44.

15. George Washington to Henry Lee, 26 August 1794, in PGWP 16:601–2.

16. George Washington to Burgess Ball, 25 September 1794, in PGWP 16:723.

17. George Washington to Edmund Randolph, 16 October 1794, in PGWP 17:72.

18. George Washington, Sixth Annual Message to Congress, 19 November 1794, in PGWP 17:186.

19. James Madison to James Monroe, 4 December 1794, in PJM 15:406.

20. On the Jay Treaty, see Jerald A. Combs, *The Jay Treaty: Political Battleground of the Founding Fathers* (Berkeley: University of California Press, 1970); and Todd Estes, *The Jay Treaty Debate, Public Opinion, and the Evolution of Early American Political Culture* (Amherst: University of Massachusetts Press, 2008).

21. George Washington to Alexander Hamilton, 29 July 1795, in PGWP 18:458.

22. Ibid., 18:459.

23. George Washington to Edmund Randolph, 29 July 1795, in PGWP 18:464.

24. George Washington to Patrick Henry, 9 October 1795, in PGWP 19:37.

25. George Washington to Charles Carroll of Carrollton, 1 May 1796, in FO.

26. Quoted in Rhodehamel, *George Washington: The Wonder of the Age*, 287.

27. George Washington to Thomas Jefferson, 6 July 1796, in PTJ 29:142–43.

28. Thomas Jefferson, Notes on a Conversation with Edmund Randolph, after 1785, in PTJ 28:568.

29. John Jay to George Washington, 18 April 1796, in FO.

30. George Washington to John Jay, 8 May 1796, in FO.

31. George Washington to Thomas Jefferson, 6 July 1796, in PTJ 29:142.

32. George Washington to Charles Cotesworth Pinckney, 8 July 1796, in FO.

33. George Washington to Timothy Pickering, 27 September 1795, in PGWP 18:740.

CHAPTER 3. SET UP A BROOMSTICK

1. On the Farewell Address, see Avlon, *Washington's Farewell*; Ellis, *Founding Brothers*, chap. 4; and Matthew Spalding and Patrick J. Garrity, *A Sacred Union of Citizens: George Washington's Farewell Address and the American Character* (Lanham, MD: Rowman and Littlefield, 1996).

2. Jeffry Morrison remarks that as "a joint production by Washington, Madison, Hamilton, and John Jay, the latter three authors of *The Federalist Papers*," the Farewell Address could be viewed as "the single best summation of the elite political mind of the founding era." Jeffry H. Morrison, *The Political Philosophy of George Washington* (Baltimore: Johns Hopkins University Press, 2009), 15.

3. For a still-indispensable volume incorporating the various drafts of the address and a facsimile of Washington's final manuscript, see Victor Hugo Paltsits, *Washington's Farewell Address* (New York: New York Public Library, 1935).

4. George Washington, Farewell Address, 19 September 1796, in FO.

5. As Ron Chernow writes, Washington's "real passions and often fiery opinions were typically confined to private letters rather than public utterances. During the Revolution and his presidency, the public Washington needed to be upbeat and inspirational, whereas the private man was often gloomy, scathing, hot-blooded, and pessimistic." Chernow, *Washington: A Life*, xx.

6. George Washington, First Draft for a Farewell Address, in Paltsits, *Washington's Farewell Address*, 168.

7. George Washington, Farewell Address, 19 September 1796, in FO.

8. Ibid.

9. Ibid.

10. See Thomas Jefferson, First Inaugural Address, 4 March 1801, in PTJ 33:150.

11. George Washington, Farewell Address, 19 September 1796, in FO.

12. On Washington and slavery, see François Furstenberg, *In the Name of the Father: Washington's Legacy, Slavery, and the Making of a Nation* (New York: Penguin, 2006); Philip D. Morgan, "'To Get Quit of Negroes': George Washington and Slavery," *Journal of American Studies* 39.3 (December 2005), 403–29; L. Scott Philyaw, "Washington and Slavery," in *Companion to George Washington*,

ed. Lengel, 104–20; Mary V. Thompson, *"The Only Unavoidable Subject of Regret": George Washington, Slavery, and the Enslaved Community at Mount Vernon* (Charlottesville: University of Virginia Press, 2019); Dorothy Twohig, "'That Species of Property': Washington's Role in the Controversy over Slavery," in *George Washington Reconsidered*, ed. Don Higginbotham (Charlottesville: University of Virginia Press, 2001), 114–38; and Henry Wiencek, *An Imperfect God: George Washington, His Slaves, and the Creation of America* (New York: Farrar, Straus and Giroux, 2003).

13. George Washington to Robert Lewis, 18 August 1799, in PGWR 4:256.

14. George Washington to John Francis Mercer, 9 September 1786, in PGWC 4:243; and George Washington to Robert Morris, 12 April 1786, in PGWC 4:16.

15. George Washington to Alexander Spotswood, 23 November 1794, in PGWP 17:207; and George Washington to Lawrence Lewis, 4 August 1797, in PGWR 1:288.

16. John Bernard, *Retrospections of America, 1797–1811* (New York: Harper and Brothers, 1887), 91.

17. George Washington to Jonathan Trumbull, 3 March 1797, in FO.

18. On Washington's retirement years, see Jonathan Horn, *Washington's End: The Final Years and Forgotten Struggle* (New York: Scribner, 2020). I am grateful to Horn for allowing me to read his fine book prior to publication.

19. On the Quasi-War, see Alexander DeConde, *The Quasi-War: The Politics and Diplomacy of the Undeclared War with France, 1797–1801* (New York: Charles Scribner's Sons, 1966).

20. George Washington to William Heath, 20 May 1797, in PGWR 1:149; and George Washington to David Humphreys, 26 June 1797, in PGWR 1:219.

21. George Washington to Alexander White, 1 March 1798, in PGWR 2:113.

22. Thomas Jefferson to Edward Rutledge, 24 June 1797, in PTJ 29:456.

23. George Washington to Thomas Pinckney, 28 May 1797, in PGWR 1:158.

24. George Washington to Charles Carroll of Carrollton, 2 August 1798, in PGWR 2:483.

25. Ellis, *His Excellency: George Washington*, 247–48.

26. George Washington to James McHenry, 4 July 1798, in PGWR 2:377.

27. George Washington to James McHenry, 5 July 1798, in PGWR 2:384.

28. On the Alien and Sedition Acts, see John C. Miller, *Crisis in Freedom: The Alien and Sedition Acts* (New York: Little, Brown, 1951); and James Morton Smith, *Freedom's Fetters: The Alien and Sedition Laws and American Civil Liberties* (Ithaca, NY: Cornell University Press, 1966).

29. George Washington to Alexander Spotswood, 22 November 1798, in PGWR 3:217.

30. George Washington to Marquis de Lafayette, 25 December 1798, in PGWR 3:281–82.

31. George Washington to William Vans Murray, 26 December 1798, in PGWR 3:287.

32. On the Virginia and Kentucky Resolutions, see William J. Watkins Jr., *Reclaiming the American Revolution: The Kentucky and Virginia Resolutions and Their Legacy* (New York: Palgrave Macmillan, 2004).

33. George Washington to Patrick Henry, 15 January 1799, in PGWR 3:319–20.

34. George Washington to Bushrod Washington, 5 May 1799, in PGWR 4:51.

35. George Washington to Jonathan Trumbull Jr., 30 August 1799, in PGWR 4:275–76.

36. George Washington to Jonathan Trumbull Jr., 21 July 1799, in PGWR 4:202–3.

37. As John Rhodehamel writes, "The ongoing partisan conflict was the definitive repudiation of Washington's ideal of a republican nation governed by a concurring elite of virtuous statesmen." Rhodehamel, *George Washington: The Wonder of the Age*, 296.

38. George Washington, Farewell Address, 19 September 1796, in FO.

39. George Washington, First Inaugural Address, 30 April 1789, in PGWP 2:175.

40. George Washington to James McHenry, 17 November 1799, in PGWR 4:410.

CHAPTER 4. NO MAN'S IDEAS

1. Neither Hamilton nor Adams has been the subject of a loving many-volume scholarly biography the way the Virginians Washington, Jefferson, and Madison have. The closest that exists for Hamilton is Broadus Mitchell's two-volume study (*Alexander Hamilton* [New York: Macmillan, 1957–62]), which is strong on Hamilton's Treasury activities but relatively perfunctory about the period after he left office. The best biography of Hamilton is Ron Chernow, *Alexander Hamilton* (New York: Penguin, 2004). Also useful are Forrest McDonald, *Alexander Hamilton: A Biography* (New York: W. W. Norton, 1979); John C. Miller, *Alexander Hamilton and the Growth of the New Nation* (New York: Harper and Row, 1959); and Clinton Rossiter, *Alexander Hamilton and the Constitution* (New York: Harcourt, Brace and World, 1964).

2. Alexander Hamilton, Remarks on Signing the Constitution, 17 September 1787, in PAH 4:253.

3. Miller, *Alexander Hamilton and the Growth of the New Nation*, 118.

4. For similar points, see F. McDonald, *Alexander Hamilton*, 96; and Rossiter, *Alexander Hamilton and the Constitution*, 225.

5. See Gerald Stourzh, *Alexander Hamilton and the Idea of Republican Government* (Stanford, CA: Stanford University Press, 1970), 109. For an extended argument that this kind of "internationalist" reasoning undergirded the project of the Constitutional Convention and the founding more broadly, see David C. Hendrickson, *Peace Pact: The Lost World of the American Founding* (Lawrence: University Press of Kansas, 2003).

6. See Michael P. Federici, *The Political Philosophy of Alexander Hamilton* (Baltimore: Johns Hopkins University Press, 2012), 152; Rossiter, *Alexander Hamilton and the Constitution*, 166; and Karl-Friedrich Walling, "Alexander Hamilton on

the Strategy of American Free Government," in *History of American Political Thought*, ed. Bryan-Paul Frost and Jeffrey Sikkenga (Lanham, MD: Lexington, 2003), 171.

7. Alexander Hamilton, *Federalist*, no. 15 (1 December 1787), in PAH 4:357; and *Federalist*, no. 22 (14 December 1787), in PAH 4:410–11.

8. Address of the Annapolis Convention, 14 September 1786, in PAH 3:689.

9. George Washington, diary entry, 17 September 1787, in *The Diaries of George Washington*, ed. Donald Jackson and Dorothy Twohig (Charlottesville: University Press of Virginia, 1976–79), 5:185.

10. There are five versions of Hamilton's 18 June speech: Hamilton's own notes and the notes recorded by James Madison, Robert Yates, John Lansing Jr., and Rufus King. All of them are collected in PAH 4:178–207.

11. Alexander Hamilton, Constitutional Convention Speech on a Plan of Government, 18 June 1787, in PAH 4:184.

12. Ibid., 4:192.

13. Alexander Hamilton, Plan of Government, 18 June 1787, in PAH 4:208.

14. Alexander Hamilton, Constitutional Convention Speech on a Plan of Government, 18 June 1787, in PAH 4:201.

15. Ibid., 4:192–93.

16. Ibid., 4:198.

17. Ibid., 4:191.

18. Alexander Hamilton, Remarks on the Abolition of the States, 19 June 1787, in PAH 4:211.

19. See Miller, *Alexander Hamilton and the Growth of the New Nation*, 157.

20. The former possibility is suggested by Broadus Mitchell, the latter by Jacob Cooke. See Broadus Mitchell, *Alexander Hamilton: Youth to Maturity, 1755–1788* (New York: Macmillan, 1957), 392; and Jacob Ernest Cooke, *Alexander Hamilton* (New York: Charles Scribner's Sons, 1982), 49.

21. Alexander Hamilton, Constitutional Convention Speech on a Plan of Government, 18 June 1787, in PAH 4:202.

22. Ibid., 4:186.

23. Alexander Hamilton, Remarks on the Term of Office for Members of the Second Branch of the Legislature, 26 June 1787, in PAH 4:218.

24. Alexander Hamilton to George Washington, 3 July 1787, in PAH 4:224.

25. Alexander Hamilton, Remarks on the Election of the President, 6 September 1787, in PAH 4:243.

26. Alexander Hamilton, Remarks on Signing the Constitution, 17 September 1787, in PAH 4:253.

27. See Rossiter, *Alexander Hamilton and the Constitution*, 59.

28. Alexander Hamilton, *Federalist*, no. 1 (27 October 1787), in PAH 4:304.

29. Alexander Hamilton, *Federalist*, no. 23 (18 December 1787), in PAH 4:412.

30. Alexander Hamilton, *Federalist*, no. 70 (15 March 1788), in PAH 4:599.

31. Alexander Hamilton, *Federalist*, no. 85 (28 May 1788), in PAH 4:717.

32. Alexander Hamilton, Conjectures about the New Constitution, 17–30 September 1787, in PAH 4:276–77.

CHAPTER 5. STRUGGLING TO ADD ENERGY

1. On the efforts of not just Hamilton but the Federalists more broadly to bolster the federal government, see Max M. Edling, *A Revolution in Favor of Government: Origins of the U.S. Constitution and the Making of the American State* (Oxford: Oxford University Press, 2003).

2. John Avlon claims that in fact Hamilton "was perhaps the most powerful unelected man ever to serve in a president's administration." Avlon, *Washington's Farewell*, 72. On the "alliance" that Hamilton forged with Washington, see Stephen F. Knott and Tony Williams, *Washington and Hamilton: The Alliance That Forged America* (Naperville, IL: Sourcebooks, 2015). For an account that adds Adams as a central figure, see Carol Berkin, *A Sovereign People: The Crises of the 1790s and the Birth of American Nationalism* (New York: Basic Books, 2007).

3. On Hamilton's views and aims with regard to political economy, see Peter McNamara, *Political Economy and Statesmanship: Smith, Hamilton, and the Foundation of the Commercial Republic* (Dekalb: Northern Illinois University Press, 1998).

4. Alexander Hamilton, Report Relative to a Provision for the Support of Public Credit, 9 January 1790, in PAH 6:106.

5. As Richard Brookhiser notes, "Hamilton's reports were not discrete projects. They formed a coherent design. Settling America's debts would fortify its credit; credit would allow manufactures to develop; a diverse and flourishing economy would generate the revenue that would ensure the debt's proper funding." Richard Brookhiser, *Alexander Hamilton, American* (New York: Simon and Schuster, 1999), 101.

6. George Washington to David Humphreys, 20 July 1791, in PGWP 8:359.

7. Thomas Jefferson to Pierre Samuel Du Pont de Nemours, 18 January 1802, in PTJ 36:391. It was Jefferson's habit to begin most sentences with lowercase letters, and I have retained this idiosyncrasy in the text.

8. Rossiter, *Alexander Hamilton and the Constitution*, 80.

9. Alexander Hamilton, Opinion on the Constitutionality of an Act to Establish a Bank, 23 February 1791, in PAH 8:97.

10. Ibid., 8:105.

11. Rossiter, *Alexander Hamilton and the Constitution*, 189.

12. Alexander Hamilton to Edward Carrington, 26 May 1792, in PAH 11:426–29, 442.

13. Ibid., 11:443–44.

14. On Hamilton's views on foreign policy more broadly, see John Lamberton Harper, *American Machiavelli: Alexander Hamilton and the Origins of U.S. Foreign Policy* (Cambridge: Cambridge University Press, 2004); and Peter

McNamara, "Alexander Hamilton on the Rights of War and Peace: A Strong Republic for an Enlightened Era," in *American Grand Strategy: War, Justice, and Peace in American Political Thought*, ed. Bryan-Paul Frost, Paul Carrese, and Stephen Knott (Baltimore: Johns Hopkins University Press, forthcoming). I am grateful to McNamara for sharing his essay with me prior to publication.

15. Alexander Hamilton to Edward Carrington, 26 May 1792, in PAH 11:439.
16. These debates can be found in Morton J. Frisch, ed., *The Pacificus-Helvidius Debates of 1793–1794* (Indianapolis: Liberty Fund, 2007).
17. See Morton J. Frisch, *Alexander Hamilton and the Political Order: An Interpretation of His Political Thought and Practice* (Lanham, MD: University Press of America, 1991), 26.
18. Alexander Hamilton, *Tully*, no. 3 (28 August 1794), in PAH 17:160.
19. Alexander Hamilton to Angelica Church, 23 October 1794, in PAH 17:340.
20. On Hamilton as a lawyer, see Kate Elizabeth Brown, *Alexander Hamilton and the Development of American Law* (Lawrence: University Press of Kansas, 2017).
21. Chernow, *Alexander Hamilton*, 481.
22. Alexander Hamilton to Rufus King, 21 February 1795, in PAH 18:279.
23. Ibid., 18:278.
24. Alexander Hamilton to Robert Troup, 13 April 1795, in PAH 18:329.
25. Alexander Hamilton, Address on the Jay Treaty, 30 July 1795, in PAH 18:526.
26. Alexander Hamilton, *Defence*, no. 38 (9 January 1796), in PAH 20:22.
27. Thomas Jefferson to James Madison, 21 September 1795, in PTJ 28:475.
28. Miller, *Alexander Hamilton and the Growth of the New Nation*, 442.

CHAPTER 6. THE FRAIL AND WORTHLESS FABRIC

1. John Adams to James Lloyd, 17 February 1815, in FO.
2. Alexander Hamilton, *Warning*, no. 1 (27 January 1797), in PAH 20:490.
3. Alexander Hamilton, *Stand*, no. 1 (30 March 1798), in PAH 21:381–82.
4. Alexander Hamilton, the "Reynolds Pamphlet," 25 August 1797, in PAH 21:238.
5. Alexander Hamilton to Rufus King, 8 April 1797, in PAH 21:27.
6. Alexander Hamilton to Theodore Sedgwick, 2 February 1799, in PAH 22:453.
7. Alexander Hamilton to Rufus King, 6 February 1799, in PAH 22:465–66.
8. Alexander Hamilton to Jonathan Dayton, October–November 1799, in PAH 23:604. See also Harper, *American Machiavelli*, 235–36.
9. Alexander Hamilton to James McHenry, 27 June 1799, in PAH 23:227.
10. Alexander Hamilton to Elizabeth Hamilton, 24 May 1800, in PAH 24:525.
11. Alexander Hamilton to James McHenry, 15 May 1800, in PAH 24:490.
12. Abigail Adams to Thomas Boylston Adams, 12 July 1800, in FO.
13. Alexander Hamilton to John Jay, 7 May 1800, in PAH 24:465.
14. Alexander Hamilton to unknown, 8 November 1796, in PAH 20:376–77.
15. Alexander Hamilton, *Stand*, no. 7 (21 April 1798), in PAH 1:442.

16. Alexander Hamilton to Theodore Sedgwick, 4 May 1800, in PAH 24:453.
17. Alexander Hamilton to Theodore Sedgwick, 10 May 1800, in PAH 24:475.
18. Alexander Hamilton, *Letter from Alexander Hamilton, concerning the Public Conduct and Character of John Adams, Esq. President of the United States*, 24 October 1800, in PAH 25:186.
19. Ibid., 25:233.
20. Chernow, *Alexander Hamilton*, 623; and Elkins and McKitrick, *Age of Federalism*, 736.
21. Alexander Hamilton to James A. Bayard, 6 August 1800, in PAH 25:58; and Alexander Hamilton to Oliver Wolcott Jr., 16 December 1800, in PAH 25:257.
22. Alexander Hamilton to James A. Bayard, 16 January 1800, in PAH 25:319–20.
23. Thomas Jefferson, First Inaugural Address, 4 March 1801, in PTJ 33:149.
24. Alexander Hamilton, Address to the Electors of the State of New York, 21 March 1801, in PAH 25:365.
25. Robert Troup to Rufus King, 8 August 1801, in PAH 25:376n3.
26. Alexander Hamilton, *Examination*, no. 1 (17 December 1801), in PAH 25:454.
27. Alexander Hamilton, *Examination*, no. 9 (18 January 1802), in PAH 25:501.
28. Alexander Hamilton, *Examination*, no. 12 (23 February 1802), in PAH 25:529–30, 535.
29. Alexander Hamilton to Gouverneur Morris, 29 February 1802, in PAH 25:544.
30. Alexander Hamilton to James A. Bayard, 6 April 1802, in PAH 25:587.
31. Alexander Hamilton to James A. Bayard, [16–21] April 1802, in PAH 25:606.
32. Chernow, *Alexander Hamilton*, 659.
33. Alexander Hamilton to Rufus King, 3 June 1802, in PAH 26:14–15.
34. Alexander Hamilton to Charles Cotesworth Pinckney, 29 December 1802, in PAH 26:71.
35. On the Louisiana Purchase, see Peter J. Kastor, *The Nation's Crucible: The Louisiana Purchase and the Creation of America* (New Haven, CT: Yale University Press, 2004); and John Kukla, *A Wilderness So Immense: The Louisiana Purchase and the Destiny of America* (New York: Anchor Books, 2004).
36. John C. Hamilton, *Life of Alexander Hamilton: A History of the Republic of the United States of America* (1879), quoted in PAH 26:310.
37. Alexander Hamilton, Speech at a Meeting of Federalists in Albany, 10 February 1804, in PAH 26:189.
38. On the duel and the Hamilton-Burr rivalry, see Ellis, *Founding Brothers*, chap. 1; Thomas Fleming, *Duel: Alexander Hamilton, Aaron Burr, and the Future of America* (New York: Basic Books, 1999); and John Sedgwick, *War of Two: Alexander Hamilton, Aaron Burr, and the Duel That Stunned the Nation* (New York: Berkley Books, 2015). For a superb study of the role of duels and "affairs of honor" during the founding period more broadly, see Joanne B. Freeman, *Affairs of Honor: National Politics in the New Republic* (New Haven, CT: Yale University Press, 2001).
39. Alexander Hamilton to Theodore Sedgwick, 10 July 1804, in PAH 26:309.

CHAPTER 7. SUCH SELFISHNESS AND LITTLENESS

1. The most detailed biography of Adams is Page Smith's two-volume study (*John Adams* [Garden City, NY: Doubleday, 1962]). The best one-volume overviews include John Ferling, *John Adams: A Life* (Knoxville: University of Tennessee Press, 1992); James Grant, *John Adams: Party of One* (New York: Farrar, Straus and Giroux, 2005); and David McCullough, *John Adams* (New York: Simon and Schuster, 2001). Also excellent is Gordon Wood's dual biography of Adams and Jefferson: Wood, *Friends Divided*.

2. As Clinton Rossiter remarks, "no other man in that glorious age of learned statesmen ranged farther afield for instruction and inspiration. One need only peek at random in the 'Defence of the Constitutions' and watch the long parade of philosophers and historians go slogging by to realize that Adams was a scholar with few equals in his time." Clinton Rossiter, "The Legacy of John Adams," *Yale Review* 46 (1957), 533.

3. John Adams, Notes for an Oration at Braintree, spring 1772, in *Diary and Autobiography of John Adams*, ed. L. H. Butterfield (Cambridge, MA: Harvard University Press, 1961), 2:58.

4. John Adams, *Novanglus*, no. 3 (6 February 1775), in PJA 2:245.

5. John Adams to Zabdiel Adams, 21 June 1776, in AFC 2:21; and John Adams to Mercy Otis Warren, 16 April 1776, in PJA 4:124.

6. Adams, *Defence of the Constitutions of Government*, 4:555, 553.

7. Ibid., 4:555.

8. John Adams to Mercy Otis Warren, 16 April 1776, in PJA 4:124.

9. John Adams to Mercy Otis Warren, 8 January 1776, in PJA 3:398.

10. John Adams to Mercy Otis Warren, 19 August 1807, in FO.

11. Hence scholars who rely principally on the *Defence* in their interpretation of Adams's thought sometimes claim that he eventually changed his mind about the importance of virtue for republican government, once he realized that it was unrealistic to expect that the people would reliably put the nation's well-being ahead of their own. See, for instance, C. Bradley Thompson, *John Adams and the Spirit of Liberty* (Lawrence: University Press of Kansas, 1998), esp. 192–201; and Robert Webking, "Virtue and Individual Rights in John Adams' *Defence*," *Interpretation* 13.2 (May 1985), 177–93. J.G.A. Pocock claims, in stark contrast, that Adams's *Defence* was "perhaps the last major work of political theory written within the unmodified tradition of classical republicanism." J.G.A. Pocock, *The Machiavellian Moment: Florentine Political Thought and the Atlantic Republican Tradition* (Princeton, NJ: Princeton University Press, 1975), 526.

12. Adams, *Defence of the Constitutions*, 6:208, 166.

13. Ibid., 208, 219.

14. John Adams to Abigail Adams, 27 January 1795, in AFC 10:361. On John and Abigail's marriage, see Joseph J. Ellis, *First Family: Abigail and John Adams*

(New York: Vintage, 2010); and Edith B. Gelles, *Abigail and John: Portrait of a Marriage* (New York: Harper Perennial, 2009).

15. John Adams to Massachusetts Militia, 11 October 1798, in FO.
16. John Adams to Benjamin Rush, 2 February 1807, in FO.
17. John Adams to Benjamin Rush, 28 August 1811, in FO.
18. John Adams to Thomas Jefferson, 21 December 1819, in FO.
19. The most influential statement of this position can be found in Gordon S. Wood, *The Creation of the American Republic, 1776–1787* (Chapel Hill: University of North Carolina Press, 1969), 567–92. For an even more detailed case, see John R. Howe Jr., *The Changing Political Thought of John Adams* (Princeton, NJ: Princeton University Press, 1966).
20. John Adams to Mercy Otis Warren, 8 January 1776, in PJA 3:398.
21. John Adams, *Novanglus*, no. 5 (20 February 1775), in PJA 2:287.
22. "The Earl of Clarendon" to "William Pym," 20 January 1766, in PJA 1:163; and John Adams, *Novanglus*, no. 4 (13 February 1775), in PJA 2:265.
23. Howe, *Changing Political Thought of John Adams*, 45.
24. John Adams to Abigail Adams, 3 July 1776, in AFC 2:28.
25. John Adams, diary entry of 16 July 1786, in *Diary and Autobiography of John Adams*, 3:195–96.
26. John Adams to Abigail Adams, 14 August 1776, in AFC 2:96–97.
27. The Report of a Constitution or Form of Government for the Commonwealth of Massachusetts, ca. 28–31 October 1779, in PJA 8:260.
28. John Adams to Mercy Otis Warren, 8 January 1776, in PJA 3:398.
29. John Adams to Mercy Otis Warren, 16 April 1776, in PJA 4:124–25.
30. John Adams to Joseph Hawley, 25 August 1776, in PJA 4:495.
31. John Adams to unknown, 27 April 1777, in PJA 5:163.
32. John Adams to Abigail Adams, 22 September 1776, in AFC 2:131.
33. John Adams to William Gordon, 8 April 1777, in PJA 5:149.
34. John Adams to Zabdiel Adams, 21 June 1776, in AFC 2:21.
35. John Adams to Abigail Adams, 3 July 1776, in AFC 2:28.
36. On the influence that Adams's *Thoughts on Government* had on a number of the state constitutions, see Richard Alan Ryerson, *John Adams's Republic: The One, the Few, and the Many* (Baltimore: Johns Hopkins University Press, 2016), 159, 179–80. John Ferling writes that "of all the millions of words that Adams wrote and published, none came close to rivaling the impact or the enduring influence of this pamphlet." Ferling, *John Adams*, 155.
37. See Lorraine Smith Pangle and Thomas L. Pangle, *The Learning of Liberty: The Educational Ideas of the American Founders* (Lawrence: University Press of Kansas, 1993), 2.
38. John Adams to Robert R. Livingston, 18 July 1783, in PJA 15:138.
39. John Adams to Arthur Lee, 24 March 1779, in PJA 8:16.
40. John Adams to Abigail Adams, 12 April 1778, in AFC 3:9–10.
41. John Adams to Samuel Adams, 15 August 1785, in PJA 17:336.

42. John Adams to Elbridge Gerry, 25 April 1785, in PJA 17:42–43.
43. John Adams to James Warren, 9 January 1787, in PJA 18:538.
44. John Adams to Thomas Jefferson, 9 October 1787, in PJA 19:183.

CHAPTER 8. HIS ROTUNDITY

1. Wood, *Creation of the American Republic*, 568.
2. For suggestions that there is more method to the stylistic madness in the *Defence* than is generally supposed, see John E. Paynter, "The Rhetorical Design of John Adams's *Defence of the Constitutions of . . . America*," *Review of Politics* 58.3 (Summer 1996), 531–60; and C. Thompson, *John Adams and the Spirit of Liberty*, esp. 126–27.
3. John Adams, *Novanglus*, no. 5 (20 February 1775), in PJA 2:287.
4. John Adams, *Defence of the Constitutions of Government*, 6:10.
5. Ibid., 4:401.
6. Ibid., 6:96.
7. Wood, *Creation of the American Republic*, 574.
8. John Adams to James Warren, 9 January 1787, in PJA 18:539.
9. Adams, *Defence of the Constitutions of Government*, 4:290. On Adams's attempts to limit the problems posed by these aspiring aristocrats and oligarchs, see Luke Mayville, *John Adams and the Fear of American Oligarchy* (Princeton, NJ: Princeton University Press, 2016).
10. As Richard Ryerson notes, "a belief in the necessity of a strong executive in any free, orderly, and effective government runs through the entire course of John Adams's political thought, from his early writings in the 1760s to his last letters during his retirement." Ryerson, *John Adams's Republic*, 403.
11. For discussion, see C. Thompson, *John Adams and the Spirit of Liberty*, chap. 12.
12. Gordon S. Wood, *Revolutionary Characters: What Made the Founders Different* (New York: Penguin, 2006), 190.
13. John Adams to Thomas Jefferson, 10 November 1787, in PJA 19:212. Darren Staloff writes that "while [Madison] has often been credited as the father of the United States Constitution, that document bears far more similarity to the prescriptions in Adams's *Defense* and his previously drafted Massachusetts Constitution of 1780 than to Madison's own Virginia Plan." Darren Staloff, *Hamilton, Adams, Jefferson: The Politics of Enlightenment and the American Founding* (New York: Hill and Wang, 2005), 195.
14. John Adams to Thomas Jefferson, 6 December 1787, in PJA 19:228–29.
15. Ibid., 19:228–29.
16. John Adams to Cotton Tufts, 12 February 1788, in PJA 19:270.
17. John Adams to John Jay, 16 December 1787, in PJA 19:235.
18. John Adams to Abigail Adams, 30 May 1789, in AFC 8:364.
19. John Adams to François Adriaan van der Kemp, 27 March 1790, in FO.
20. John Adams to Roger Sherman, 18 July 1789, in FO.

21. John Adams to Nathaniel Peaslee Sargeant, 22 May 1789, in FO.
22. John Adams to John Trumbull, 23 January 1791, in FO.
23. John Adams to Henry Marchant, 3 March 1792, in FO.
24. John Adams to Oliver Wolcott Jr., 24 September 1798, in FO.
25. John Adams to Roger Sherman, 20 July 1789, in FO.
26. John Adams to Benjamin Rush, 18 April 1790, in FO.
27. John Adams to Thomas Jefferson, 29 July 1791, in FO.
28. John Adams to Nathaniel Hazard, 10 March 1792, in FO.
29. John Adams to Charles Adams, 17 May 1794, in AFC 10:183.
30. John Adams to William Stephens Smith, 19 June 1791, in FO.
31. John Adams to Winthrop Sargent, 24 January 1795, in FO.
32. John Adams to George Washington, 17 May 1789, in FO.
33. See James Madison to Thomas Jefferson, 23 May 1789, in PJM 12:182–83.
34. See Andy Trees, "John Adams and the Problem of Virtue," *Journal of the Early Republic* 21.3 (Autumn 2001), esp. 411.
35. John Adams to Benjamin Rush, 28 July 1789, in FO.
36. John Adams to William Tudor Sr., 14 June 1789, in FO.
37. John Adams to Benjamin Rush, 24 July 1789, in FO.
38. John Adams to Benjamin Rush, 9 June 1789, in FO.
39. John Adams to Benjamin Rush, 9 June 1789, in FO.
40. John Adams, "The 32nd Discourse on Davila," ed. Zoltán Haraszti, in *William and Mary Quarterly* 11.1 (January 1954), 90.
41. On Adams's presidency, see Ralph Adams Brown, *The Presidency of John Adams* (Lawrence: University Press of Kansas, 1975); and Kurtz, *Presidency of John Adams*.
42. John Adams, Inaugural Address, 4 March 1797, in FO.
43. John Adams to Abigail Adams, 17 March 1797, in AFC 12:33.
44. John Adams to Elbridge Gerry, 30 May 1797, in FO.
45. John Adams to Benjamin Rush, 30 September 1805, in FO.
46. John Adams to James Lloyd, 28 January 1815, in FO.
47. On the presidential election of 1800, see John Ferling, *Adams vs. Jefferson: The Tumultuous Election of 1800* (Oxford: Oxford University Press, 2004); and Edward J. Larson, *A Magnificent Catastrophe: The Tumultuous Election of 1800, America's First Presidential Campaign* (New York: Free Press, 2007).
48. John Adams to François Adriaan van der Kemp, 28 December 1800, in FO.
49. John Adams to Joseph Ward, 4 February 1801, in FO.
50. John Adams to Elbridge Gerry, 7 February 1801, in FO.
51. John Adams to Samuel Smith, 7 February 1801, in FO.

CHAPTER 9. THE BRIGHTEST OR THE BLACKEST PAGE

1. For a superb analysis of Adams's retirement years, see Joseph J. Ellis, *Passionate Sage: The Character and Legacy of John Adams* (New York: W. W. Norton, 1993).
2. John Adams to François Adriaan van der Kemp, 24 July 1802, in FO.

3. John Adams to Abigail Amelia Adams Smith, 26 September 1802, in FO.

4. John Adams to John Quincy Adams, 6 December 1804, in FO.

5. John Adams to Benjamin Rush, 18 April 1808, in FO.

6. John Adams to Benjamin Rush, 6 February 1805, in FO.

7. For a collection of these letters, see John A. Schutz and Douglass Adair, eds., *The Spur of Fame: Dialogues of John Adams and Benjamin Rush, 1805–1813* (Indianapolis: Liberty Fund, 2001).

8. John Adams to Benjamin Rush, 19 September 1806, in FO.

9. John Adams to Benjamin Rush, 28 December 1807, in FO.

10. John Adams to Benjamin Rush, 20 June 1808, in FO.

11. John Adams to Benjamin Rush, 18 April 1808, in FO.

12. John Adams to Thomas Foxcroft, 13 February 1807, in FO.

13. John Adams to John Quincy Adams, 18 March 1815, in FO.

14. John Adams to James Lloyd, 31 March 1815, in FO.

15. John Adams to Joseph Reed, 11 February 1784, in PJA 16:29; and John Adams to Benjamin Rush, 14 March 1809, in FO.

16. John Adams to Joseph Ward, 6 June 1809, in FO.

17. John Adams to Benjamin Rush, 13 October 1810, in FO.

18. John Adams to Benjamin Rush, 27 December 1810, in FO.

19. John Adams to John Quincy Adams, 25 January 1811, in FO.

20. John Adams to Josiah Quincy III, 9 February 1811, in FO.

21. John Adams to Benjamin Rush, 11 February 1810, in FO.

22. John Adams to Benjamin Rush, 28 August 1811, in FO.

23. Staloff, *Hamilton, Adams, Jefferson*, 230. On the Adams-Jefferson relationship, see Joanne B. Freeman, "Jefferson and Adams: Friendship and the Power of the Letter," in *The Cambridge Companion to Thomas Jefferson*, ed. Frank Shuffelton (Cambridge: Cambridge University Press, 2009), 168–78; Merrill D. Peterson, *Adams and Jefferson: A Revolutionary Dialogue* (Oxford: Oxford University Press, 1976); and Wood, *Friends Divided*. For a collection of the correspondence between them, see Lester J. Cappon, ed., *The Adams-Jefferson Letters: The Complete Correspondence between Thomas Jefferson and Abigail and John Adams* (Chapel Hill: University of North Carolina Press, 1959).

24. John Adams to Thomas Jefferson, 15 July 1813, in FO.

25. John Adams to Thomas Jefferson, February 1814, in FO.

26. See Ferling, *John Adams*, 425–26; and Howe, *Changing Political Thought of John Adams*, 236–39.

27. On the war, see Donald R. Hickey, *The War of 1812: A Forgotten Conflict* (Urbana: University of Illinois Press, 2012); J.C.A. Stagg, *Mr. Madison's War: Politics, Diplomacy, and Warfare in the Early American Republic, 1783–1830* (Princeton, NJ: Princeton University Press, 1983); and Alan Taylor, *The Civil War of 1812: American Citizens, British Subjects, Irish Rebels, and Indian Allies* (New York: Vintage, 2010).

28. John Adams to Benjamin Rush, 18 July 1812, in FO.

29. John Adams to Thomas Jefferson, 5 July 1813, in FO.

30. John Adams to Benjamin Rush, 7 July 1812, in FO.
31. Thomas Jefferson to James Madison, 30 January 1787, in PTJ 11:92–93; and John Adams to Abigail Adams, 3 July 1776, in AFC 2:28.
32. John Adams to John Quincy Adams, 16 October 1814, in FO.
33. John Adams to Thomas McKean, 30 October 1814, in FO.
34. John Adams to John Quincy Adams, 2 September 1815, in FO.
35. John Adams to Benjamin Rush, 23 March 1809, in FO.
36. John Adams to François Adriaan van der Kemp, 13 July 1815, in FO.
37. John Adams to Thomas McKean, 26 November 1815, in FO.
38. John Adams to Thomas Jefferson, 2 February 1817, in FO.
39. John Adams to Richard Sharp, 27 April 1817, in FO.
40. John Adams to David Sewall, 22 May 1821, in FO.
41. John Adams to Thomas Jefferson, 13 November 1815, in FO.
42. John Adams to Thomas Jefferson, 16 December 1816, in FO.
43. John Adams to John Quincy Adams, 31 December 1817, in FO.
44. John Adams to Thomas Jefferson, 21 December 1819, in FO.
45. John Adams to John Jay, 18 March 1822, in FO.
46. Ellis, *Passionate Sage*, 235.
47. Wood, *Friends Divided*, 409.
48. John Adams to Robert J. Evans, 8 June 1819, in FO.
49. John Adams to Thomas Jefferson, 3 February 1821, in FO.
50. John Adams to Thomas Jefferson, 21 December 1819, in FO.
51. John Adams to Louisa Catherine Johnson Adams, 23 December 1819, in FO; and John Adams to Louisa Catherine Johnson Adams, 13 January 1820, in FO.
52. John Adams to Robert Walsh Jr., 18 January 1820, in FO.
53. On the intertwined careers of Adams and his son, see Nancy Isenberg and Andrew Burstein, *The Problem of Democracy: The Presidents Adams Confront the Cult of Personality* (New York: Viking, 2019).
54. Josiah Quincy, *Figures of the Past: From the Leaves of Old Journals* (Boston: Roberts Brothers, 1888), 74.
55. John Adams to John Adams, 19 February 1825, in FO.
56. John Adams to Abigail Adams, 3 July 1776, in AFC 2:30.
57. John Adams to Abigail Adams, 17 May 1776, in AFC 1:411.
58. See Ellis, *Passionate Sage*, 65.
59. On the Jubilee, see Andrew Burstein, *America's Jubilee: How in 1826 a Generation Remembered Fifty Years of Independence* (New York: Alfred A. Knopf, 2001).
60. John Adams to John Whitney, 7 June 1826, in FO.
61. Ellis, *Founding Brothers*, 247.

CHAPTER 10. WEATHERING THE STORM

1. The Jefferson literature is breathtakingly vast, even in comparison with the considerable literatures devoted to the other figures covered in this book. Dumas

Malone's six-volume study (*Jefferson and His Time* [Boston: Little, Brown, 1948–81]) is a classic, though too forgiving of Jefferson's flaws. Among the innumerable one-volume overviews, some of the standouts include R. B. Bernstein, *Thomas Jefferson* (Oxford: Oxford University Press, 2003); John P. Boles, *Jefferson: Architect of American Liberty* (New York: Basic Books, 2017); Joseph J. Ellis, *American Sphinx: The Character of Thomas Jefferson* (New York: Vintage, 1998); Annette Gordon-Reed and Peter S. Onuf, *"Most Blessed of the Patriarchs": Thomas Jefferson and the Empire of the Imagination* (New York: Liveright, 2016); Jon Meacham, *Thomas Jefferson: The Art of Power* (New York: Random House, 2013); and Merrill D. Peterson, *Thomas Jefferson and the New Nation: A Biography* (Oxford: Oxford University Press, 1970).

2. On Jefferson and the democratic virtues, see Jean M. Yarbrough, *American Virtues: Thomas Jefferson on the Character of a Free People* (Lawrence: University Press of Kansas, 1998).

3. Thomas Jefferson, The Response, 12 February 1790, in PTJ 16:179.

4. On the lifelong collaboration and friendship between Jefferson and Madison, see Lance Banning, *Jefferson and Madison: Three Conversations from the Founding* (Lanham, MD: Madison House, 1995); Andrew Burstein and Nancy Isenberg, *Madison and Jefferson* (New York: Random House, 2010); Annette Gordon-Reed, "The Resonance of Minds: Thomas Jefferson and James Madison in the Republic of Letters," in *Cambridge Companion to Thomas Jefferson*, ed. Shuffelton, 179–92; Adrienne Koch, *Jefferson and Madison: The Great Collaboration* (Oxford: Oxford University Press, 1950); and Peter S. Onuf, *Jefferson and the Virginians: Democracy, Constitutions, and Empire* (Baton Rouge: Louisiana State University Press, 2018), chap. 3. For a collection of the correspondence between them along with extensive commentary, see James Morton Smith, *The Republic of Letters: The Correspondence between Thomas Jefferson and James Madison*, 3 vols. (New York: W. W. Norton, 1995).

5. Thomas Jefferson, First Inaugural Address, 4 March 1801, in PTJ 33:149, 151.

6. See Merrill D. Peterson, *The Jefferson Image in the American Mind* (Charlottesville: University Press of Virginia, 1998).

7. Wood, *Empire of Liberty*, 277.

8. For an argument that Jefferson's legendary optimism was balanced by a healthy dose of pessimism from the very beginning, see Maurizio Valsania, *The Limits of Optimism: Thomas Jefferson's Dualistic Enlightenment* (Charlottesville: University of Virginia Press, 2011). On Jefferson's views of history and progress, see Hannah Spahn, *Thomas Jefferson, Time, and History* (Charlottesville: University of Virginia Press, 2011).

9. Thomas Jefferson to James Madison, 30 January 1787, in PTJ 11:92–93.

10. Thomas Jefferson to Richard Price, 1 February 1785, in PTJ 7:630.

11. Thomas Jefferson to Edward Carrington, 4 August 1787, in PTJ 11:678.

12. Thomas Jefferson to John Adams, 30 August 1787, in PTJ 12:69; and Thomas Jefferson to John Adams, 12 November 1787, in PTJ 12:350–51.

13. Thomas Jefferson to John Adams, 12 November 1787, in PTJ 12:351.
14. Thomas Jefferson to James Madison, 20 December 1787, in PTJ 12:442.
15. Thomas Jefferson to James Madison, 31 July 1788, in PTJ 13:442.
16. Thomas Jefferson to Francis Hopkinson, 13 March 1789, in PTJ 14:650.
17. Thomas Jefferson to David Humphreys, 18 March 1789, in PTJ 14:678.
18. Thomas Jefferson to Gideon Granger, 13 August 1800, in PTJ 32:95–96.
19. Thomas Jefferson to George Washington, 23 May 1792, in PTJ 23:537–38.
20. Thomas Jefferson to George Washington, 9 September 1792, in PTJ 24:353.
21. Thomas Jefferson to William Branch Giles, 31 December 1795, in PTJ 28:566.
22. Thomas Jefferson to Archibald Stuart, 4 January 1797, in PTJ 29:252.
23. Dumas Malone, *Jefferson the Virginian* (Charlottesville: University of Virginia Press, [1948] 2005), xxviii.
24. Thomas Jefferson to Marquis de Lafayette, 16 June 1792, in PTJ 24:85. On Jefferson's friendship with Lafayette, see Tom Chaffin, *Revolutionary Brothers: Thomas Jefferson, the Marquis de Lafayette, and the Friendship That Helped Forge Two Nations* (New York: St. Martin's, 2019).
25. Thomas Jefferson to Thomas Paine, 19 June 1792, in PTJ 20:312.
26. Thomas Jefferson to William Short, 3 January 1793, in PTJ 25:15.
27. Thomas Jefferson to Philip Mazzei, 25 April 1796, in PTJ 29:82.
28. Thomas Jefferson to John Taylor, 4 June 1798, in PTJ 30:388–89.
29. Thomas Jefferson, Fair Copy of the Kentucky Resolutions, before 4 October 1798, in PTJ 30:548.
30. Thomas Jefferson to James Madison, 23 August 1799, in PTJ 31:174.
31. Thomas Jefferson to Robert R. Livingston, 23 February 1799, in PTJ 31:57.
32. This is a point stressed in Gary Wills, *"Negro President": Jefferson and the Slave Power* (New York: Houghton Mifflin, 2003).
33. Thomas Jefferson to Spencer Roane, 6 September 1819, in FO.
34. On Jefferson's "revolution of 1800," see Susan Dunn, *Jefferson's Second Revolution: The Election Crisis of 1800 and the Triumph of Republicanism* (Boston: Houghton Mifflin, 2004); Joanne B. Freeman, "A Qualified Revolution: The Presidential Election of 1800," in *A Companion to Thomas Jefferson*, ed. Francis D. Cogliano (Oxford: Wiley-Blackwell, 2011), 145–63; James Horn, Jan Ellis Lewis, and Peter S. Onuf, eds., *The Revolution of 1800: Democracy, Race, and the New Republic* (Charlottesville: University of Virginia Press, 2002); and Peter S. Onuf, *Jefferson's Empire: The Language of American Nationhood* (Charlottesville: University Press of Virginia, 2000), chap. 3.
35. Thomas Jefferson to Robert Morris, 6 March 1801, in PTJ 33:201.
36. Thomas Jefferson to John Dickinson, 6 March 1801, in PTJ 33:196.
37. Thomas Jefferson to Marquis de Lafayette, 13 March 1801, in PTJ 33:270.
38. Thomas Jefferson to Joseph Priestley, 21 March 1801, in PTJ 33:393–94.
39. Thomas Jefferson to James Warren, 21 March 1801, in PTJ 33:398–99.
40. Thomas Jefferson to Samuel Adams, 29 March 1801, in PTJ 33:487.
41. Thomas Jefferson to Elbridge Gerry, 29 March 1801, in PTJ 33:490–91.

42. Thomas Jefferson, First Inaugural Address, 4 March 1801, in PTJ 33:149; and Thomas Jefferson to Levi Lincoln, 25 October 1802, in PTJ 38:566.

43. On Jefferson's presidency, see Forrest McDonald, *The Presidency of Thomas Jefferson* (Lawrence: University Press of Kansas, 1976); and Robert M. S. McDonald, "The (Federalist?) Presidency of Thomas Jefferson," in *Companion to Thomas Jefferson*, ed. Cogliano, 164–83.

44. See esp. Jeremy D. Bailey, *Thomas Jefferson and Executive Power* (Cambridge: Cambridge University Press, 2007). On Jefferson and the notion of discretionary executive power, see Benjamin A. Kleinerman, *The Discretionary President: The Promise and Peril of Executive Power* (Lawrence: University Press of Kansas, 2009).

45. Ellis, *American Sphinx*, 271.

46. On the Embargo Act, see Burton Spivak, *Jefferson's English Crisis: Commerce, Embargo, and the Republican Revolution* (Charlottesville: University Press of Virginia, 1979). On Jefferson's foreign policy more generally, see Robert W. Tucker and David C. Hendrickson, *Empire of Liberty: The Statecraft of Thomas Jefferson* (Oxford: Oxford University Press, 1990).

47. F. McDonald, *Presidency of Thomas Jefferson*, 164.

48. Thomas Jefferson, Eighth Annual Message to Congress, 8 November 1808, in FO.

49. Thomas Jefferson to the Citizens of Washington, DC, 4 March 1809, in PTJR 1:13.

50. Thomas Jefferson to Pierre Samuel Du Pont de Nemours, 2 March 1809, in FO. On Jefferson's personal life during his retirement, see Alan Pell Crawford, *Twilight at Monticello: The Final Years of Thomas Jefferson* (New York: Random House, 2008). See also Andrew Burstein, "Jefferson in Retirement," in *Companion to Thomas Jefferson*, ed. Cogliano, 218–33.

51. Thomas Jefferson to Marquis de Lafayette, 14 February 1815, in PTJR 8:265.

CHAPTER II. THE KNELL OF THE UNION

1. Among the many works on the founders' treatment of, and relationship with, the American Indians, see esp. Colin G. Calloway, *The Indian World of George Washington: The First President, the First Americans, and the Birth of the Nation* (Oxford: Oxford University Press, 2019).

2. Sean Wilentz, *No Property in Man: Slavery and Antislavery at the Nation's Founding* (Cambridge, MA: Harvard University Press, 2018), 25.

3. There are seemingly countless works on this tortured relationship, but some good extended treatments include Douglas R. Egerton, "Race and Slavery in the Era of Jefferson," in *Cambridge Companion to Thomas Jefferson*, ed. Shuffelton, 73–82; Joseph J. Ellis, *American Dialogue: The Founders and Us* (New York: Alfred A. Knopf, 2018), chap. 1; Paul Finkelman, "Jefferson and Slavery: 'Treason against the Hopes of the World,'" in *Jeffersonian Legacies*, ed. Peter S. Onuf (Charlottesville: University Press of Virginia, 1993), 181–221; Gordon-Reed and

Onuf, *"Most Blessed of the Patriarchs,"* esp. chaps. 2–3; and John Chester Miller, *The Wolf by the Ears: Thomas Jefferson and Slavery* (New York: Free Press, 1977).

4. On Jefferson's relationship to his own slaves and on Monticello as a working plantation, see Lucia Stanton, *"Those Who Labor for My Happiness": Slavery at Thomas Jefferson's Monticello* (Charlottesville: University of Virginia Press, 2012). On the now-settled controversy over Jefferson's relationship to Sally Hemings, see Annette Gordon-Reed, *Thomas Jefferson and Sally Hemings: An American Controversy* (Charlottesville: University of Virginia Press, 1997); and Annette Gordon-Reed, *The Hemingses of Monticello: An American Family* (New York: W. W. Norton, 2008).

5. Thomas Jefferson, "Original Rough Draught" of the Declaration of Independence, 11 June 1776, in PTJ 1:426.

6. See Thomas Jefferson, *Notes on the State of Virginia*, ed. William Peden (Chapel Hill: University of North Carolina Press, 1955), 137–38; and Thomas Jefferson, Draft of a Constitution for Virginia, May–June 1783, in PTJ 6:298.

7. Thomas Jefferson, Report of the Committee on an Ordinance for the Western Territory, 1 March 1784, in PTJ 6:604.

8. See William M. Wiecek, *The Sources of Antislavery Constitutionalism in America, 1760–1848* (Ithaca, NY: Cornell University Press, 1977), 60.

9. Jefferson, *Notes on the State of Virginia*, 162–63.

10. John Adams to Thomas Jefferson, 22 May 1785, in PJA 17:116–17.

11. Thomas Jefferson to Jean Nicolas Démeunier, 26 June 1786, in PTJ 10:64.

12. Jefferson, *Notes on the State of Virginia*, 163.

13. Thomas Jefferson to Jean Nicolas Démeunier, 26 June 1786, in PTJ 10:64.

14. Thomas Jefferson to Richard Price, 7 August 1785, in PTJ 8:356–57.

15. Winthrop Jordan concluded many decades ago that Query 14 of Jefferson's *Notes on the State of Virginia* "constituted, for all of its qualifications, the most intense, extensive, and extreme formulation of anti-Negro 'thought' offered by any American in the thirty years after the Revolution." Winthrop D. Jordan, *White over Black: American Attitudes toward the Negro, 1550–1812*, 2nd ed. (Chapel Hill: University of North Carolina Press, 1968), 481.

16. See esp. Jefferson, *Notes on the State of Virginia*, 138–43.

17. Peterson, *Thomas Jefferson and the New Nation*, 262.

18. Finkelman, "Jefferson and Slavery," 208.

19. Thomas Jefferson to Edward Coles, 25 August 1814, in PTJR 7:604.

20. Thomas Jefferson to Thomas Humphreys, 8 February 1817, in PTJR 11:61.

21. Thomas Jefferson to James Heaton, 20 May 1826, in FO.

22. On the Missouri crisis, see Richard H. Brown, "The Missouri Crisis, Slavery, and the Politics of Jacksonianism," *South Atlantic Quarterly* 65 (Winter 1966), 55–72; Don E. Fehrenbacher, "The Missouri Controversy and the Sources of Southern Separatism," *Southern Review* 14 (1978), 653–67; and Robert Pierce Forbes, *The Missouri Compromise and Its Aftermath: Slavery and the Meaning of America* (Chapel Hill: University of North Carolina Press, 2007).

23. Thomas Jefferson to John Holmes, 22 April 1820, in FO.
24. Thomas Jefferson to Albert Gallatin, 26 December 1820, in FO.
25. Thomas Jefferson to John Adams, 22 January 1821, in FO.
26. Thomas Jefferson to Albert Gallatin, 26 December 1820, in FO.
27. Thomas Jefferson to Marquis de Lafayette, 26 December 1820, in FO.
28. Thomas Jefferson to Charles Pinckney, 30 September 1820, in FO.
29. Thomas Jefferson to Albert Gallatin, 26 December 1820, in FO.
30. Thomas Jefferson to Charles Pinckney, 30 September 1820, in FO.
31. Thomas Jefferson to John Holmes, 22 April 1820, in FO.
32. See esp. Forbes, *The Missouri Compromise and Its Aftermath*, 103–6; and Stuart Leibiger, "Thomas Jefferson and the Missouri Crisis: An Alternative Interpretation," *Journal of the Early Republic* 17.1 (spring 1997), 121–30.
33. Thomas Jefferson to John Adams, 10 December 1819, in FO.
34. Thomas Jefferson to Hugh Nelson, 7 February 1820, in FO.
35. Thomas Jefferson to Hugh Nelson, 12 March 1820, in FO.
36. Thomas Jefferson to Mark Langdon Hill, 5 April 1820, in FO.
37. Thomas Jefferson to William Short, 13 April 1820, in FO.
38. See Merrill D. Peterson, ed., *Visitors to Monticello* (Charlottesville: University Press of Virginia, 1989), 90–91.
39. Thomas Jefferson to Albert Gallatin, 26 December 1820, in FO.
40. Thomas Jefferson to Richard Rush, 27 December 1820, in FO.
41. Thomas Jefferson to James Breckenridge, 15 February 1821, in FO.
42. Thomas Jefferson to Spencer Roane, 9 March 1821, in FO.
43. Thomas Jefferson to Richard Rush, 14 August 1821, in FO; and Thomas Jefferson to Henry Dearborn, 17 August 1821, in FO.
44. Thomas Jefferson to Richard Rush, 1822 to 1823, in FO.

CHAPTER 12. A CONSOLIDATION OR DISSOLUTION OF THE STATES

1. On the decline of Virginia, see Susan Dunn, *Dominion of Memories: Jefferson, Madison, and the Decline of Virginia* (New York: Basic Books, 2007).
2. Staloff, *Hamilton, Adams, Jefferson*, 240.
3. See Robert E. Shalhope, "Thomas Jefferson's Republicanism and Antebellum Southern Thought," *Journal of Southern History* 42.4 (November 1976), 529–56.
4. Thomas Jefferson to Isaac H. Tiffany, 26 August 1816, in PTJR 10:349.
5. Thomas Jefferson to John Taylor, 28 May 1816, in PTJR 10:88.
6. Thomas Jefferson to John Melish, 13 January 1813, in PTJR 5:564.
7. Thomas Jefferson to Robert Selden Garnett, 14 February 1824, in FO. See also Thomas Jefferson to John Melish, 13 January 1813, in PTJR 5:564.
8. Thomas Jefferson to John Adams, 28 October 1813, in PTJR 6:565.
9. Thomas Jefferson to John Tyler, 26 May 1810, in PTJR 2:421.
10. Thomas Jefferson to Joseph C. Cabell, 2 February 1816, in PTJR 9:438.

11. Thomas Jefferson to John Tyler, 26 May 1810, in PTJR 2:421.

12. See Onuf, *Jefferson and the Virginians*, 3.

13. Thomas Jefferson to Benjamin Austin, 9 January 1816, in PTJR 9:335.

14. Thomas Jefferson to Charles Yancey, 6 January 1816, in PTJR 9:329.

15. Thomas Jefferson to Albert Gallatin, 16 October 1815, in PTJR 9:95; and Thomas Jefferson to John Taylor, 28 May 1816, in PTJR 10:86.

16. See Drew R. McCoy, *The Elusive Republic: Political Economy in Jeffersonian America* (Chapel Hill: University of North Carolina Press, 1980).

17. On the lifelong battle between Jefferson and Marshall, see James F. Simon, *What Kind of Nation: Thomas Jefferson, John Marshall, and the Epic Struggle to Create a United States* (New York: Simon and Schuster, 2002). On Jefferson and the judiciary more broadly, see David N. Mayer, *The Constitutional Thought of Thomas Jefferson* (Charlottesville: University Press of Virginia, 1994), chap. 9.

18. In 1823, Jefferson wrote that "I read but a single newspaper, Ritchie's Enquirer, the best that is published, or ever has been published in America." Thomas Jefferson to William Short, 8 September 1823, in FO. As Robert Shalhope notes, "a once open-minded and voracious reader" had by this point come "to trust only an outspokenly prosouthern newspaper." Shalhope, "Thomas Jefferson's Republicanism and Antebellum Southern Thought," 553.

19. Thomas Jefferson to Thomas Ritchie, 25 December 1820, in FO.

20. Thomas Jefferson to Spencer Roane, 9 March 1821, in FO.

21. Thomas Jefferson to John Wayles Eppes, 23 October 1821, in FO; and Thomas Jefferson to William Taylor Barry, 2 July 1822, in FO.

22. Miller, *Wolf by the Ears*, 211.

23. Thomas Jefferson to Spencer Roane, 6 September 1819, in FO.

24. Thomas Jefferson to John Wayles Eppes, 23 October 1821, in FO.

25. Thomas Jefferson to Samuel Kercheval, 12 July 1816, in PTJR 10:226–27.

26. Thomas Jefferson to Spencer Roane, 6 September 1819, in FO.

27. Thomas Jefferson to Thomas Ritchie, 25 December 1820, in FO.

28. Thomas Jefferson to William Taylor Barry, 2 July 1822, in FO; see also Thomas Jefferson to John Wayles Eppes, 23 October 1821, in FO.

29. Thomas Jefferson to Edward Livingston, 25 March 1825, in FO.

30. Thomas Jefferson to Marquis de Lafayette, 14 May 1817, in PTJR 11:353–54.

31. Thomas Jefferson to Marquis de Lafayette, 28 October 1822, in FO.

32. Thomas Jefferson to Albert Gallatin, 29 October 1822, in FO.

33. Thomas Jefferson to William Johnson, 27 October 1822, in FO.

34. Thomas Jefferson to William Johnson, 12 June 1823, in FO.

35. Thomas Jefferson to John Adams, 15 February 1825, in FO.

36. Thomas Jefferson to William Harris Crawford, 15 February 1825, in FO.

37. Thomas Jefferson, Solemn Declaration and Protest of the Commonwealth of Virginia, 24 December 1825, in FO.

38. Dumas Malone, *The Sage of Monticello* (Charlottesville: University of Virginia Press, [1981] 2005), 356.

39. Thomas Jefferson to William Branch Giles, 26 December 1825, in FO.
40. Thomas Jefferson to William Gordon, 1 January 1826, in FO.
41. Thomas Jefferson to William Johnson, 27 October 1822, in FO.
42. Thomas Jefferson to Claiborne W. Gooch, 9 January 1826, in FO.
43. Thomas Jefferson to Roger Weightman, 24 June 1826, in FO.
44. See Douglass Adair, "Rumbold's Dying Speech, 1685, and Jefferson's Last Words on Democracy, 1826," *William and Mary Quarterly* 9.4 (October 1952), 521–31.

CHAPTER 13. NO CHEERING PROSPECT

1. See Jeff Broadwater, *George Mason, Forgotten Founder* (Chapel Hill: University of North Carolina Press, 2006), chap. 10; and John Kukla, *Patrick Henry: Champion of Liberty* (New York: Simon and Schuster, 2017), chap. 27.
2. Samuel Adams to John Scollay, 30 December 1780, in *The Writings of Samuel Adams*, ed. Harry A. Cushing (New York: G. P. Putnam's Sons, 1904–8), 4:238. See also Mark Puls, *Samuel Adams: Father of the American Revolution* (New York: Palgrave Macmillan, 2006), chap. 15; and George Athan Billias, *Elbridge Gerry: Founding Father and Republican Statesman* (New York: McGraw-Hill, 1976), chap. 20.
3. See John Keane, *Tom Paine: A Political Life* (London: Bloomsbury, 1995), chap. 12.
4. Benjamin Rush to Granville Sharpe, 8 October 1801, in John A. Woods. "The Correspondence of Benjamin Rush and Granville Sharpe, 1773–1809," *Journal of American Studies* 1.1 (April 1967), 35.
5. Benjamin Rush to John Adams, 19 February 1805, in FO.
6. Benjamin Rush to John Adams, 13 June 1808, in FO.
7. Benjamin Rush to John Adams, 27 June 1812, in FO. See also Stephen Fried, *Rush: Revolution, Madness, and the Visionary Doctor Who Became a Founding Father* (New York: Broadway Books, 2018), pt. 2.
8. On Morris's role and impact at the convention, see James J. Kirschke, *Gouverneur Morris: Author, Statesman, and Man of the World* (New York: Thomas Dunne Books, 2005), chap. 5.
9. Gouverneur Morris, *The Diary and Letters of Gouverneur Morris*, ed. Anne Cary Morris (New York: Charles Scribner's Sons, 1888), 2:542–43.
10. Ibid., 566.
11. Ibid., 582. See also William Howard Adams, *Gouverneur Morris: An Independent Life* (New Haven, CT: Yale University Press, 2003), chap. 14.
12. John Jay to William P. Beers, 18 April 1807, in William Jay, *The Life of John Jay, with Selections from His Correspondence* (New York: J. and J. Harper, 1833), 2:309–10.
13. John Jay to Judge Peters, 24 July 1809, in ibid., 2:315. See also Walter Stahr, *John Jay: Founding Father* (New York: Diversion Books, 2012), chap. 15.
14. James Monroe to John C. Calhoun, 7 January 1829, in *The Writings of James Monroe*, ed. Stanislaus Murray Hamilton (New York: G. P. Putnam's Sons,

1898–1903), 7:187. See also Harry Ammon, *James Monroe: The Quest for National Identity* (Charlottesville: University Press of Virginia, 1990), chaps. 30–31.

15. John Marshall to Edward Everett, 3 November 1830, in *The Papers of John Marshall*, ed. Charles F. Hobson et al. (Chapel Hill: University of North Carolina Press, 1974–2006), 11:389.

16. John Marshall to Joseph Story, 25 December 1832, in ibid., 12:249.

17. John Marshall to Joseph Story, 22 September 1832, in ibid., 12:238.

18. John Marshall to Joseph Story, 6 October 1834, in ibid., 12:422. See also Joel Richard Paul, *Without Precedent: Chief Justice John Marshall and His Times* (New York: Riverhead Books, 2018), chaps. 30–33.

19. There are a handful of other reasonably prominent founders who showed little sign of disillusionment. However, most of these figures either died fairly early on, within a few years of the Constitution's ratification—such as Roger Sherman (who died in 1793), John Hancock (1793), and James Wilson (1798)—or disengaged from national politics in the same period for health or other reasons, such as John Dickinson and Edmund Randolph.

CHAPTER 14. FAR FROM DESPONDING

1. Madison too has been the subject of much study, by historians, political theorists, and legal scholars alike. Irving Brant's six-volume biography (*James Madison* [Indianapolis: Bobbs-Merrill, 1941–61]) resembles Dumas Malone's six-volume biography of Jefferson in both its classic status and its largely uncritical admiration for its subject. Brant devotes scarcely one hundred pages (out of around three thousand) to Madison's two-decade retirement. The best one-volume treatments include Noah Feldman, *The Three Lives of James Madison: Genius, Partisan, President* (New York: Random House, 2017); Ralph Ketcham, *James Madison: A Biography* (New York: Macmillan, 1971); and Jack N. Rakove, *James Madison and the Creation of the American Republic*, 3rd ed. (New York: Pearson Longman, 2006).

2. Abraham Lincoln, Address before the Young Men's Lyceum of Springfield, Illinois, 27 January 1838, in *The Collected Works of Abraham Lincoln*, ed. Roy P. Basler (New Brunswick, NJ: Rutgers University Press, 1953), 1:108.

3. James Madison to George Washington, 16 April 1787, in PJM 9:383.

4. See Forrest McDonald, *Novus Ordo Seclorum: The Intellectual Origins of the Constitution* (Lawrence: University Press of Kansas, 1985), 208–9. Similarly, Andrew Burstein and Nancy Isenberg write that "Madison was not particularly successful at the Constitutional Convention, certainly not in the way Americans have been taught and certainly not enough to warrant the title 'Father of the Constitution.'" Burstein and Isenberg, *Madison and Jefferson*, xix. Greg Weiner likewise argues that "Madison is miscast as the father of the Constitution" and that he would be "better understood as the attending physician at its birth—and, later, as its tutor." Greg Weiner, *Madison's Metronome: The Constitution, Majority*

Rule, and the Tempo of American Politics (Lawrence: University Press of Kansas, 2012), xi.

5. James Madison to Thomas Jefferson, 6 September 1787, in PJM 10:163–64.

6. See James Madison to Thomas Jefferson, 24 October 1787, in PJM 10:205–20.

7. Rakove, *James Madison and the Creation of the American Republic*, 61.

8. The literature on Madison's contributions to *The Federalist* is enormous, but a good starting place is Michael Zuckert, "James Madison in *The Federalist*: Elucidating 'The Particular Structure of This Government,'" in *A Companion to James Madison and James Monroe*, ed. Stuart Leibiger (New York: Wiley-Blackwell, 2013), 91–108.

9. For overviews of the debate, see Jeremy D. Bailey, *James Madison and Constitutional Imperfection* (Cambridge: Cambridge University Press, 2015), chap. 1; and Alan Gibson, "The Madisonian Madison and the Question of Consistency: The Significance and Challenge of Recent Research," *Review of Politics* 64.2 (Spring 2002), 311–38. The most detailed case that Madison remained fairly consistent throughout the 1780s and 1790s can be found in Lance Banning, *The Sacred Fire of Liberty: James Madison and the Founding of the Federal Republic* (Ithaca, NY: Cornell University Press, 1995). The classic case for greater inconsistency between the two periods is Gordon S. Wood, "Is There a 'James Madison Problem'?," in *Liberty and American Experience in the Eighteenth Century*, ed. David Womersley (Indianapolis: Liberty Fund, 2006), 425–47. For a judiciously balanced analysis, see Jack N. Rakove, *A Politician Thinking: The Creative Mind of James Madison* (Norman: University of Oklahoma Press, 2017), esp. 153–54.

10. James Madison, "A Candid State of Parties," in *National Gazette*, 22 September 1792, in PJM 14:372.

11. On Madison's presidency, see Robert Allen Rutland, *The Presidency of James Madison* (Lawrence: University Press of Kansas, 1990). On the adulation of Madison at the close of his presidency, see Drew R. McCoy, *The Last of the Fathers: James Madison and the Republican Legacy* (Cambridge: Cambridge University Press, 1989), chap. 1.

12. James Madison to US Congress, 3 December 1816, in FO.

13. For a superb analysis of Madison's retirement years, see McCoy, *Last of the Fathers*. Ralph Ketcham, *The Madisons at Montpelier: Reflections on the Founding Couple* (Charlottesville: University of Virginia Press, 2009), which draws heavily on Ketcham's biography, is strong on Madison's personal life during his final years.

14. James Madison to Thomas Jefferson, 17 February 1825, in PJMR 3:475.

15. James Madison to Spencer Roane, 2 September 1819, in PJMR 1:500–501.

16. James Madison to Thomas Jefferson, 27 June 1823, in PJMR 3:83.

17. James Madison to Spencer Roane, 6 May 1821, in PJMR 2:318.

18. James Madison to Robert Walsh Jr., 27 November 1819, in PJMR 1:557–58.

19. James Madison to Marquis de Lafayette, 25 November 1820, in PJMR 2:159.

20. See Jeff Broadwater, *James Madison: A Son of Virginia and a Founder of the Nation* (Chapel Hill: University of North Carolina Press, 2012), 205–6.

21. James Madison, Speech in Virginia Convention, 2 December 1829, in FO.
22. James Madison to Edward Coles, 29 August 1834, in FO; and James Madison to Edward Coles, 15 October 1834, in FO.
23. On the nullification crisis, see Richard E. Ellis, *The Union at Risk: Jacksonian Democracy, States' Rights, and the Nullification Crisis* (Oxford: Oxford University Press, 1987); and William W. Freehling, *Prelude to Civil War: The Nullification Controversy in South Carolina, 1816–1836* (Oxford: Oxford University Press, 1966).
24. See McCoy, *Last of the Fathers*, chap. 4; and James H. Read, "Madison's Response to Nullification," in *James Madison: Philosopher, Founder, and Statesman*, ed. John R. Vile, William D. Pederson, and Frank J. Williams (Athens: Ohio University Press, 2008), 269–83.
25. James Madison to Edward Coles, 29 August 1834, in FO.
26. James Madison to Richard Rush, 17 January 1829, in FO.
27. James Madison to Nicholas P. Trist, 15 May 1832, in FO.
28. See Kevin R. Gutzman, "A Troublesome Legacy: James Madison and 'The Principles of '98,'" *Journal of the Early Republic* 15.4 (Winter 1995), 569–89.
29. See Onuf, *Jefferson's Empire*, 144–45.
30. John Marshall to Joseph Story, 15 October 1830, in *Papers of John Marshall*, ed. Hobson et al., 11:384–85.
31. James Madison to Andrew Stevenson, 10 February 1833, in FO.
32. James Madison to Henry Clay, 2 April 1833, in FO.
33. Much has been written on Madison and slavery, but a good starting place is Jeff Broadwater, "James Madison and the Dilemma of American Slavery," in *Companion to James Madison and James Monroe*, ed. Leibiger, 306–23.
34. James Madison to Marquis de Lafayette, 1 February 1830, in FO.
35. James Madison to Ralph Randolph Gurley, 29 December 1831, in FO.
36. James Madison to Robert J. Evans, 15 June 1819, in PJMR 1:472.
37. James Madison to Thomas R. Dew, 23 February 1833, in FO.
38. Alan Gibson writes that "ultimately, Madison's late writings do not show him to be an alienated, irascible, and irrational old man. He emerges instead as a soothing and insightful sage, Aristotle's prudential statesman. James Madison kept the republican faith." Alan Gibson, "Madison's Thinking in the Later Years," *Review of Politics* 53.3 (Summer 1991), 558.
39. James Madison to Peyton Grymes and others, June 1834, in FO.
40. James Madison, On Nullification, December 1834, in FO.
41. James Madison to Hubbard Taylor, 15 August 1835, in FO.
42. James Madison to Levi Woodbury, 29 December 1835, in FO.
43. James Madison to unknown, March 1836, in FO.
44. James Madison to George Tucker, 22 June 1836, in FO.
45. Harriet Martineau, *Retrospect of Western Travel* (London: Saunders and Otley, 1838), 2:4, 7, 17.

CHAPTER 15. GROUNDS FOR HOPE

1. Edward Coles to Hugh Blair Grisby, 23 December 1854, quoted in McCoy, *Last of the Fathers*, 21.
2. James Madison to Robert Walsh Jr., 27 November 1819, in PJMR 1:558. As Kevin Gutzman writes, "For even-tempered James Madison, this was agitated writing." Kevin R. C. Gutzman, *James Madison and the Making of America* (New York: St. Martin's, 2012), 338.
3. James Madison, *Federalist*, no. 38 (12 January 1788), in PJM 10:369–70.
4. James Madison to unknown, December 1834, in FO.
5. James Madison, *Federalist*, no. 10 (22 November 1787), in PJM 10:265.
6. James Madison, "Parties," in *National Gazette*, 23 January 1792, in PJM 14:197. On this and the other essays that Madison wrote for the *National Gazette* in the early 1790s, see Colleen A. Sheehan, *James Madison and the Spirit of Republican Self-Government* (Cambridge: Cambridge University Press, 2009); and Colleen A. Sheehan, *The Mind of James Madison: The Legacy of Classical Republicanism* (Cambridge: Cambridge University Press, 2015).
7. James Madison, Speech at the Virginia Ratifying Convention, 10 June 1788, in PJM 11:163.
8. James Madison, *Federalist*, no. 37 (11 January 1788), in PJM 10:361.
9. James Madison, On Nullification, December 1834, in FO.
10. James Madison to Andrew Bigelow, 2 April 1836, in FO.
11. McCoy, *Last of the Fathers*, 39.
12. See ibid., chap. 4.
13. James Madison, Outline on the Federal Constitution, 1 September 1829, in FO.
14. Madison's original, 1787 records of the convention's proceedings can be found—along with other delegates' records of the convention—in Farrand, *Records of the Federal Convention of 1787*. A version that incorporates his pre-1820s revisions can be found in Adrienne Koch, ed., *Notes of Debates in the Federal Convention of 1787* (Athens: Ohio University Press, 1966). For the closest approximation of the transcript that Madison hoped to leave behind at the end of his life, see Lloyd, *Debates in the Federal Convention of 1787*. On Madison's revisions, see Mary Sarah Bilder, *Madison's Hand: Revising the Constitutional Convention* (Cambridge, MA: Harvard University Press, 2015), though Bilder's claims should be tempered by Jack Rakove, "A Biography of Madison's Notes of Debates," *Constitutional Commentary* 23 (2016), 317–49. Madison was not entirely consistent about whether he believed the intentions of the delegates who attended the convention should be used as a basis for constitutional interpretation; for discussion, see Bailey, *James Madison and Constitutional Imperfection*, chap. 7; and Jack N. Rakove, *Original Meanings: Politics and Ideas in the Making of the Constitution* (New York: Alfred A. Knopf, 1996), chap. 11.

15. James Madison, sketch of the origin of the Constitutional Convention, ca. 1835, in FO.
16. James Madison, Advice to My Country, 1834, in FO.

EPILOGUE. A VERY GREAT SECRET

1. Josiah Quincy III to John Adams, 29 January 1811, in FO.
2. John Adams to Josiah Quincy III, 9 February 1811, in FO.
3. Thomas Jefferson to Samuel Kercheval, 12 July 1816, in PTJR 10:226.
4. George Washington to Bushrod Washington, 9 November 1787, in PGWC 5:422.
5. James Madison, *Federalist*, no. 14 (30 November 1787), in PJMC 10:288.
6. See, for instance, Morris P. Fiorina, *Unstable Majorities: Polarization, Party Sorting, and Political Stalemate* (Stanford, CA: Hoover Institution Press, 2017); and Frances E. Lee, *Insecure Majorities: Congress and the Perpetual Campaign* (Chicago: University of Chicago Press, 2016).
7. Larry M. Bartels, "Uninformed Votes: Information Effects in Presidential Elections," *American Journal of Political Science* 40.1 (February 1996), 194. The classic work on the decline in civic engagement is, of course, Robert D. Putnam, *Bowling Alone: The Collapse and Revival of American Community* (New York: Simon and Schuster, 2000).
8. Chernow, *Alexander Hamilton*, 6. Similarly, Darren Staloff writes that Hamilton's "vision of a strong federal government with an independent judiciary and a vigorous executive has become second nature to most Americans. . . . No other founding father or leader of the early republic grasped as clearly and embraced as unflinchingly the modern world we have inherited. To that extent at least, as modern Americans in the most powerful country on earth, we are the children of Alexander Hamilton." Staloff, *Hamilton, Adams, Jefferson*, 125–26.
9. See, for instance, the Gallup poll at https://news.gallup.com/poll/1669/General-Mood-Country.aspx.
10. On the likelihood that the United States will remain the world's sole superpower even in the face of China's rise, see the work by my former colleague at Tufts University, Michael Beckley, *Unrivaled: Why America Will Remain the World's Sole Superpower* (Ithaca, NY: Cornell University Press, 2018).
11. On Jefferson and his university, see John A. Ragosta, Peter S. Onuf, and Andrew J. O'Shaughnessy, eds., *The Founding of Thomas Jefferson's University* (Charlottesville: University of Virginia Press, 2019); and Alan Taylor, *Thomas Jefferson's Education* (New York: W. W. Norton, 2019).

INDEX

secession: Civil War as expression
of, 224; Northern threats of, 99–100,
137; nullification crisis as motivation for, 214; Republican threats
of, 12; as response to consolidation
of government power, 187–91;
Southern threats of, 42, 139,
170. *See also* dissolution of
Union
Second Continental Congress, 144
sectional conflicts: Jefferson on, 4, 10,
151, 154, 172–78; legacy of, 227;
Missouri crisis and, 143; slavery as
source of, 171–75; Washington on
danger of, 47
Sedgwick, Theodore, 90, 92, 100
Shalhope, Robert, 259n18
Shays's Rebellion, 64, 151
Sherman, Roger, 121, 261n19
Short, William, 155, 176–77
slave codes, 164
slave rebellions, 205
slavery: abolition of, 50, 143, 167–69,
171, 205; Adams and, 50, 143, 165;
colonization of freed slaves proposed as solution for, 143, 164, 167,
172, 174, 214–15, 217; Constitution
and, 170–72; diffusion theory of,
173–74, 210; in early years of America, 162–63; Founding Fathers and,
50; Jefferson and, 50, 143–44, 163–75,
193; Madison and, 173, 210, 214–15,
217; Missouri crisis and, 143–44;
Monroe and, 173; the South and,
32, 162–75; Washington and, 49–51,
168
slave trade, 163–64, 168, 170
Society of the Cincinnati, 114
Sons of Liberty, 38
South: political influence of, 157,
170, 198–99; secession threats of,
12, 42, 139, 170, 224; and slavery, 32,
162–75. *See also* sectional conflicts

South America, 91, 136
South Carolina, and nullification crisis,
212, 222
Sparta, 104, 197
Staloff, Darren, 250n13, 265n8
Stamp Act (1765), 38, 105
states: Adams and the constitutions
of, 105, 109, 111–12, 116–19, 145;
federal government's relations
with, 56, 64–65, 68, 79, 90, 99, 121,
182, 184–85, 190, 207–8, 210, 212–13;
Hamilton's attitude toward, 67,
79, 90; Jefferson's attitude toward,
181–82; Madison's attitude toward,
208, 209, 222
Story, Joseph, 200

Talleyrand-Périgord, Charles-Maurice
de, 53
Tallmadge, James, and Tallmadge
amendment, 170–72
tariffs, 188, 189, 212–13
Taylor, John, 184
three-fifths principle, for political
representation, 157, 170, 181,
199
treason, 12, 33, 41, 53, 81, 92
Treaty of Paris, 105, 112–13
Trist, Nicholas, 213
Troup, Robert, 83, 95
Trumbull, Jonathan, 57
Turner, Nat, 205
Twelfth Amendment, 18

US Congress: financial authority
of, 74; Hamilton's vision for,
63, 67; and internal improvements,
181, 183, 188, 189; Madison's vision
for, 206, 220; representation in,
206; states' authority in relation
to, 184, 200; and tariffs, 188, 189,
212–13. *See also* US House of
Representatives; US Senate

Also by
DENNIS C. RASMUSSEN

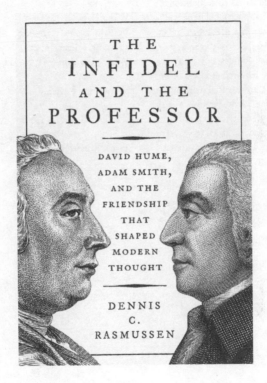

PRINCETON UNIVERSITY PRESS

Available wherever books are sold.
For more information visit us at www.press.princeton.edu

DETAIL OF THE RISING SUN CHAIR

Catalog INDE 11826. National Park Service. Courtesy of Independence National Historical Park.

FEARS OF A SETTING SUN